CHARLES LEERHSEN

A TRUE TALE OF MYSTERY, MAYHEM, AND THE BIRTH OF THE INDY 500

BLOOD AND SMOKE

SIMON & SCHUSTER

NEW YORK   LONDON   TORONTO   SYDNEY

Simon & Schuster
1230 Avenue of the Americas
New York, NY 10020

First Simon & Schuster hardcover edition May 2011

SIMON & SCHUSTER and colophon are registered trademarks
of Simon & Schuster, Inc.

For information about special discounts for bulk purchases,
please contact Simon & Schuster Special Sales at
1-866-506-1949 or business@simonandschuster.com.

The Simon & Schuster Speakers Bureau can bring authors to
your live event. For more information or to book an event,
contact the Simon & Schuster Speakers Bureau at
1-866-248-3049 or visit our website at www.simonspeakers.com.

Designed by Ruth Lee-Mui

Manufactured in the United States of America

10   9   8   7   6   5   4   3   2   1

Library of Congress Cataloging-in-Publication Data

Leerhsen, Charles.
  Blood and smoke : a true tale of mystery, mayhem, and the birth of the Indy 500 /
Charles Leerhsen.
      p.   cm.
  Includes bibliographical references and index.
  1. Indianapolis Speedway Race.   2. Automobile racing—United States.
I. Title.
GV1033.5.I55L44 2011
796.7206'877252—dc22   2010051942

ISBN 978-1-4391-4904-1
ISBN 978-1-4391-5364-2 (ebook)

FOR ADELE LEERHSEN, MY MOM

CONTENTS

Behind them was a past forever destroyed, still quivering on its ruins with all the fossils of the centuries of absolutism; before them the dawn of a vast horizon, the first glimmerings of the future; and between these two worlds, like the ocean that separates the Old World from young America, something vague and floating, a stormy sea full of wreckage, traversed from time to time by some far-off white sail or some ship puffing heavy smoke—in short, the present century.

—ALFRED DE MUSSET,
The Confession of a Child of the Century

Gentlemen, start your coffins.

—JIM MURRAY, *Los Angeles Times*

BLOOD AND SMOKE

PRELUDE

ALL THESE YEARS later his heart still swells with pride for his father, who won the Indianapolis 500-mile race. When he opens the door of his place down near Orlando, the son doesn't so much greet you as present you with his smooth and pleasant face, turning it a bit this way then that, wanting you to notice how closely he resembles Dad. You gasp obligingly, and he smiles, as in a card trick.

The son says he is waiting for the cleaning lady but the house is immaculate. The father was fastidious, small-built, and dapper with a pencil mustache—like a lot of race car drivers of his day—and the house is a fitting shrine to him, though he never lived here himself. Scattered throughout the rooms are framed photographs of Dad, miniature automobiles, laminated documents, scrapbooks with crumbling clippings from long-gone barbershop magazines (*Argosy, Saga, True*) and even yellower telegrams of congratulation. When you win the Indianapolis 500, people start laminating your documents, and it just goes on from there.

ONCE, ACROSS VAST swaths of America, the race was the most anticipated event on the calendar apart from Christmas. Every Memorial Day as many as 400,000 spectators packed themselves into the Speedway, a two-and-a-half-mile rectangle (with curved corners) located not in Indianapolis, technically, but in Speedway, Indiana (pop. 12,594), a suburb about five miles northwest of the capital. The mobs were no doubt drawn to the race in part by the loud and sexy cars and the (usually) quiet and (by definition) sexy men who drove them at speeds of 75, then 150, and, as the years went by, well above 200 miles per hour. Americans love cars, of course, and speed and competition, and sunshine and pork tenderloin sandwiches, but no one has ever been able to explain exactly why so many people feel so passionately about this particular race, which involves esoteric machines and arcane feats of mechanical engineering as well as the occasional fiery death—and which does not even determine the championship of the Indy car circuit. "I don't know why Indy became such a phenomenon," former Speedway president Joe Cloutier once said, "but I do know it's a fragile formula that we don't want to mess with."

Until 1986 not messing with the formula meant keeping the best-attended sports event in America off live national TV, the better to preserve that robust gate. So in the '60s and '70s, as the cool, low-slung roadsters gave way to fierce-looking rear-engine racers, and the Speedway found itself flooded with future immortals like A.J. Foyt (four wins), Al Unser (four) and his brother Bobby (three), Johnny Rutherford (three), and Mario Andretti (just one, but God what great hair), the only way for most people to see the race as it happened was to "see" it on radio. Crowding around the portable at the Memorial Day picnic, shushing each other while announcers Sid Collins and later Paul Page described the action, became for millions a rite of late middle-American spring. Indeed like most other things forbidden to the eye, the race in this accidental way gained a potent extra allure.

To win the Indy 500 was a glorious, life-changing event that severely tested the winner's ability to handle money, media, and awe. "The stakes for a driver are so high, in terms of money and prestige, that it heightens the danger," Sam Posey, who finished fifth in the 1972 Indy 500, once said. "There's never a moment that you relax at the Speedway, never a moment when you get past the possibility of something really insane happening. I mean, who cares if you win at Trenton?" Winning the 500 was a distinction comparable to being the heavyweight champion in the era before that division was merely a merry-go-round of revolving Russians. You walked into a restaurant and someone sent drinks to your table and every once in a while someone threw a drink in your face—the ultimate compliment, really, when your only offense was being just too much for the drink flinger to handle—your famous face now a glorious bump, like that of all the other winners, on the silver Borg-Warner trophy. The radio monologist Jean Shepherd, who grew up in Hammond, Indiana, observed in the early 1970s that all retired Indy winners have "a sadness around their eyes, because they know they can never win the 500 again." The rush of victory at the place they call the Brickyard does seem highly addictive. Two winners, Floyd Roberts and Bill Vukovich, died on the track while trying for a second and third Indy, respectively. The 1924 "co-winner," Lora Corum, hanged himself—though that is a complicated story, his suicide coming many years after the disgrace of being fired after the 109th lap by car owner Fred Duesenberg, who replaced him on the spot with the more aggressive Joe Boyer (who won the race but died on another track just a few months later). Even if winning at Indy doesn't change you forever it will change forever the way other men see you. It will change the way women see you, too. The father of the son in Orlando, for example, was married five times.

Baby boomers, those masters and slaves of nostalgia, will point to the '60s and '70s as the best of times at Indy, but the matter is hardly settled. You could make a case for the 1980s, an era of dramatic duels (see, for example, Danny Sullivan's 1985 "spin-and-win" victory over Andretti, and the ballsy wheel-brush with which Emerson Fittipaldi finally shook off Al Unser Jr. with four laps to go in '89) and sleek, curvaceous cars that looked like they were going 230 mph when they were sitting in the pits (the record for the fastest race lap, set in 1996, is 236.103 mph). These one-off speed machines would later be outlawed by a governing body, the Indy Racing League, concerned about safety, yes, but perhaps just as much about the cost to the car owners of constantly pushing the borders of technology and design. Still, the very real possibility that the machines in those years might at any moment become airborne and fly into the stands seemed to scare away no one. Quite the opposite, actually. Not only would 400,000 come to watch the race in the mid-'80s, but nearly 200,000 routinely turned out the day before (Carburetion Day, as it is still known, though no Indy car has had a carburetor since 1991) to see the final tune-ups. Perhaps the one legitimate knock against the '80s as the true Glory Days is that the then new generation of drivers—a group led by Bobby Rahal, Tom Sneva, and especially Rick Mears, who won four 500s between '79 and '91—were more competent than charismatic, the vanguard of the all too vanilla era lying just around the next turn.

A lack of pungent personalities was not a problem in the '40s and '50s: *the* key decades in the opinion of many Indy aficionados. Of course it was easier to discern and distinguish the human players in those days of open-top roadsters and visor-less, chin-strapped helmets that looked like hollowed-out cannonballs. But the members of what some would call Indy's Greatest Generation do truly qualify as self-sacrificing, forward-looking men on a mission: namely, to save the hallowed Speedway from the crumbling, weed-choked mess it had become after closing in 1941 in the wake of a wartime ban on auto sports. The conventional wisdom had Eddie Rickenbacker, the World War I fighter ace and Congressional Medal of Honor winner who had been the principal owner of the Indianapolis Motor Speedway since 1927, selling the property to developers intent on melding it into the general postwar suburban sprawl. But former driver Wilbur Shaw—a Hoosier who had won the big race in '37, '39, and '40—led a search for a savior, and found one in Terre Haute's Tony Hulman, a forty-four-year-old Yale graduate and heir to the Clabber Girl baking powder fortune. Hulman bought the bare ruined rectangle for $750,000 and, with Shaw serving as president of the Speedway, spearheaded a renovation that allowed racing to resume in 1946. Drivers like Mauri Rose (three wins) and the Mad Russian, Bill Vukovich (two), created a new racing culture that would eclipse the proud but primitive era (1912–1929) that until then had been known semiofficially as the Golden Years.

THE FATHER OF the man in Orlando did his driving before all that, before even the epic 1912 race in which the great Ralph DePalma gallantly got out and pushed his Mercedes down the homestretch after leading for 194 of the 200 laps and breaking down on mile 497. The photograph of that Sisyphean finish, reproduced in hundreds of local newspapers (the only mass media in those pre-radio days), helped the Speedway certify its status as a kind of Olympus–cum–service pits, a place where gods cavort and larger-than-life things occur. Two years later, in 1914, the race already had the mythic quality it would carry into the next century, and the weekly *Motor Age* was describing it as "a pageant of motion, a spectacle of action, a fete of frenzy and a melodrama of speed—it is color, excitement, uncertainty, despair and triumph crowded into seven hours of a May day."

But the 1912 Indy was not the first Indianapolis 500-mile race. That happened a year earlier, on May 30, 1911, a month after a great fire destroyed much of Bangor, Maine, a week after the New York Public Library opened for business, and the day before the White Star Line's new flagship, RMS *Titanic,* was launched on a test run from the Harland and Wolff shipyard in Belfast. Many buffs classify that first 500 as its own discrete era, and if they think of it at all consider it a strange day when death and a bizarre post-race controversy tainted what might have been a glorious and historic moment, leaving thousands to wonder what exactly their eyes had just witnessed. Eventually, official decisions were rendered, backs were slapped, a body was buried, and the cross fire of accusations more or less subsided—but the controversy concerning the result of the first Indy 500 never really got resolved. Resentment and doubt festered in the hearts and minds of those who were directly involved until the day they died, sometimes boiling over in the presence of a family member or surprised reporter who had thought he was writing a warm and fuzzy Where Are They Now piece about some genial old Stutz Bearcat–driving gent.

Over the years, the events of May 30, 1911, also became fodder for legions of Indy 500 buffs who still periodically pick up the topic in Internet forums or at vintage car rallies, bat it around a bit, then move on in frustration, having no new information to support their particular point of view. The odd truth is that except for a couple of rather sloppily executed magazine pieces published at least two decades ago, the events of that Indianapolis afternoon have for these last hundred years never been subject to anything like a thorough journalistic look-see. To discover what is possible to know about the first 500-mile race, and to shed light on the curious and now largely forgotten early automobile racing scene, is the dual mission of this book.

For now, at the outset, let us agree on this: rather than lose a bar bet, you should say, if the question is who won the first Indy 500, and the money is sitting right there under the beer glass, that the answer is Ray Harroun. No reference book, or relevant Web site, would disagree with you, and you might even be correct. Harroun's streamlined yellow Marmon Wasp finished the 1911 race in six hours, forty-two minutes, and eight seconds, averaging 74.6 miles per hour (the average speed record is now 185.981 mph). That put him one minute and forty-three seconds ahead of the luxurious white Lozier that "Smiling" Ralph Mulford had driven all the way from Detroit to the Indy starting line. These results and numbers are taken, by the way, from the official record of the Indianapolis Motor Speedway, and there is no reason to be suspicious of them—unless you are the sort of person who might wonder why they were not produced on the spot, in sync with the statutory snap of the checkered flag, but rather over the course of two days and nights of closed-door meetings in a downtown Indianapolis hotel, and not until the Speedway's founding president, Carl Graham Fisher, ordered all the scoring sheets and judges' notes destroyed.

THE RACE TODAY is either in a post-heyday or pre-comeback state, depending on your general attitude toward life and whether you are employed by the marketing arm of the Indianapolis Motor Speedway. Some Indy traditions survive unchanged (the 6:00 A.M. explosive charge that signals the opening of the gates; Jim Nabors warbling "Back Home Again in Indiana"; the Speedway's Vatican approach to information dispersal, which means among other things that attendance figures are always approximate). Other rituals have experienced some light revision (it is now, almost always, "*Ladies* and gentlemen, start your engines," and the winner's obligatory glass of milk is sponsored by the American Dairy Association). But in more recent years much of what former Speedway president Cloutier called "the delicate formula" has been seriously messed with. Since 1971, the race has taken place not necessarily on Memorial Day—or Decoration Day, as the holiday was known at the time of the first Indy—but on the Sunday of Memorial Day weekend. That is largely a concession to television, as is a starting time (since 2005) of 1:00 P.M. or noon (as opposed to the original 10:00 A.M.), meaning that to many fans the race now unfolds in a different and much less interesting light. Who knew this crowd was so painterly?

Most of the major changes, however, trace back to a mid-'90s schism in the world of open-wheel racing that had the effect of diluting the Indy talent pool (a dentist raced in the 500 one year) and ushering in the age of slower/safer cars, which look clunkier and sound wimpier, in the opinion of many fans who have long since gone over to NASCAR. Certainly, not all developments have been for the worse: a few intriguing—and, it would seem, highly marketable—personalities have surfaced in the last decade. Yet despite the presence of three-time winner Helio Castroneves, a dreamboat Brazilian driver who also cha-chaed to glory on *Dancing with the Stars*, and Danica Patrick, who has demonstrated that she is much more than just a very pretty face, TV ratings for the race have dropped precipitously, and are now passing through hockey territory on their way to the land of women's basketball.

IT WOULD BE difficult—and impolite, and pointless—to raise the issue of a diminished Indy 500, or the matter of the controversial finish, with Dick Harroun, the ninety-four-year-old man sitting on his bed in Orlando, with an open scrapbook in his lap, talking about his long-departed dad. "Dad was the first to use strategy to win a race—tire strategy!" he is saying, enthusiastically. "He went to Firestone and asked them how fast he could go without blowing a tire and they said 75 miles per hour. So he stuck to that speed, letting whoever wanted to pass him by in the early stages, and in the end he made fewer pit stops and guess what—he won the race!"

Ray's Marmon was also the only one of the forty cars in the first 500 built as a single-seater. It was the custom in those days for every race car to have a "riding mechanic" who would check the gauges, manually pump fuel and water, and let the driver know when other cars were coming up on his right or left, the better to avoid collisions. Dick says that his father designed the car with one seat primarily for humanitarian reasons: "There were so many accidents in those days that Dad thought that if something happened to his car it would be better if one man, not two, were involved in the wreck. At the end of the day there would be, you know, one less widow." That is a son's story. The way the tale usually goes, the other drivers thought a one-seater was unfairly advantageous to Ray because it was streamlined and lighter, and dangerous for all concerned because it lacked a lookout. During qualifying week, they threatened to boycott the 500 should the Marmon be allowed to start. Ray then went back to the garage, or so the story goes, and worked up a crude rearview mirror, which he mounted on the Marmon to mollify his rivals, at least about the matter of his not being able to see who was coming from behind. Either way you tell it, though, Ray comes out the hero. "You see, Dad was an engineer at heart," Dick says, "not just a driver."

Dick, born in 1915, is too young to have witnessed his father's one Indy 500, but he had an older brother, Ray Jr., who at the age of eleven saw it with their mother, Edith. "It must have been very exciting for them to be there," Dick says. "Halfway through the race, fans in the grandstand had figured out that he was Ray Harroun's son, and they started yelling at the people standing up in front, 'Sit down so this boy can see his father win the 500-mile sweepstakes!'" Dick heard this story from his mother; he never met his only sibling, who was killed, by an automobile, while playing ball in a Chicago street two years later.

Dick probably didn't have the happiest of childhoods. In an era before divorce was common, he grew up in Detroit with his single mother while Ray, who had quit driving on the day he won the Indy 500, saying it was too dangerous, pursued a career in the automobile business, sometimes working for others, sometimes for himself, and traveling frequently. Dick says that his father invented the automobile bumper (they were fancy add-ons in the 1910s, like custom horns and mud flaps), and for a while, just before the First World War, Ray ran the Harroun Motor Company, which manufactured a mid-priced sedan called the Harroun. "There were times," Dick says, "when Dad was in the money." Those times, alas, did not include the long final chapter of Ray's life, when he and his much younger fifth wife were living in a trailer in Anderson, Indiana, thirty-nine miles from the scene of his defining, if sometimes disputed, triumph, surviving on his $116 monthly

Social Security check. But Dick is right about his father having a passion for automobile engineering. The day Ray died—in 1968, at the age of eighty-nine—he was sitting in the kitchen of his trailer and, says Dick, "working on a variable-ratio power steering unit that would have made going around turns a lot safer for everyone."

In times of chicken and in times of feathers, as they used to say, Ray always tried to be a good father to Dick, in his fashion. In 1922, when Ray made a business trip to Los Angeles, he took along Dick, then seven, and the two got a tour of several Hollywood movie studios. On the set of *Grandma's Boy* at General Service Studios they met the comedian Harold Lloyd, who was shooting a scene involving farm animals escaping from a truck and running amok, which Dick still chuckles about to this day. From there they proceeded to Paramount, where they saw Rudolph Valentino dressed as a matador for his famous silent movie *Blood and Sand.* In Dick's memory, the studio had built a full-scale bullring on its back lot for the most celebrated actor of his day. In the middle of the ring stood a bored-looking bull, tightly chained to stakes in the ground so he would be less likely to harm Valentino as the actor passed his cape over him in close-ups. During a break in the shooting a publicist whispered something in Valentino's ear and the actor's face lit up in astonishment. Then, making a vague gesture toward director Fred Niblo (whom he famously disliked), he strode off in the direction of the Harrouns.

"I'll never forget the way he treated us," says Dick. Valentino tousled Dick's hair, bent to pinch his cheek, and asked if he would like to pet the bull. Then, standing erect, the great Latin Lover looked directly into the eyes of the man who might have billed himself as the great Spartansburg, Pennsylvania, Lover—and clasped both of Ray's hands in his own.

"Oh, my, my," Valentino said, as if in a rapture, "the 500 miles!"

PART ONE

A SPEEDWAY IS BORN

UNTIL THE MOMENT that one ran over his breastbone, Clifford Littrell had been exceedingly fond of automobiles. To be sure, a lot of young people were car-crazy in 1909, endlessly debating the relative merits of the National, the Pierce-Arrow, and the Knox, fogging the windows at the McFarlan showroom with their Sweet Caporal–scented sighs, scanning the glossy pages of *The Horseless Age* for gossip about rumored innovations like windshields and black tires (as opposed to the standard, tiresome off-white)—and digging through bins at dry goods emporiums for the latest in silk driving scarves (for men) or the kind of cunning little riding bonnet sported by Lottie Lakeside in the hit Broadway musical *The Motor Girl.* But Littrell was no mere enthusiast.

No, this poor fellow—whom we come upon writhing in the bustling intersection of Capitol Avenue and Vermont Street in Indianapolis, Indiana, at 11:30 on the sunny, sticky morning of Tuesday, August 17— had dedicated his life to what was then known as autoism. At the age of twenty-seven, he had risen from the position of molder in a metal factory to what was then known as a mechanician. His main job was to road-test motorcycles, which is what some Americans who disdained the French word *automobile* (because it was French) then called cars. It was still so early in the motor age, you see—three years before the Stutz

Bearcat and four before the Duesenberg—that people hadn't quite worked out the terminology.

A corpse was a corpse, though, and the prospect of seeing one caused a crowd to gather. Littrell was no one they knew, they could see, yet no mysterious stranger, either, having just come loose from the noisy caravan of men and equipment heading to the not-quite-finished Indianapolis Motor Parkway—or rather *Speedway*, as they had been calling it these last couple of months—some five miles northwest of town. A long line of Jacksons, Marmons, Amplexes, Buicks, and other cars had been traveling there, circus-train-style, the better to attract attention and whip up curiosity as they prepared for a historic event: the first racing meet in America conducted on a track built specifically for automobiles. Thousands of auto industry people—executives, salesmen, and common laborers like Littrell—had flocked to Indianapolis that week for three days of competition that would begin the next afternoon and culminate in the first edition of the 300-mile Wheeler-Schebler race on Saturday, August 21.

Littrell worked for Stoddard-Dayton of Dayton, Ohio, one of more than a thousand auto manufacturers then trying to grab a share of the booming U.S. market. Most of those car companies were tiny operations—some were virtual one-man shops—but Stoddard-Dayton ranked among the largest, with several hundred employees. Littrell had started there about five years before, when the company, instead of turning out "Touring cars with Speed and Symmetry in every line," as their literature boasted, was instead still making mowers, hay rakes, and harrows. That morning he had been perched on the rear of the company's highly touted No. 19 race car as it rolled out of the garage. It was a precarious spot, atop the gas tank with no handle to grasp, but the trip to the Speedway seemed relatively short, and the traffic, a mix of horse-drawn and motorized vehicles, was moving sluggishly; he thought he would be all right. Then he remembered a wrench he had left behind, and, without informing the driver, he braced himself to hop off the vehicle, figuring he would grab the tool, catch up to the car, and quickly clamber back aboard. Just at that moment, though, the traffic jam eased a bit, the No. 19 car surged forward, and Littrell, who had been poised to jump, tumbled to the street, landing on his back. Brakes, like automobile lingo, were a work in progress in those early months of the Taft administration, and the car behind him could not stop in time to avert disaster. One witness said the sound was "that of a coconut being cleaved."

The ambulance that came for Littrell was a brand-new electric-powered Waverly with a butter-soft black leather driver's seat and an interior of polished poplar, the kind of elegant, expensive ($3,000) vehicle already becoming increasingly rare following the introduction of the plebeian Model T Ford ($850) in 1908. Befitting a city that aspired to open a clear lead over Detroit as an automobile manufacturing center, Indianapolis had two motorized ambulances in those days, proudly publicized in the press. That the unknown Samaritan who called for help that morning had summoned the one from the Methodist Hospital, and not the motor ambulance belonging to the Flanner and Buchanan funeral home, is perhaps a testament to the optimism that percolated through the town of 233,000 on the eve of the Speedway's debut. Or maybe it was just wishful thinking. Once the word spread about Littrell's accident, his well-being would concern a circle far beyond his immediate family, back in their humble digs on Dayton's Wyoming Street. Some of the most powerful men in Indianapolis would stop what they were doing and pray that the Lord not take the beloved husband of Jesse and the devoted father of two-year-old Helen—at least not until Sunday, by which time the crowds and the out-of-town newspapermen would have moved on.

One couldn't blame the town fathers and the Speedway founders for hoping to avoid unseemly incidents that might mar the mood. A lot was at stake for the spunky Circle City over the next few days, and to have a young autoist mangled by one of the very machines that everyone had come to celebrate would be something sure to get tongues a-clucking. If the papers played it as a random accident that was one thing; plenty of car wrecks made the pages of the town's four dailies each day, usually with too much information about heads sliced cleanly open and knees crushed to a papery translucence. But should the Littrell incident turn into some sentimental tabloid trope about how "Death had visited the race meeting even before the first cars were cranked up for competition" and so on, as it easily might—well, that no doubt would set off the biggest round of I-told-you-so's since the day in 1897 when the first automobile arrived in Indianapolis (it was a Benz, shipped from Germany) and, against much good advice, carriage maker Charles Black took it for a trial spin and promptly smashed a horse cart parked outside the Grand Hotel and two plate glass shopwindows on Washington Street. More than that, Littrell's death, should it occur, would provide political leverage to certain voices in the community who equated an auto racing track with the Seventh Circle of Hell, and wanted no such diabolical venue in Indianapolis.

WHILE SCIENTIFIC MARKET research was still in its infancy, it was clear from tavern-talk and newspaper stories that America was sharply divided on the subject of automobile racing. To put that controversy in context, let's recall first, though, that the nation just then was palpitating through the first torrid stages of a love affair with organized sports. Entrepreneurs and politicians had established that horse racing, boxing, and baseball—the three most popular pastimes in the first decade of the twentieth century—could, if presented properly, stir civic pride, keep young men out of trouble, and enliven the local economy. The relatively new games of football and basketball were meanwhile coming on strong as school sports. Indiana, for its part, already had thriving men's and women's basketball leagues that mixed college and YMCA (and YWCA) teams, and a baseball club, the Indianapolis Indians, who in 1909 were the reigning champs of the American Association, eclipsing their cross-state rivals, the Muncie Fruit Jars. But Indianapolis— twenty-third on the list of American cities in terms of economic clout, and hell-bent on cracking the top ten—badly needed what today would be called a marquee event to attract out-of-towners and help the city overcome its image as a burg somehow both sleazy and dull.

Earlier that year, Mayor Charles A. Bookwalter, borrowing from the writings of Saint Paul, had ordered the proud phrase "I am a citizen of no mean city" inscribed on the cornerstone of the new city hall. Bookwalter, a practical politician known for his tolerance of downtown gin mills, whorehouses, and gambling dens, was also a strong believer in sports as a tool of urban advancement; a former president of the American Bowling Congress, Bookwalter had brought the titans of tenpins to Indianapolis for the ABC Tournament in 1903, and the event had attracted a fair-sized "family" audience to Tomlinson Hall. For those looking to burnish the city's reputation as a place where Big Things happened, and crowds flocked, sports was obviously one way to go. But was an *automobile speedway* really the project around which the good citizens of Indianapolis wanted to rally?

Was auto racing, for that matter, really even a *sport*?

It was a fair question.

A large problem with auto racing for many people (then and now) was that machines, not athletes, provided the muscle and the quickness. A short stroll through the pit area at, say, the one-mile Indiana State Fairgrounds track, where car races in Indianapolis had previously occurred, could have told you that most professional autoists were not athletes in the conventional sense of the term. A star driver like Ralph DePalma believed in calisthenics, a balanced diet, and abstaining from alcohol while preparing for a race (he sometimes consumed nothing but bread and milk for several days before a competition), but DePalma was a singular driver in any number of ways. In terms of personal habits and physical presence, the cherubic, cigar-chomping Barney Oldfield and the ungainly, pear-shaped Louis Chevrolet were more the norm for race car men—though the point is really that there was no norm.

Which was absolutely fine for many fans for whom the cars were sexy and interesting enough to compensate for any failure on the part of the drivers to resemble Greek deities. Americans at that moment were poised on the edge of a historic domestic decision. Or maybe "poised" isn't the right word for a multitude in an emotional roil over the question of when to finally bid adieu to Old Dobbin and take the plunge into the motor age, to convert the old stable into a garage. Differentiating among the mind-boggling number of auto makes was difficult but key for those for whom a car might be the largest financial commitment they would ever make. Racing—which put the latest products to the test and let the chips (as well as the drive chains and connecting rods) fall where they may—was one good way of getting the information people sorely needed, the closest thing a car shopper had in those days to *Consumer Reports.* Leading manufacturers favored the practice, too, because they felt that it got clutched customers off the dime. As Henry Ford himself said, "The way to sell cars is to race them."

And yet there were severe limits on what one could glean from the racing game. After almost fifteen years of fitful evolution, auto racing in 1909 remained an inchoate muddle, capable of yielding few hard truths. As an attraction at fairs and horse tracks it sometimes worked, and sometimes failed miserably to pull in fans. Even its staunchest backers admitted that the sport—or whatever it was—suffered from a lack of structure: it had no dependable schedule, no regular season, no annual rallying point unless you counted the Vanderbilt Cup, a road race far out on Long Island—and no clear and consistent rules about how much you could soup up your supposedly stock vehicle. Statistics were kept haphazardly if at all, and the timing and charting of events was often highly subjective when it wasn't utter chaos. Gimmicks were often the order of the day, with promoters staging races in which drivers picked up and dropped off female passengers, or tried to see how far they could go in twenty-four hours of constant circling; in 1908 a Brooklyn-born choirmaster named Ralph Mulford emerged as the steely-bunned king of these round-the-clock marathon grinds. But a lot of what was called auto racing then was really just barnstorming, a distant cousin of vaudeville in which a field of five or six drivers would tour the country, staging what was essentially a fixed race at every stop. "Fixed" in this context, however, does not suggest something entirely predictable or in full working order. Just because it wasn't difficult to guess the intended winner of an event billed as "Barney Oldfield and His Traveling All Stars" didn't mean that tires, gears, centrifugal force, and fate wouldn't conspire to produce a bloody or even deadly day at the races.

Which was, of course, why a lot of people came to the auto races. Not to see death, exactly, in most cases—but to spend some time luxuriating in its titillating possibility.

IT WOULD BE difficult to exaggerate the dangerousness of racing in a vintage 1909 automobile. "A man prominently identified with motor racing said that he would as soon ask a man to stand against a wall and be shot at with a Winchester as ask him to drive in a track race," said an editorial in the *Detroit Daily News* in 1909. Explosive tire blowouts were common, oil leakage routine, and so you often had cars careening out of control on a well-lubricated surface. Vehicles frequently flipped over, or "turned turtle" as they said in those days, usually crushing the driver and "riding mechanicians" (the term didn't shed its vestigial syllable until about 1912), poor souls—or total idiots, or immoral thrill seekers, depending on your point of view—who had no seat belts, roofs, roll bars, or hard helmets to protect them. Nor were the drivers' and RMs' chances much better when, following a collision or blowout, they flew from their seats and sailed into walls, trees, fences, buildings, infield ponds, or seas of startled onlookers. No one kept stats on deadly racing wrecks, but they occurred so often that drivers sometimes took up a collection the night before an event for the next day's newly minted widows, whoever they might turn out to be. Some bookmakers offered propositions that allowed you to bet on a particular driver to win, live, or die. (Wagers were seldom accepted on the fate of riding mechanicians, who, for all practical purposes, didn't count; though killed at a significantly greater rate than the drivers—who at least had the steering wheel to hang on to when things got hairy—RMs often went unnamed in newspaper accounts of their own demise.)

Because of all the carnage racing produced, a good many people thought the sport-not-a-sport debate missed the point, and that car competitions ought simply to be declared illegal. Some towns formally banned auto racing, while elsewhere mobs reminiscent of the torch-bearing villagers in *Frankenstein* chased touring drivers and their crew-members out of town. More than a few localities went so far as to hire a professional rainmaker, hoping he could create a cloudburst on race day that would force a possibly life-saving cancellation. A man named Ned Broadwell made a handsome living in the Midwest in the early 1900s both by trying to cause rainouts at race meets and accepting bribes from auto racing promoters to get lost.

THE ANTI-RACING FORCES in Indianapolis had spoken out strongly after Carl Fisher announced, in the winter of 1908, that he and his partners would begin construction of the Indianapolis Motor Parkway, and Mayor Bookwalter had heard them out—and then gone about the business of helping the founders of the Speedway, as it would be retitled after a few months, get the necessary approvals and permits. By the spring of '09, all seemed to be going well at the construction site, or so the press releases said. The track would open as scheduled on June 5 of that year, Bookwalter proudly told whoever would listen, and soon the world would know, he was sure, that auto racing, if packaged and presented properly, could be an exciting but safe and decidedly high-class endeavor every bit as worthy of public acceptance as the Sport of Kings, America's Pastime, or the Manly Art of Self-Defense. And this, the mayor felt, besides being a triumph in itself, would help Indianapolis establish a reputation as the Car Capital of the U.S.A.

But the optimistic projections of Bookwalter—who was perhaps still feeling exhilarated from the injection of campaign funds he had received from the Speedway's backers—were one thing. The true facts told a different, more sobering, tale.

For Fisher and his three co-founders—Arthur Newby, James Allison, and Frank Wheeler—launching the Indianapolis Motor Speedway was proving to be much less fun than they had imagined when, with a clink of highball glasses, they kicked in a total of $250,000 to buy 320 acres of what had been the old Pressley farm (no relation, but the owner did have a daughter named Elva) the year before. Back then the affluent amigos saw the Speedway as a mere sideline to their regular endeavors, a valuable addition to the community and the Indiana auto industry, to be sure, but also an amusing, high-profile way of flexing their celebrated Midas touches. Almost immediately, though, their lark had turned into a bear of a project and they had found themselves mired in quotidian but crucial issues relating to racetrack construction—most notably, the problem of getting a sufficient quantity of the particular kind of gleaming white stones that their chief engineer had chosen for the racing surface. They needed 90,000 cubic yards to cover the planned 60-foot-wide, two-and-a-half-mile-long course, and, because the surface was what would elevate the Speedway above the cindery, poorly graded horse tracks that autoists hitherto had been racing on—and thus be the key component in allowing a sometimes primitive spectacle to be presented as civilized sport—Fisher had spent the winter and spring of '09 identifying, visiting, and striking deals with eighteen different firms in and around Indiana that stocked that particular grade and shade of gravel.

The Speedway, in general, had necessitated much more day-to-day decision making and hands-on managing of people and resources than the partners had anticipated. Seven days a week for five months, five hundred men and three hundred mules had toiled long hours, hauling in thousands of wagonloads of track bedding and surfacing material. The same workforce also had built a twelve-thousand-seat grandstand and forty-two other structures including cafés, clubhouses, refreshment stands, judges' booths, restrooms, and a press shack from which the word could go forth about the wonders of the Indianapolis Motor Speedway, America's answer to the year-old but already famous Brooklands course in Surrey, England, the first built-for-auto-racing venue in the world.

Throughout the construction period, the word did go out relentlessly and at times weirdly, thanks to publicity chief Ernest A. Moross, a tall, lean former bicycle racer whose official title at the Speedway was director of contests. While composing propaganda pieces for various newspapers—publicists often published under their own bylines in those days—Moross maintained an unvarying regimen: he would roll a sheet of paper into his typewriter, light a cigarette, then allow himself to be transported to the land of purple prose. In the *Indianapolis Star* of August 14, 1909, he promised "Competition such as been dreamed of will be witnessed when cars representing almost every country in the world will whirl by piloted by demons of speed and unrest." Hyping the infelicitously titled Wheeler-Schebler race, which was named after a carburetor company owned in part by Speedway founder Frank Wheeler, he called it "a battle of giants at which the pygmies will be torn in twain as if by mountain chains." In Moross's defense, no one knew just how receptive the citizens of Indianapolis would be to the idea of auto racing at the Speedway, so it made sense, in a way, to go with the hard sell and err on the side of shredded pygmies. (By the same logic, he could also be forgiven for asserting elsewhere that "the town was booked up solid" for the race meet, although "many fine accommodations" remained available.) But Moross, like Fisher, may simply have been burnt out by mid-August of '09, having spent the last few months tied to his desk as if by mountain chains, working like a demon of unrest. The man was exaggerating, spinning, and outright fibbing as fast as he could, doing heavy-duty damage control in the wake of two shakedown events that had caused flop sweat to blossom across a number of prominent brows.

IT WOULD BE difficult to designate the bigger of the two disasters that preceded the Speedway's first auto racing meet, though the more colossally boring was clearly the hot-air balloon races, held on the unseasonably sultry Saturday of June 5. This should not have surprised anyone, really, since competitive gasbagging had been on the downslide since the late eighteenth century, when the invention of the passenger balloon by the Montgolfier brothers of Annonay, France, had ignited an all too brief vogue for joining the Mile-High Club. But Fisher, though born poor, had a collection of eccentric-rich-guy passions, one of which involved the vehicles he liked to call "cloud racers." The previous October he had arranged for a 40,000 cubic foot balloon to carry one of his new-model Stoddard-Daytons over Indianapolis — with him in the driver's seat. Fisher, perhaps the most successful auto dealer in the country that year, guessed that the stunt would generate more interest than signs or ads about the car's new state-of-the-art oil pump and "double ignition system," and he was correct. "Five thousand unbelieving people watched the start at the plant of the Indianapolis Gas Company," the *Star* reported, "and saw the automobile securely hitched to the balloon to take the place of the customary basket. . . . Cheers from the thousands and hats waved in the air marked the start of the flight . . . [and] more than 100 cameras held by persons in the crowd were snapped several times." The car hovered about a hundred feet above the downtown area for an hour and forty minutes before landing softly in Southport, about eight miles away. How much the stunt helped sales can never be known, but Fisher had such fun that he resolved to get a balloonist's license and compete in a race that his Speedway (then still in the dreaming stages) would one day present. "Carl Fisher holds license No. 17 for balloon pilots in America," his friend Will Rogers wrote in his syndicated newspaper column soon afterward. "I didn't know you could pilot one — I thought the wind did that."

Just as Will Rogers's jokes couldn't all be gems, Carl Fisher's aeronautical exploits weren't uniformly riveting. He had sold the idea of a balloon race to his fellow founders as a way to generate revenue without disrupting work on the track surface, which was at that late date still far from finished. (The balloonists would use only the infield, as a launching point.) Naturally, Fisher couldn't resist taking part in the competition: he and his "aeronautical advisor," Capt. George F. Bumbaugh, would travel in a large red balloon Fisher had christened the *Indiana.* But the event was a hard sell from the start. Although statistics showed ballooning to be about as dangerous as duckpins, Moross did his best to wring melodrama from the lives of the pilots. "Pathetic partings were exchanged between some of the men before they left their families," said a story he planted in the June 4 *Star.* "Wives and children feared to bid goodbye to the men because of the possibility of fatal damage in such a daring undertaking. Mrs. Lambert and Mrs. Honeywell both pleaded with their husbands in vain to restrain them from entering, according to reports by friends."

The day actually started out promisingly for the promoters: an estimated forty thousand pilgrims clogged the roads to the Speedway. Ultimately, however, only about 3,500 paid the 50-cent to one-dollar admission, the rest realizing that they could see just as well, if not better, reclining in pastures or perching on tree limbs just outside the grounds. Not that anyone saw much more than nine huge balloons slowly disappearing into a scorching, featureless sky at the urging of their rather stodgy-looking pilots (a silk top hat tumbled sadly from the stratosphere as the modest throng began to disperse). It was all so very 1789, or at any rate so pre-1903, the year the Wright brothers made their historic powered flight at Kitty Hawk, and rendered ballooning a quaint curiosity. Prizes were to be awarded for distance traveled and hours spent aloft, but the results wouldn't be known for days, by which time the populace had long since moved on to other, more engaging matters, like, say, combing their hair and chopping celery. (Then and now, balloon races became interesting only when the contestants were blown over Southern states, where people shot at them.) Most people never noticed Fisher's claim that his *Indiana* had stayed aloft for a world-record 48 hours, 50 minutes—or that, after witnesses came forward to say they had seen him on the ground during that interval, he confessed that he and Bumbaugh had in fact landed periodically so he could "stretch my limbs and smoke a cigar."

Although Moross feigned amazement over the results of the balloon races, insisting they were an aesthetic and financial success beyond description (as so many things for him were) and speculating publicly about future air shows involving the Wright brothers and others, the communal yawn over the Speedway's inaugural event was more than a bit disconcerting to the founders and others concerned with the facility's fate. True, this wasn't the big midsummer auto racing meet, but the fact remained that the Indianapolis Motor Speedway had thrown open its gates with considerable fanfare, and few Hoosiers with four bits in their pocket had seemed to give a hoot.

2

NEXT UP ON the Speedway's agenda: motorcycles!

In theory it was a smart idea to have one more preliminary event before the place opened "for real" on August 18, for all the crowd control, food service, and plumbing-related reasons a casual observer might imagine. In practice, however, the two-day motorcycle meet scheduled for August 13 and 14 was good news only for Carl Fisher's scotch supplier. The central problem was that, unlike balloonists, motorcycle racers need a track on which to conduct their noisy business. And if you define a track as a firm, smooth, and stable surface over which vehicles can move easily, then that's not something that the Indianapolis Motor Speedway had with only a few days to go before its official launch date. As the members of the Federation of American Motorcyclists poured into Indianapolis for what was for them an event of historic magnitude, this failing weighed heavily on the minds and livers of the already beleaguered Founding Four.

The vehicles overseen by the FAM were essentially motorcycles as we know them today—two-wheeled motorized bikes—but ridden by men who were clearly not the spiritual forebears of the Hells Angels. While they liked to rev up their lightweight, 5 to 7 horsepower Indians, Harley-Davidsons, and Flying Merkels and tear around a track, the men of the FAM stood for sportsmanship, camaraderie, and safety first. A highly social lot, they tended to enjoy having banquets, making speeches, and presenting plaques and trophies to one another almost as much as racing, or so it seemed. When the FAM agreed to hold its seventh annual national convention in Indianapolis in conjunction with the motorcycle meet, the town fathers knew just how to welcome the five hundred not-so-wild-ones: they draped the downtown in red, white, and blue bunting and scheduled four days of parades, photo opportunities, and lemonade luncheons. Jake DeRosier, the almost jockey-size thirty-year-old "world champion motorcyclist" (a title that seems to have been bestowed upon him by Moross), was feted as if he were Enrico Caruso, the racehorse Dan Patch, or one of the other superstars of the day.

But if the members of the FAM aren't smiling in any of the photographs taken during those gala pre-meet festivities—and they don't appear to be—there is ample reason. An advance party from the organization, while attempting to hold an impromptu practice session at the Speedway on Friday, August 6, had discovered the place's scary little secret: although the grandstand and other structures appeared ready and even eager for action in their crisp green and white trim, the course itself was an unmade bed of dirt, rocks, and taroid (a mix of pitch and oil).

It was clear at that point to even the founders themselves that they had tried to do way too much far too quickly. They had given themselves only five months to build their Speedway and their original plan had called for a rectangular outer track of two and a half miles surrounding an equally long "road course" that would snake its way irregularly through the infield and connect with the rectangle at the top of the homestretch, near turn four. But all hope of finishing the road course by mid-August had been abandoned by early summer, and the day the FAM folks arrived they saw that Fisher's tendency to think too grandly extended to the main course as well.

The track as conceived by engineer Park Taliaferro Andrew was an elaborate—and unprecedented—parfait: two inches of large gray gravel laid upon the natural red-clay soil of Marion County, followed by two inches of limestone covered with taroid, followed by two more inches of slightly smaller, taroid-drenched gravel, topped off with another two inches of the dry white stones Fisher had spent so much time procuring, each layer being steamrollered repeatedly to pack it down hard. Andrew had claimed that for a price less than asphalt, macadam, or brick, this unique method provided a course that was faster, easier on cars, and more durable than the concrete track at Brooklands, which reportedly had begun crumbling in places after just a few months' use. After looking over the plans, Fisher had granted his enthusiastic approval. It would be "like solid rock," Moross assured the press, and "as smooth as a floor."

Andrew also claimed that the Speedway surface would be much safer than the road courses and the horse tracks the drivers were accustomed to because his method supposedly eliminated dust. It was "the fatal dust," wrote Moross, which was "so rapidly decimating the number of skilled pilots," sending them "embalmed and battered into speed oblivion." Translation: dust—or the grit or cinders blown by the wind or kicked up by the cars in front of you—became a potentially deadly factor as one reached racing speeds of 60 to 80 miles per hour. In an age when drivers (and their riding mechanicians) sat high off the ground in windshield-less cockpits, insidious racetrack dust could rip a man's face to bloody ribbons, crack or work its way around the edges of his goggles, and invade his eyes, blinding him to slow-moving or broken-down vehicles ahead. More than a few spectators could tell tales of witnessing fatal wrecks in which drivers plowed at full speed into disabled cars that the fans could see clearly from their 50-cent seats in the grandstand. When, as sometimes happened, a worried mother beseeched a race organizer to bar her speed-crazy son from driving, it was, whether she knew it or not, dust, and not a scalding steel engine, a blown tire, or the battle-scarred (and sometimes bloodstained) wall around some poorly graded racetrack curve that was her darling boy's deadliest enemy.

But effective though the gravel-and-taroid technique might (or might not) have been, it took a long time to install such a track—more days (it would later become apparent) than the founders had remaining on their schedule. Motorcycle practice on August 6 was out of the question, and a spokesman for the FAM informed Fisher that the race meeting nine days hence would most likely need to be canceled. Fisher knew they weren't negotiating, just stating a fact. He could see the fear in their eyes (the cyclists usually raced on hard-packed sand beaches or smooth little wooden velodromes they inherited after the 1890s bicycle racing boom fizzled) and they could see the fear in his (the Speedway had been counting on fifty thousand paying customers for the two days of motorcycle competition, and the FAM's refusal to race could make the American Automobile Association think twice about sanctioning the automobile meet scheduled for the following week).

Fisher may have been quaking in the odd, self-designed patent leather strap-on slippers he favored for most occasions (he liked to keep his feet well ventilated, he said, even in winter)—but he didn't have much choice about a course of action. Rather than argue with the motorcyclists, he employed the sort of diplomatic skills he didn't always exhibit when dealing with various authority figures around Indianapolis and his often disgruntled girlfriends (he was sued for breach of promise ten times). Visiting the leaders of the FAM in their suite at the Dennison Hotel, he forthrightly acknowledged the sad state of the Speedway, and promised, as one of the principal owners of Prest-O-Lite, a company that made acetylene headlamps for motorized vehicles, that work would continue around the clock, thanks to one hundred gas-powered lanterns that he would have hauled in and placed at strategic intervals along the course. "The Speedway will positively be in finished condition and ready for record time," he announced, through Moross, to the local papers.

All the wattage in the world wouldn't have helped, though, because no amount of tamping and steamrolling could get the sundry components of the track to cohere. The night before the Friday the 13th opening of the motorcycle meet, FAM officials, on their way back to their headquarters at the Dennison from a (Fisher-arranged) outing to attend a vaudeville show at the German House, fell into a discussion about whether they ought to consider moving their races to the track at the Indiana State Fairgrounds, the very venue that the Speedway was supposed to supersede. It was hardly an outrageous notion, given that in practice runs the track kept breaking away under the motorcyclists' tires, and that some members of the grounds crew were predicting that the annual plague of snails that hit the Pressley farm about that time each year was fixing to erupt, adding a stratum of snail-slime to the taroid-and-gravel mixture. Still, when a *Star* reporter staking out the hotel got wind of their thinking, and reached Fisher by telephone for a reaction, he continued to insist that everything would be fine by race time, and refused to consider canceling. Just that afternoon, Fisher noted, the acclaimed motorcyclist Ed Lingenfelder had gone twenty-five miles around the Speedway in twenty-five minutes and reported no problems (at least not formally). "We have double the force of men working day and night smoothing out the remaining defects," Fisher said in a written statement that had scant truth but more than a little Moross in it. "There is no reason why records cannot be broken. The races on the track tomorrow will demonstrate the truth of this assertion, as the practices have already done."

Fisher's statements about Lingenfelder were accurate as far as they went. But he neglected to mention several things: that the motorcyclist's time that day was a full *five minutes* slower than DeRosier's record for the same distance; that afterward Lingenfelder had stalked off the course, saying it was far too abrasive for motorcycle tires—and that other cyclists had complained that day that the roughness made it impossible for them to hold on to their handlebars. These omissions show that Fisher knew how dangerous his course was, but chose to push forward anyway. Like other unfettered capitalists of that era, he could be careless with other people's lives.

Fortunately for all concerned, a steady, light rain fell on Friday morning, and Fisher jumped at the excuse to postpone the first day's racing until Saturday, and shift the second day's card to Monday afternoon (racing was prohibited on Sundays). As a gesture of peace, and a means of keeping the FAM executives away from the still bustling construction site, Fisher invited his already well-wined-and-dined guests to a boxing smoker on Friday night in West Lafayette. As the group watched Colored Jimmy Backburn outpoint Young Tholman, Young Cohen draw with Young Forbes, and Indiana featherweight champ Young Donnelly defeat the amazingly neither colored nor young Frank Edler, they puffed on cigars with a custom FAM band that Fisher had passed out with an only slightly too wide smile.

■ ■ ■

SOMETIMES A CIGAR is just a cigar, but at the Speedway on Saturday dozens of "brawny young men" who were "stripped to the waist" because of the intense heat "swung heavy mallets" and tamped down gravel with "thick beams" while others sat astride "champing motorcycles," waiting for the competition to start. The scene as described by the Indianapolis dailies sounds like Christopher Street of a summer evening. Not everyone was feeling macho, though, especially after what happened to one of the first men to go out for a practice run. At just past noon, Albert Gibney, a twenty-three-year-old motorcycle cop on the Indianapolis police force who had entered himself in an amateur event, was taking a turn at about 60 miles per hour on his Reading Standard (not his work bike) when he lost control, flew off, and rolled some 200 feet over the moonscape passing as a racing track. The local papers waxed waggish about the irony, describing Patrolman Gibney as "bogey of the speed fiends of the city" and "the bane of scorchers [speeders]." The *Star* said little about his extensive internal injuries and painful lacerations (he would be hospitalized for six weeks) while breezily noting that he had been "temporarily laid up for repairs." Coverage of Gibney's accident also revealed just how blasé—or naive—many people in those days were about motor sports: the *Indianapolis Sun*, noting that Gibney was hand-pumping oil into his engine (a necessity in those days) as he took the turn, described the procedure as "a process which requires no slackening of speed, but which does require the use of one hand."

After Gibney went down, many riders, already worried about the roughness of the track, and the surprisingly timid banking on the Speedway turns, muttered among themselves that they wouldn't start— or if they did they wouldn't push themselves or their bikes very hard. Some Speedway officials confronted the grousers and called them "yellow," the papers said, but quite a few motorcyclists proved as good as their word: only nine of thirteen entrants came to the wire for the first race, ten of twenty-nine in the second, nine of fifteen in the third, and so on; no accidents had occurred to that point, but neither had anyone gone close to a record time despite the unusually long course on which they were racing. When track maintenance work caused a forty-five-minute delay after the fourth race, a large percentage of the crowd—

which had reached only about 3,500 at its peak (not even many snails showed up)—went home.

Those who left early missed the Kodak moment when exactly no riders came out for the sixth race, which was supposed to be the afternoon's feature event, a 10-miler for the top pros. Some of the remaining fans booed. Storming into the pits, Fisher called upon the racers to consider the paying public, or what was left of it, and when that didn't work he scratched his chin for a moment or two, then proposed a 10-mile match race pitting the Champion of the West, Lingenfelder (he was champion of nothing and a native of Chicago but was living in Los Angeles at the time), against DeRosier, a French Canadian who had moved to Massachusetts and thus qualified as Champion of the East (as well as, in Moross's opinion, the world). Before those two could say yes or no a band was playing patriotic marches and Moross was standing before the grandstand with his megaphone held aloft, declaiming their names and some partially true facts about them in the direction of scattered weenie vendors—since the heavily German population of Indianapolis called hot dogs "weenies" in those days—and mostly empty seats.

As sorry as the scene was, being chosen for single combat appealed to the riders' egos. Lingenfelder, who had been already dressed in his trademark all-white racing togs, rode out proudly; DeRosier also cut an impressive figure, wearing bright red tights and a jersey with an American flag sewn to the back. At Lingenfelder's request, an assistant had tied his feet to the cranking pedals of his German-made NSU motorcycle, a terribly risky tactic that ensured he'd stay attached to the machine despite the bumpy surface, but which left him with no chance to bail out.

Clearly the so-called Western Champ was bent on winning—he got off aggressively and was holding a lead of about one motorcycle length after the first lap. But they were going far too fast for DeRosier's taste. As the two swept down the backstretch for the second time, the Eastern Champ pulled his Indian within shouting distance of Lingenfelder and urged him "for God's sake take it easy." Lingenfelder responded by lowering his chest against the handlebars, gunning his engine, and pulling away. He was still lengthening his lead when, as they came around turn four and passed under the pedestrian bridge about 250 yards from the grandstand, DeRosier's front tire blew to pieces, and a chunk of it got lodged in his cycle's front fork. The bike bucked like a mustang, and he flew onto the track and slid, on his flag-draped back, almost a hundred feet over sharp gravel behind his snarling, slithering machine. Lingenfelder said later that he could hear his opponent's screams above their cycles' combined roar.

DeRosier would survive, albeit barely (to die in another wreck at another track a few years later). But some of the spectators were traumatized by the violence they had witnessed at such close range, and had to be led to the Speedway's hospital tent for sherry and talk therapy. The program ended shortly thereafter, with the pathetic announcement that not just the rest of that day's card but also Monday's slate of races had been canceled.

3

Competition is indispensable to progress.

—JOHN STUART MILL

JAKE DEROSIER WAS still in the hospital, and still hemorrhaging, the morning that Cliff Littrell went down at the intersection of Capitol and Vermont. But though it had been less than a week since the FAM meet came to its inglorious ending, no one was talking about DeRosier or any of the other motorcyclists anymore, just as people around Indianapolis had largely neglected to check the sports page agate type for results of the balloon races a few days after they transpired so vaporously back in June. It was almost as if the evil genius Moross had pulled off a mind-wipe of the populace, allowing the Speedway to launch a fresh propaganda campaign each time it presented a different sort of show.

But that is giving the empurpled publicist far too much credit. As common sense will tell you, and as the Speedway's early paid attendance figures clearly demonstrated, not all kinds of racing have an equal pull on the public, and some, *pace* those tens of thousands who stole a peek at the balloons from surrounding farmland, hold almost no appeal at all. As they met most mornings around their table at Pop Haynes's restaurant on North Pennsylvania Street, the founders may have expressed grave concern about the impending opening, they may have signaled for a little gin in their tomato juice, but the public did not sense the weight of their concerns. Rather than seeing the

Speedway as having stumbled out of the starting gate, most people, if they thought anything at all about the venture, assumed that it hadn't really begun in earnest yet.

Automobile racing, everyone understood, was the endeavor that would decide the place's fate. As a business, auto racing, as we have already seen, was no sure thing in 1909, but any reasonable observer would have called it a decent bet—a new and glamorous and controversial sport (let us call it) with considerable upside potential. If Fisher and his fellow founders could harness civic spirit, whip up curiosity about the state-of-the-art cars and the colorful characters who drove them, and trade on the potent idea of danger while minimizing actual carnage—well, then, their Speedway would almost certainly flourish. And that would do much more than make four rich men richer and give the sports-minded citizenry an occasional alternative to boxing matches, basketball tournaments, and baseball games: it would ensure that Indiana's four-hundred-odd auto manufacturers had something that no other state yet had in an age when consecutive miles of paved road were still difficult to come by—a decent testing ground for cars. That, in turn, could help Indianapolis elbow aside Detroit and become the motor capital of America. All this and a few hundred jobs depended on the success of the Speedway, whose founders needed most immediately to keep optimism alive by shifting the focus away from their still unstable racing surface—and, now, the broken body of Littrell.

So far so good. The positive part of their plan—the selling of auto racing as the Next Big Thing—had begun months before, and, in contrast to the track work, it was proceeding apace. By midsummer, Moross (a much better schmoozer than writer) had bonded with practically every journalist in town over "Scotch highs" and mint juleps. Eager to give the scriveners something to write about besides gravel and taroid, he took them for spins around the Speedway, steering artfully to avoid the more bone-jarring stretches. One day he issued a quite modern-seeming "tale of the tape"–type fact sheet concerning the brand-new but somehow already "prestigious" Wheeler-Schebler trophy, noting that it was eight feet tall, made of sterling silver, estimated to weigh 500 pounds troy weight, designed by Tiffany, and valued at $10,000 (though contemporary Speedway documents show it cost

$8,600). On another occasion he announced that President William Howard Taft had been invited to attend the automobile races on opening day. (Taft was known to be a bit of a car nut, at least compared to his predecessor, Theodore Roosevelt, who still had a "No Automobiles Allowed" sign on the front gate of his home in Oyster Bay, Long Island.) The White House failed to RSVP, but that didn't matter. The overriding message was that auto racing was no longer just a country-fair attraction, a hybrid of sport and sideshow designed to con the yokels. It was, or would soon be, classy, big-time stuff.

Moross was also prescient about the power of celebrity, a not yet widely understood concept; he had been Barney Oldfield's personal manager for several years, and had noted with interest how modern cosmopolitans gathered around the stage doors of vaudeville theaters just to see headliners like Houdini, Eddie Cantor, and Eva "That's Why They Call Me Tabasco" Tanguay come and go. This led him to conclude that there was hidden gold in the service pits in the form of battle-scarred men who had been out in the world learning about life, as opposed to spending long hours in a gymnasium juggling Indian clubs or tossing medicine balls, like the studiously conditioned stars of more conventional sports. Construction of the Speedway had barely started when he began bringing in luminaries from the auto racing world to beguile the local writers.

On a cold, gray day in early March of 1909, Moross introduced Lewis Strang to the Indianapolis press. Although his name, like those of virtually all the early drivers, has faded from public consciousness, Strang, twenty-four years old when he toured the Speedway's construction site, was one of the most famous—and flamboyant—racers of his day. He won a lot (the prestigious Briarcliff, New York, Savannah, Georgia, and Lowell, Massachusetts, road races) and wrecked a lot and seemed to live in a movie version of his own life, full of mayhem but devoid of dire consequences. He could veer off the course and mow down a fence, plowing through a crowd of "chauffeurs and tire people" and "knocking them high in the air" (as he did at Brighton Beach in 1907), but then, having caused no lasting damage (to himself at least), come back a day after a calamity "swathed in bandages" (as he did in 1909 in Chattanooga, following an injury at Birmingham) and drive "like a demon, though the dust was thick" to a roundly cheered victory. (Unattributed quotes here and elsewhere are taken from contemporary newspaper or automobile trade journal accounts.) That same night, to cap off an already good story, he might get pulled over for speeding in some far-flung hick town—or be seen smooching with his wife-to-be, the naughty Ziegfeld Follies siren Louise Alexander.

Strang was short and feisty with a kind of up-from-the-gutter elegance, a precursor to James Cagney. Raised by his widowed mother in a tenement in Manhattan's seedy, muddy Longacre Square (soon to become Times Square), he dropped out of school early and was working as a stenographer at the age of fifteen. Strang was among the few drivers of that era who did not begin his racing career on a bicycle, but instead went directly into cars, taking a job as a chauffeur with H. O. Havemeyer, the rapacious "Sugar King," in 1905 and two years later signing on as a mechanic with his uncle Walter Christie, later to be known for his brilliance as a designer of tanks for the Russian and British armies. (After he had made his fortune, Christie observed, "It is no shame to be poor, but it is damn inconvenient.") Christie at that time was campaigning a controversial "Freak Racer" that had two engines, giving it front- *and* rear-wheel drive; it was doubly powerful and, in the opinion of some, doubly dangerous—essentially a very fast tank. The Freak, or Double-Ender, would sometimes be disqualified at the starting line at events where the much discussed rule requiring all cars to be "stock"— that is, virtually identical to models that the public could purchase—was enforced more rigidly (it was not sold in any showroom).

But Strang, who had quickly worked his way from the mechanician's to the driver's seat, won enough races with the oversized auto, in the U.S. and Europe, to make himself one of the top names on the makeshift racing circuit. He soon found it necessary never to leave home without a pocketful of coins, which, when a crowd gathered around him, he would toss in the air, creating a diversion, as his fans scrambled for the money, that allowed him to make an escape. Sometime in early 1908, at a Broadway nightspot, his burgeoning cloud of charisma bumped up against that of the hard-hearted, two-timing, and thoroughly irresistible Ms. Alexander. Thunder ensued.

The well-publicized courtship of Strang and Alexander was tempestuous from the start, with him going back and forth on his vow to quit racing for her sake, and her standing him up at the altar at least once after their post-Broadway-curtain, 1:30 A.M. wedding had been announced in the *New York Times*—likely because she was still married to wealthy garmento Edward H. Lowe, aka the "Shirt King." Alexander, who was born Jennie Spaulding in Hartford, Kentucky, was in many ways typical of the women whom that first wave of race drivers fell for—only to discover that it was really just their cars they liked fast. Besides the Ziegfeld shows, in which she had relatively minor parts, Alexander seemed to specialize in the kind of roles that caused critics to assure readers that she was, despite initial appearances, not in fact nude but wearing flesh-colored tights; she may own the record for causing the term "flesh-colored tights" to appear in newsprint. Not long after she finally married Strang, Alexander was named in the divorce suit of the man with whom she was performing a sultry "vampire dance" in a Manhattan cabaret show. Meanwhile, during one of the periods when Strang had quit racing to attend to their troubled marriage, she ordered him to go back on the track and make enough money to buy her a player piano—which he did, but in a gesture that seemed designed to salvage his dignity, he insisted on calling it a "pianola."

One day when Strang was experimenting with aeronautics, as many drivers did back then, he tumbled out of a biplane as it was ascending, fell several dozen feet, and landed hard on his back, probably suffering a concussion. The first person to reach him as he lay dazed on the tarmac was a reporter who informed him that Alexander wanted a divorce so she could marry Joseph Pani, a Broadway restaurateur who claimed to have introduced broccoli to the U.S. (The credit or blame rightly belongs to Thomas Jefferson.) "Two knockouts together—this is the limit!" Strang supposedly said.

Even if his more extravagant marital woes still lay ahead of him on the day he came to Indianapolis, clad in a smartly cut navy blue overcoat and gray rolled-brim fedora, to meet the press, Strang was already an A-list star. That the Hoosier writers loved him was apparent the minute Moross brought him out. He dazzled them with his clothes, his stories of past exploits ("I drove my first lap like a real fiend," he said of the previous year's Briarcliff run. "I guess the others shut down in the fog but I kept on it and at one time nearly went over"), and his street-suave demeanor. When someone asked about his first accident he winked and said it was "in 1904 when I hit an elevated post on Third Avenue in New York." Strang the interlocutor displayed the same coolness he possessed in the driver's seat, an attitude that, according to at least one journalist, gave him an advantage over the "hot-blooded Latins"—by which was meant almost anyone from across the Atlantic.

When Strang asked Moross if he could see the "scale model" of the Speedway that management had placed near the Crawfordsville Pike (now 16th Street) entrance to stimulate public interest in the project, the press corps trotted along behind him for the long walk over, and a photographer snapped Strang bending a bit stiffly, hands on knees, pretending to inspect what is really not much more than an eight-foot-long chalk outline of the proposed course carved into the March mud. Viewed strictly in aesthetic terms, the photo is drab and static, the image of a man in well-shined shoes contemplating an oversized on-deck circle. Still, "The Vision," as it became known after it was published a few days later in the *Sun,* would stir hope and curiosity in the people of Indianapolis, and quickly become part of the Speedway iconography. (The photograph that ran in the *Sun* is slightly different from the one that most Indy buffs think of as "The Vision"; it shows Strang standing straight up.)

MOROSS'S PUBLICITY CAMPAIGN had been, then, alternately crude and cunning. He sometimes found himself preaching to the proverbial choir—car-loving folks who salivated at the thought of the spectacle Fisher and his pals were promising—and, just as often, fending off naysayers (and neigh-lovers) who predicted that anything to do with automobiles was bound to resolve in bloody doom. But what did all that add up to in terms of audience response? How much Cracker Jack needed to be laid in, how many ticket rippers taken on, how urgent was the need for the founders to start developing some crackerjack excuses in case the crowds were motorcycle-meeting size? Early in the summer, when it was becoming ever clearer that the center of the operation, the track itself, would not hold, Fisher grew pessimistic; at one point he canceled his plan to put a saloon in the grandstand, a sign that he was operating out of fear, and trying to be as inoffensive as possible, although, as we shall see, inoffensiveness was not his forte. A part of him may have hoped for a lackluster response, on the theory that the fewer witnesses to his disaster of a racing strip, the better; let the mobs come, he may have thought, when he was better prepared. No one could say for certain if Fisher was right to keep his expectations low—until the moment in mid-August when a white-gloved bellman walked across the lobby of the Claypool Hotel in downtown Indianapolis and slipped a demure "No Vacancy" sign in the front window. And then it was official: Fisher's long-nurtured dream of a robustly attended auto meet was, for better or worse, coming true.

Long a bellwether for Indianapolis business, the 495-room Claypool—which boasted "more bathtubs than any hotel in the country" and dishes washed by "the art of electricity"—declared itself sold out for August 19 through 21. Almost simultaneously, the *Sun* reported that "more than 200 homes have been booked to the limit of accommodations." The *Star* said "Indianapolis hotels have never been so thronged with business," and noted that one downtown hostelry was squeezing as many as seventeen people into a single room. "Interest in the races has spread over the country, and there will be thousands of people from out of the state here to witness the events. A constant stream of autoists arrived in the city yesterday and today hundreds are arriving on trains, foreshadowing one of the largest crowds that ever attended a western motor event."

Sales of tickets at the Speedway's downtown box office were said by the *Star* to be "very heavy." Railroads announced they were putting on extra cars (the entire 1,300-person Stoddard-Dayton workforce, and about four hundred others, were coming from Dayton alone); the St. Elmo Steak House (still doing business today in the name of the patron saint of sailors at the landlocked corner of Georgia and South Illinois) was laying in extra bottles of Hunter rye whiskey behind its tiger oak bar. Besides the mob from Dayton, the single biggest contingent—at least five hundred people—came from Chicago, where the *Tribune* had proclaimed that "the speedway itself is a marvel" packed with "space annihilating racing machines, panting and puffing, eager to start in the grim contest with Father Time." A "fox chase" of about sixty-five cars left the Loop at 4:00 A.M. on August 18, the lead machine, a National, carrying two hundred pounds of pink and white confetti that its occupants, the automotive writers Charles P. Root and Frank Trego, tossed to the winds as they made the 225-mile trek. "Apart from several punctures," said the *Star*, "the trip was made without mishap." It was 12:30 P.M. when the National and its "honking followers" (among them, driving a 1908 Oldsmobile, was fifteen-year-old Tommy Milton, a Minnesotan who would win the Indy 500 in 1921 and '23, becoming the race's first two-time winner) arrived at the bathtub-mad Claypool.

The auto industry's response to the Speedway had been equally enthusiastic; for months, the daily mails had brought completed entry forms from the racing game's elite. (For the most part it was the car companies, not individual owners, who campaigned vehicles in those days; drivers worked under contract, or as freelancers, or, in rare instances, as salaried employees of the manufacturers.) Strang, who drove for Buick, would of course compete at the big Indianapolis meet, as would Barney Oldfield (by far the most renowned driver of his day, as well as the most frequently disciplined). Also committed were the brilliant but ill-fated driver-designer Louis Chevrolet and the impossibly handsome Ralph DePalma, who because he was born in Apulia, Italy, was assumed by the auto racing writers to be a "spaghetti fiend." ("Ralph DePalma would rather beat Barney Oldfield than eat five straight spaghetti suppers!" declared the *Star*.) Oldfield, under contract to drive a National, would also be debuting his newly acquired 200 horsepower "Blitzen Benz," which had cost him $4,000, as well as tuning up the Cleveland-made Stearns car that would be driven in an amateur event by Gilbert Van Camp, grandson of the food magnate Frank and heir to the pork-and-beans fortune. Even Henry Ford, who lately had seemed to be waffling on his idea about the connection between racing cars and selling them, announced that he would be sending a lightweight experimental vehicle with two sets of oil and gasoline tanks, one for races of ten miles or fewer, another for longer events.

ON THE SWELTERING Sunday of August 15, 1909 — the day that Pius X became the first pope to ride in a car, traveling about 5 miles per hour in a primitive Mercedes Popemobile along the Appian Way—several hundred people, most coming back from church services in Indianapolis, stopped at the Speedway to watch the drivers circling the glittering white track on their practice runs. It was an interesting moment for the spectators, for before them passed the future of transportation, the promise of speed, ease, and personal freedom—while behind them three thousand hitching posts stood waiting for horses in the facility's parking lot.

It wasn't a bad show for free, a sort of motor sports equivalent of stumbling, fifty years later, into a loft in Greenwich Village where Monk and Coltrane were jamming. Here was Oldfield himself with a red, white, and blue National, the car manufactured by the Speedway's vice president, Arthur Newby; and there in the crimson Apperson Jack Rabbit was the thirty-three-year-old "Dean of American Drivers" Herb Lytle, who had been racing since 1895, but who had been sidelined for several months after showing just how great a daredevil he truly was by eating oysters in Toledo. Whether or not that small group of spectators felt, as the historian Henry Adams did while viewing the dynamos at the 1900 Paris Exhibition, that the "moral force" of the machine age could be experienced "much as the early Christians felt the Cross," they might have agreed with Adams, after watching Len Zengel rip off a lap in 2:02 in his huge gray Chadwick, that suddenly "the planet itself seemed less impressive in its old-fashioned, deliberate, annual or daily revolution."

It was still the familiar old world in at least one way, though: the race car drivers were all white men. And yet one (white) woman did take the measure of the track that day. Marie Chomol, an editor at the *Star*, had accepted Buick's offer to take a spin around the Speedway with "Wild" Bob Burman, and under the *nom de course* (*et plume*) of Betty Blythe she filed a first-person account that ran in the paper a few days later. The thrust of her piece was that riding in a race car was a lot less glamorous than it looked:

First you hold hard and guess if you will land on the biggest pile of rocks. You turn up a disgusted nose at the oil that rains from the machine and wraps you in a cloud. You try to find another foothold for the foot that you are sure the red-hot engine is burning to a cinder. You observe with deep distaste that your hand is reeking with nasty oil and you suspect that what is left of your face is likewise decorated. You find yourself inquiring sarcastically of the driver how he knows precisely where all the rough spots are.

Finally, swerving away from excess snark, she observed,

> I felt quite safe and at home with Mr. Burman at the wheel. There was some consolation in knowing that if anything happened to me it would also happen to him, and I was of the opinion that he was not anxious to have anything happen to him on the eve of the greatest motor races ever.

The greatest motor races ever. They hadn't transpired yet—but to the readers of the *Indianapolis Star* that's already what they were. Whether scholars can credit the fine hand of Moross, or just the momentum that often overcomes the hype-inclined media, as race week dawned the newspapers fell into line like Floradora Girls. "Great Auto Carnival!" trumpeted the *New York Tribune*. "Fastest Cars and Most Daring Drivers in the Country Will Compete," said the *New York Times*. "Eyes of Automobile Enthusiasts of Two Hemispheres on Indianapolis," noted the *Indianapolis News*.

Stories about the still troubled racing surface simply did not exist. Except for a line here and there about the track "not being perfect," and a picture and text block about the Speedway's ambulance corps, the advance coverage avoided any allusion to the unpleasant possibility of track-induced troubles. The hundreds of shirtless men still pouring gravel and pitch, still shoveling and tamping the top layer while race cars whizzed around them, the relentless parade of seething steamrollers—all that might as well have been invisible. "The stranger who visits Indianapolis may well imagine that the city is wrapped in the throes of speed mania," the *Star* said. It was only if she made her way into the deepest depths of the *Star*'s lengthy final pre–opening day puff piece that the careful reader might come upon this startling sentence, presented without context or explication:

"Carl G. Fisher yesterday made a statement to the effect that he wished it were possible to postpone the race meeting."

4

I'd rather be dead than dead broke.

—BARNEY OLDFIELD

NOT EVERYONE WHO came to Indianapolis for the big auto racing party in August of 1909 was going to get out alive. Any professional race car driver could have told you that and—this is where those men differed significantly from their coevals in other sports—*would* have told you that, or anything else you might want to know, if you had just walked up and asked his opinion. Drivers back then were the newspaperman's dream; they liked to talk, and they didn't give you any blah-blah about staying focused and taking it one race at a time. They were risk-prone, publicity-conscious (yet often heartbreakingly naive) young men unaffected by the peer pressure that often keeps team-sport athletes from expressing themselves in a candid and interesting manner—boxers on wheels. Of course, and also like boxers, some of their colorful personality traits could be attributed to head injuries they had sustained along the way. Told that he had only a few moments to live after his car turned turtle and crushed him on a road course near Kansas City, Ned Crane, who had never won a race in more than one hundred starts, propped himself up on one elbow and said, "Tell them the greatest driver of them all is dead!" But for whatever reason nothing was off limits with them, not even their personal lives. Talk about being good copy—they often *brought up* the subject of women and their latest woman troubles to anyone with a notebook hanging around the garages. A fundamentally different breed of sportsman than we know today, they were at once more macho and more delicate, crying if they were saddened or enraged, screaming if they were frightened or in pain, and passing out if they were extremely hot, hungry, or exhausted.

Although superstitious as a rule—in the Savannah Grand Prize race of 1908, the Italian Felice Nazzaro fastened a horseshoe to the floorboards of his Fiat, only to be passed on the final lap by teammate Louis Wagner, a Frenchman who had *two* horseshoes concealed under his seat—they often spoke publicly about their premonitions of disaster, and of their acceptance of death as a part of the racer's bargain. "One hardly knows why one takes such chances," sighed Ferenc Szisz, a Hungarian driver described by one sportswriter of the day as "that man of rapid name." "I guess it hasn't been my turn yet," the German Emil Stricker once said as he was being carried off a Long Island road course on a stretcher following an accident in which his car had jumped a ditch, cut down two adolescent trees, and collided with a fence, launching him and his mechanician thirty or so feet in the air. "When it is my time, I won't complain. Look, in every race somebody gets it."

That was not precisely true, of course. Someone did not die in every single automobile race. But the shadow of death hung over every starting line just as it did every bugle call to arms, and in a program such as the Speedway was presenting in its opening meet—more than a dozen races, with two at a distance of 250 miles or more—the odds were strongly against a fatality-free three days, even if you failed to take into consideration the unstable racing surface. This is why the more straitlaced members of the community felt so anxious in mid-August of 1909, why an ambulance corps was standing by in the Speedway's infield, and why John J. Blackwell, a local undertaker who held the position of county coroner, took what some saw as an unseemly interest in the Speedway proceedings.

Blackwell's behavior first came under question shortly after 2:30 A.M. on Thursday, August 19, when Cliff Littrell, after lingering for almost two days and even talking fairly lucidly to his sister at times, expired from his extensive internal injuries. So it goes. Before the family could be asked its wishes, indeed before Littrell's wife, Jesse, had even reached

Methodist Hospital, Coroner Blackwell had swooped in, held a hasty "inquest," dragooned a doctor into performing an autopsy at which he assisted, and sent the body along to his funeral home for processing prior to its return to Dayton. The job of county coroner was then a plum of the political patronage system, awarded with the understanding that the undertaker who held it would channel business in his own direction and benefit financially in that way. But the next day's *Star* raised the question of why an autopsy needed to be performed when it was possible, from observing the tread marks on the deceased's chest, to tell not just how he had died, but the make of the tire that had run him over and its degree of wear. Could the fact that Blackwell received $25 per autopsy have influenced his decision? The coroner huffily denied the suggestion, and said that he performed the autopsy because you just never know what you'll learn from such procedures.

And the lesson in this particular case? asked the admirably persistent *Star*.

The fifty-year-old Blackwell hemmed and dithered, then puffed himself up, and finally, showcasing the brogue he had retained from his boyhood in Ireland, said, "I learned that I was more than a bit surprised that this gentleman lived as long as he did."

INDIANAPOLIS AT THIS point was no pure little prairie haven. It is true that for many decades the Great Squirrel Invasion of 1822 (pretty simply explained: millions of them ran through town; to this day no one knows why) ranked as the most electrifying event to have occurred there, and that a Civil War soldier had confided to his diary that it was "the most boring place in the world." In the 1950s the comedian Herb Shriner used to tell a joke about an airline pilot getting on the speaker and saying, "We are now approaching Indianapolis, Indiana, where the local time is 1890." But the reality of the place has never been in sync with its reputation. The city known as "Nap Town" to the world-weary troupers of the B. F. Keith vaudeville circuit had become under the very practical Republican mayor Bookwalter something (to put it in Hoosier terms) less James Whitcomb Riley and more Theodore Dreiser.

Politics there "was no place for a timid man," wrote Sim Coy, the Democratic boss of Marion County; indeed, by the late 1800s the openly discussed price of a vote in Indianapolis was $10, according to historian John Bartlow Martin, and a bought man who didn't stay bought might find himself missing an arm or eye. As a hub for railroads and gas fields, and the men who worked on and in them, the city was also a logical locus for the sort of pleasure dens whose existence depended on bribes. In 1890, the U.S. Census Bureau noted, albeit without providing hard numbers, that Indianapolis had "nearly as many brothels as New York City," the most elegant of which was Queen Mab's, down near the train station, where, says Martin, "the girls were said to possess seminary educations and where champagne, not beer, was the standard drink."

Martin makes Indianapolis sound like a hygienic Hollywood take on the Wild West, but the city, viewed from other, probably more realistic, angles, seemed decadent in what today might be called a late–Weimar Republican sort of way. "Open-air brothels," as they were somewhat euphemistically known, blossomed in downtown alleyways, "gentlemen for hire" did a fast business in both sex and blackmail, and the town's most prominent citizen—Carl G. Fisher—gallivanted publicly with a blond beauty rumored to be barely fifteen years old. Whether or not Fisher realized it, Jane Watts was in fact a few years older than that, a generally more worldly woman than she let on. Still, in that eventful summer of '09, Fisher and Watts were a Midwestern roadshow version of Stanford White and the Girl in the Red Velvet Swing—a taboo-testing couple whose titillating, disturbing, somewhat out-of-control love affair perfectly mirrored the times.

We tend to look back on the early 1900s as an era of innocent and even slightly comic propriety, when women in corsets and men in straw boaters strode arm-in-arm down spotless sidewalks to a jaunty ragtime beat; when emotion was expressed with the twitching of a handlebar mustache or, at most, the flinging of a pie; and when every fifth storefront was a German butcher shop being exited by a dog dragging a line of sausage links. To those living through the first decades of the twentieth century, though, life was no Mack Sennett two-reeler. It was, rather, a strange and disquieting time, not just in Indianapolis, but throughout America and the Western world, an era when optimism mixed with fatalism as—thanks to first the steamship, then the railroad, then the automobile and the airplane—life kept getting faster and more nerve-racking.

The historian Barbara Tuchman has written:

> Man had entered the 19th Century using only his own and animal power, supplemented by that of wind and water, much as he had entered the 13th, or for that matter, the First. He entered the 20th with his capacities in transportation, communication, production, manufacturing and weaponry multiplied a thousandfold by the energy of machines. Industrial society gave man new powers and new scope while at the same time building up new pressures.

In his provocative and aptly titled 2008 study of the period, *The Vertigo Years*, Philipp Blom writes:

> Speed and exhilaration, anxiety and vertigo were recurrent themes of the years between 1900 and 1914, during which cities exploded in size and societies were transformed, mass production seized hold of everyday life, newspapers turned into media empires, cinema audiences were in the tens of millions, and globalization brought meat from New Zealand and grain from Canada to British dinner plates, decimating the incomes of the old landed classes and enabling the rise of new kinds of people: engineers, technocrats, city-dwellers.

To the French the nervous mood was a recurrence of the *mal du siècle* they'd endured at the start of the nineteenth century.

Besides the frightening new velocity of life, men had to deal with the rise of women—as fellow students, colleagues at work, and aspiring voters—the result being, says Blom, "an aggressive restatement of the old [masculine] values; never before had so many uniforms been seen on the street or so many duels fought, never before had there been so many classified advertisements for treatments allegedly curing 'male maladies' and 'weak nerves'; and never before had so many men complained of exhaustion and nervousness, and found themselves admitted to sanatoriums and even mental hospitals." In France during this period, the birthrate plummeted.

If Blom and Tuchman are correct, it is hardly surprising that the early race car drivers, men confronting the peculiar challenges of the Vertigo Years head-on, tended to range, on what might be called the Strung Scale, somewhere between "high" and "un." The driver Eddie Hearne, whose behavior had adhered to the usual masculine codes during his stint as a second-string quarterback at Notre Dame, was said to have sat in his car and "cried tears of rage" when he thought his pit crew was taking too long to change a tire. David Bruce-Brown, an heir to the Lorillard tobacco fortune, violently swung a tire iron at curious fans he felt had gathered too closely around him and his mechanician when they stopped to fix a flat during the 1909 Vanderbilt Cup race. Frenchman Victor Hémery, whose nickname was "The Surly One," was said by *Collier's* magazine to have thrown a "Gallic fit" after a careless smoker slightly damaged his beloved Darracq racer at a garage in Mineola, New York, in 1905.

When "Smiling" George Robertson wanted to communicate the idea "Go faster, please" to his crewmembers, he beat them with a monkey wrench. Robertson, it was said, also threw monkey wrenches at competitors who were coming up alongside and threatening to pass him in a race. While he admitted to the former charge, he denied the latter, saying once, as he grabbed a bucket of bolts that stood nearby, "*These* are what I throw at them. I might need my monkey wrench for something else, and these things are cheaper and just as good!" Flying hardware could blind or probably even kill a competitor, of course, and yet it's hard to think too poorly of Robertson, who once, when he had a comfortable lead late in the 1907 Lowell, Massachusetts, road race, made an unscheduled pit stop so he could dash into the grandstand and buy what he called "a delicious red-hot."

A few drivers—Nazzaro, Ray Harroun, and (sometimes) Strang among them—had a reputation as cool customers who, like horse racing jockeys, looked to the right and left when a race began, sizing up their competitors and making decisions about whether to go for the lead or hang back in the early going. But the majority were macho men who equated strategy with weakness, even femininity. "The flat-out, stand-on-it-and-turn-left charger," says Griffith Borgeson in his landmark *The Golden Age of the American Racing Car*, "is typically a

person of very strong, virile libido." Indeed, drivers almost by definition were unapologetic, balls-out frontrunners who couldn't control
the urge to gun to the lead as quickly as possible. "If I can keep cool
for the first three or four laps I'm all right," Hémery once said. "My
great fight is with myself. [He committed suicide in 1950.] It is a struggle to settle down to a steady pace at first and let overeager fellows do as
they please. If a car comes up behind me it is very hard for me to throttle the impulse to let my own car out. Likewise, when I see a car ahead,
I am mad until I pass it." The reader will remember that Dick Harroun,
when I visited him in Orlando, made the odd claim that his father was
"the first driver ever to use strategy in a race." That distinction certainly
doesn't go to the pride of Imlay City, Michigan, "Wild" Bob Burman,
who was unapologetic about his unwavering pedal-to-the-metal approach. "The car holds together and I win running wide open," he once
said. "Or it breaks and I lose."

AWAY FROM THE track, drivers didn't pace themselves very well, either.
Although they were on the whole shortish (fighter-pilot-size, we might
call them today) and a good number had neither money nor culture,
their profession, and the way they tended to carry themselves—stepping
out of a racer, they would fling off their dust-coated goggles, toss back
their racing scarf, and perhaps brush a squashed sparrow off their well-
tailored if oil-soaked lapel—infused them with a kind of screwball sex
appeal. As a result, as we have already seen in the case of Strang, they
often got in over their heads with women, causing themselves considerable anguish but providing sportswriters with a welter of worthy
plotlines. Louis Disbrow, who would drive in the first Indianapolis
500 and several Vanderbilt Cup races, beat a sordid double murder rap
after the bodies of his high-society girlfriend Sarah "Dimple" Lawrence
(a direct descendant of naval commander James "Don't give up the
ship!" Lawrence) and her apparent paramour Clarence Foster were
found floating in Tiana Bay, off Long Island, in 1902. After overcom-
ing a mountain of circumstantial evidence to gain an acquittal, Disbrow
may have felt invincible. He raced "like a demon," it was said, until his
late forties, promising all three of his wives that he would stop soon,
but not actually quitting until 1926, when, at the age of forty-eight, he

was declared dead — mistakenly but understandably — following a fiery smashup.

Drivers often swore before God and their local motor sports writer to stop (or win) in the name of love. In mid-May of 1911, the *Atlanta Constitution* reported that Harry Knight had promised to marry "the vivacious Hungarian actress Jennie Dollie," as soon as he won the first Indianapolis 500, then about two weeks hence. Several months later, however, after playing a hero's role in that race but finishing 30th, he told the same paper that he had "disposed of his big brown [Cole] race car" and quit driving at the request of "the beautiful Miss Madonna Wood, of Indianapolis," whose heart he had been "trying to race his way into for four years." Miss Wood said, with a giggle, that their wedding date was flexible, "depending on how lonely we get." They never married, though, and Knight was killed in a race at Columbus, Ohio, in 1912, while his fiancée — Margaret Doyle, of Cambridge City, Indiana — watched in horror.

Deadly wrecks had a way of cracking open drivers' private lives for public viewing. When Burman, who took pains to portray himself as an abstemious, nonsmoking Baptist, crashed his Peugeot and died on the road course at Corona, California, in 1916, a mysterious woman showed up at the hospital and, while Mrs. Burman was convulsed with grief, lifted a diamond pin, valued at $800 and presumed to be a good-luck charm, from an inside pocket of the deceased's jacket, her deftness suggesting that she possessed foreknowledge of the object's location. How shocking that a supposedly good Christian like Burman would believe in talismans. But how curious to learn that the woman, who was eventually noticed by Mrs. Burman, and apprehended, tearfully blamed her behavior on a certain ancient Egyptian, who she said had gained control of her mind and heart during a recent séance. Stuff like this just didn't happen to the Indianapolis Indians.

JUST WHO *WERE* these mysterious men who streamed into Indianapolis in the summer of '09 and, as the *Star* said, "chugged through the main thoroughfares with their monster automobiles in racing trim and throbbing with suppressed speed held in reserve"? A thorny question, that.

Somehow, after thousands of years of military history, it is easier to wrap one's mind around the idea of a job that requires facing death on a daily basis than it is to imagine putting on a clean shirt and tie (as many drivers did) and going off each day to be pelted with grit, oil, rocks, the better part of George Robertson's tool kit, and the occasional idiot member of a low-flying flock of birds. And all this for a salary of perhaps $50 a week, win or lose. How this peculiar subspecies of human fit into society in the eons before the advent of automobile racing, and what became of Early Driver-Man after the game grew saner and more corporate—these things scientists still do not know.

What we can say with some certainty, however, is that there were basically three types of drivers in those early years of the sport: the glamorous and gallant Europeans ("Not mere men," said *Motor Age*, "but descendants of heroes whose valor has made red the musty pages of history"); the rich Ivy League–ish boys looking for a few thrills before they settled behind a desk at the family business (David Bruce-Brown, Arthur Greiner, Spencer Wishart), and the scrappy working-class American kids desperate to avoid a life sentence at the farm or factory (Strang, Burman, Ralph Mulford).

Whatever their circumstances, the conventional wisdom had it that drivers were born and not made (though many also held that the best ones had honed their God-given talent by driving a big-city taxicab, an occupation then believed to cultivate the virtues of carefulness and patience). A good driver, said *Motor Age*, is "daring, yet conservative; he must be an excellent judge of pace [ha!], and he must know everything about the mechanical construction of the car he drives." More than anything, though, he had to be willing and able to endure tremendous physical pain and every other imaginable difficulty. "Steering those heavy cars was hard work and took a lot out of you," said the Canadian driver Ira Vail, who routinely went into longer races at 135 pounds and came out ten pounds lighter. "And the shock absorbers we had—they were Hartfords and worked like scissors—they didn't give you the soft ride that you get today on shocks. I'd come out of a race bruised, yes, and the heavier men took an awful beating. Some, like [Gaston] Chevrolet, had to wear corsets and bind themselves with tape." Eddie Miller said he was always "black and blue from tailbone to shoulders, and unable to breathe properly" by the time he saw the checkered flag.

It was just a guess, the born-not-made theory, but it sounded right: no one could teach a man how to keep going when his hands, despite gloves, were a sticky, stinging mass of broken blisters, and his eyes, despite goggles, watered and throbbed. Goggles were useful only until they were dusted or oiled over, or smashed by a stone, at which point they became a liability. "To care for their organs of sight, all drivers and mechanics had to seek medical treatment after the race," the German magazine *Rad-Welt* reported after the particularly rough 1908 Grand Prix in Dieppe, France. When a stone penetrated Christian Lautenschlager's lenses in that race, "the pieces of broken glass danced up and down in front of my eye inside the goggles" as he drove to victory. A similar inconvenience befell another driver in the Grand Prix, Victor Hémery; probably no one present ever forgot the sight of him pulling into the pits and dropping his head back so a doctor could remove "the larger shards" of glass from his left eye—then taking off again with blood running out from under the rims of his fresh goggles and into his elaborate mustache.

THE ULTIMATE CELEBRITY driver of the era, Berna Eli Oldfield, embodied elements from all three of the main feeder groups mentioned above. Barney Oldfield, as he was known no doubt even to cloistered nuns, came from the farm (in Wauseon, Ohio), had money (albeit from his own efforts, and only occasionally), and, while no debonair European, was an exotic creature constituting a culture all his own. Indeed, the odd words and phrases that crop up in his life story make it sound like a fairy tale: young Berna's first job was as a bellhop in the Boody House; he married a woman named Bessie Gooby, and when putting himself forward for an assignment, even later in life, he didn't say "I'm your man," he said "I'm your little huckleberry!" In an age when other men drove the No. 37 car, or the No. 22 or 15, he raced the 999, the Bullet, the Old Glory, the Blitzen Benz, the Golden Submarine, and the Green Dragon—saying, as he stepped into those meretricious machines, things like, "This chariot may kill me, but they will say afterwards that I was going like hell when she took me over the brink!" If he hadn't been so very bad when it came to ladies and liquor, Barney Oldfield would have been too good to be true.

Some people say of Oldfield, as some would say of Danica Patrick a hundred years later, that he got more attention than he deserved just because he stood out visually from the rest, and wasn't shy about the spotlight. It is true that "The Human Comet," as he was sometimes billed, was a pleasantly fat and often frazzled-looking figure bobbing in a sea of early-driver dapperness—as well as an unrepentant barnstormer whose traveling thrill show featured races against cars, horses, trains, track stars, and low-flying airplanes, almost all of them rigged. It is also accurate to say that whenever the American Automobile Association suspended him for competing in "outlaw" races or violating other rules he turned the punishment into publicity, usually before taking off on a tour of Mexico, where he was beyond the AAA's grouchy grasp. Still, the bulk of the evidence, both statistical and anecdotal, points to Old-field, who by 1904 had held every one-mile track record between one and 50 miles, as being the best driver of his time.

Oldfield had been a professional boxer ("The Toledo Terror") and a champion bicycle racer when he drove his first race car—his first car of any sort—in 1902. This was the 999, built by an aspiring auto manufacturer named Henry Ford with help from his partner-in-racing, yet another bicyclist named Tom Cooper, and several of their friends. Painted fire-engine red and named for the New York Central train that had made a record run between Manhattan and Chicago, the fearsome, no-frills 999 featured a four-cylinder 80 horsepower engine ("previously unheard of," Ford would later say) mounted on a big, stiff chassis. It was "built to speed, and speed alone," said *The Automobile and Motor Review*, and it demonstrated "how an automobile may be simplified by the leaving-off process." The first time Oldfield saw it he called it "a bedframe on wheels," and mocked Cooper for getting swept up in "the automobile fad."

It was not a pleasant car to drive. "The roar of those cylinders alone was enough to half kill a man," Ford admitted. Steering was accomplished awkwardly, with a tiller, not a wheel, because Ford thought it would be easier to see the position of the two-foot tiller bar in the dust-and-smoke storms that wreaked havoc in virtually every race, and thus to know whether or not the car was going straight. In addition, the vehicle's open crankcase ensured that the driver received a warm motor oil bath. After Ford took the 999 out for a few laps for the press in September of 1902, a reporter from the *Detroit Journal* observed, "His collar was yellow, his tie looked as though it had been cooked in lard, his shirt and clothes were spattered and smirched, while his face looked like a machinist's after 24 hours at his bench."

After driving it once or twice more, the thirty-nine-year-old Ford, who found himself nauseated by the sheer physical effort it took to keep the 999 on course, sold it to Cooper. Cooper, twenty-eight, drove it a couple of times, or rather tried to, and then—mindful that the car was entered the following week in a high-profile 5-mile race featuring Alexander Winton, the to-the-manor-born national champ, steering a sleek new car of his own design—called in his semi-crazy friend Oldfield, who said he was their little huckleberry. On the day of the so-called Manufacturer's Challenge Cup, at the one-mile trotting horse track in Grosse Pointe, Michigan, Oldfield, who had never driven anything more powerful than a motorized bicycle, shot immediately to the lead, skidded wildly around the turns, and came home the winner in what he would often call "the race that changed my life." That astounding victory—"Men were white-faced and breathless . . . women covered their eyes," said *The Automobile* magazine—did indeed make him a household name, but when, eight months later, he employed the 999 to break the vaunted mile-a-minute "barrier" at the state fairgrounds track in Indianapolis (at a race meeting promoted by Carl Fisher) he became something greater: a trailblazer for humankind, a bold adventurer who, having gone where no man had gone before, could now inform the masses (with the obvious aid of a ghostwriter) what it was like to travel at a speed of slightly more than 60 miles per hour:

> You have every sensation of being hurled through space. The machine is throbbing under you with its cylinders beating a drummer's tattoo, and the air tears past you in a gale. In its maddening dash through the swirling dust the machine takes on the attributes of a sentient thing. . . . I tell you, gentlemen: no man can drive faster and live!

Of course, all sorts of men, women, and children were destined to drive faster, on the way to the dry cleaners or a kids' soccer game. And in those coming decades many who would be pulled over by policemen for speeding were asked the sarcastic question that a century later still faintly echoes through the culture: *"Hey, who do you think you are, Barney Oldfield?"*

OLDFIELD'S PARTICIPATION IN the Speedway's inaugural meeting probably guaranteed several thousand admissions, but he was hardly the hottest driver of 1909. That distinction belonged to Lewis Strang. After the Indianapolis press conference in March, Strang had proceeded directly to Florida for the seventh annual Daytona races. There, on a beach smoothed and hardened by a recent heavy nor'easter, he drove his Buick 100 miles in 1:34.01-1/5, eclipsing the world record set the previous year in New Orleans by Burman. A week later Strang popped up in Atlanta, where he stole the spotlight, and frightened the swells down front, before the start of a six-day bicycle race by gunning that same Buick around a tiny (twelve laps to the mile) velodrome that was banked at a K2-ish 85 degrees. "The performance was so spectacular that the occupants of the boxes and front seats left them in panic as Strang made the first round," said the *New York Times.* "Automobilists considered the limit of daring was reached by Strang." Two months later he and the Buick were back in Indiana, winning in record time at the Crown Point road course—with a newspaper reporter in the mechanician's seat. (Buick liked to work this publicity ploy.) "Strang took some of the down grades at the rate of eighty miles an hour," wrote the anonymous *New York Tribune* correspondent, "and any irregularity in the roadbed was sufficient to send the car into the air more like an aeroplane than an automobile."

THE *BUSIEST* DRIVER of them all that year, if not quite the top one in terms of AAA points accumulated or groupies groped, was Wilfred "Billy" Bourque, a shy, twenty-six-year-old Canadian who would inadvertently play a key role in the history of the Indianapolis Motor Speedway. Bourque that spring and summer had traveled to practically every hill climb, sprint, or marathon race he found listed in the automotive weeklies. A native of West Farnham, Quebec, a confluence of five railroads about forty miles southeast of Montreal, the highly touted newcomer had for the last seven years been patiently working his way through the ranks of the Knox Automobile Company of Springfield, Massachusetts, holding lunch-bucket jobs like molder and tester, then working as a salesman for a while before being allowed to try his hand at race driving. Bourque—one of the rare non-mustachioed drivers— was not the quote machine that some of his colleagues were, and he had a seemingly uncomplicated and conventional love life, revolving around a single, longtime sweetheart, Alexina Boivin, a shopgirl at a milliner's in Springfield, whom he intended to marry that September 14 in a double ceremony with two of their best friends (double wedding ceremonies were then enjoying a brief vogue). He had the dark, square-jawed looks of a heartthrob, though—in early August, Vice President James S. Sherman, while presenting Bourque with a trophy for winning a race in Richfield Springs, New York, had called him "by far the best-looking of all the drivers"—and once the official starter said "Go!" Bourque was able to shed his mild Canadian side and display an aggressiveness that set him apart even from other so-called speed maniacs.

Two months earlier Bourque had pushed himself, his Knox, and his twenty-two-year-old rookie riding mechanic Harry Holcomb to the limit winning the 396-mile Cobe Trophy race at Crown Point (it was Holcomb's first race). *Motor Age* reported that before they left for Indianapolis, Bourque and Holcomb had been advised by a Knox vice president, William Wright, that they could speak up without fear of any consequences if they thought they needed a break from racing, and that they were also cautioned by Wright about being too hell-bent on the new Speedway. "Go out boys and do your best to win, but without taking chances," Wright said he had told them. "You boys are very dear to us and we want no wins at the sacrifice of safety. We merely want you to drive within the safety limit, but finish the contest." Bourque and Holcomb—who understood that some car manufacturers had lately begun questioning the business sense, and even the morality, of participating in races so often marred by deadly accidents, and who had in any case made a pact to quit racing the following month, on the day of Wilfred and Alexina's wedding—were said to have nodded silently in assent.

"THE DRIVERS WILL be tucked in early tonight," said the *Star*, on the eve of the race meeting, "to lay in store a good supply of sleep before the nerve racking endurance tests tomorrow." But it was not a quiet night on the streets of Indianapolis. In the early hours of Thursday, August 19— coincidentally at almost the very moment that Cliff Littrell was expiring in his hospital bed—an accident occurred at Pennsylvania and 22nd streets. George Van Camp, a forty-eight-year-old executive in the Van Camp Packing Company and the uncle of Gilbert Van Camp, the young amateur driver whose engine was being tuned by Oldfield, had been taking a late-night tour of the northern portion of the city with his friends, Mr. and Mrs. Richard Trevesian of Cleveland, who were in town for the Speedway meet and who had earlier that evening attended a "garden concert" of German singing at a hall called the Maennerchor. At 2:20 A.M., Van Camp missed seeing a "jog" or irregularity at the intersection and as a result drove what the *News* called his "large touring car" onto the lawn of a William B. Westlake and "rammed it under his porch." Van Camp and Richard Trevesian were thrown clear and landed safely, but Antoinette Trevesian flew from the backseat to the front, then somehow "bounced off the steering wheel" and hit a post on the porch, breaking her collarbone and suffering severe scalp wounds as well as internal injuries.

As she was being lifted into the horse-drawn ambulance that came from the city dispensary, her screams, said the paper, "brought out men in their night clothes." Still, Mrs. Trevesian insisted on being taken to her rooms in the Claypool for treatment, not the hospital, and the doctor who came with the ambulance had shrugged, yawned, and said fine, and so it looked like there would not be another death to link to the auto racing meet.

Ten hours to go until race one.

The final edition of the *Star* had said that "Tomorrow morning, long before daylight, the honk of touring horns is expected to waken the cocks in farmyards all around the Hoosier capital signaling the approach of motorists, who will be eager to get on the spot in ample time."

At about 10:30 that morning, Clark E. Day, an Indianapolis physician rushing to the Speedway to get a good parking spot with his wife, Ethel, and their two young daughters, ran over and killed Elmer Grampton, age six, who had been playing with a hoop in the street.

Coroner Blackwell requested that the body be brought in for an autopsy.

5

I HAVE ON my desk a brief (six pages, single-spaced) memoir of the early days of the Indianapolis Motor Speedway, never published but written, probably in the 1940s, by Louis Schwitzer, a name that may be familiar to some more advanced auto buffs. Born on Leap Day of 1880, in Bielitz, Austria, Schwitzer earned engineering degrees at the prestigious German technical universities at Darmstadt and Karlsruhe before arriving in America "with $18 in my pocket," as he liked to remember it, in 1905. Several years later he would design the four-cylinder engine of the Marmon Wasp, the car that is officially listed as the winner of the first Indianapolis 500-mile race—his journey from Mitteleuropa to mid-America thus complete. After that Schwitzer improved the design of military trucks for the U.S. Army, revolutionized automobile cooling systems, and developed the turbocharger that is now a standard component of diesel engines. By the time he died, in 1967, an esteemed member of the American Society of Automotive Engineers, and the president of the Schwitzer Corporation, a multinational automotive parts concern, few remembered that he was the same oil-stained, dust-encrusted Louie-boy who drove the winner of the first car race ever contested at Carl Fisher's new Speedway.

Truth be told, Schwitzer was a better engineer than memoirist, at least if this unpublished piece that I have counts for anything. In it, he confuses events of the 250-mile Prest-O-Lite race, conducted on the first day of the meeting, with those of the 100-mile race that happened the following afternoon, a significant bit of misremembering; and he is maddeningly unclear about his role in the first 500-mile "sweepstakes" two years later, in which he either did or did not drive for a portion of the race (the Speedway's records are unclear on the matter of substitute drivers, among other things) in the National car that finished 10th with a then well-known driver named Harry Cobe in the cockpit, about 39 minutes behind the Marmon. Schwitzer also misses the chance to properly set the scene for the 1909 opening, which was a moment worth noticing.

Probably the single most striking aspect of Day One at the Speedway was the presence of so many women, a good number of whom were already waiting when the gates swung open at 9:00 A.M. Although August 19 was a scorching Thursday in Indianapolis, women, said the *Star*, came wearing their finest "multi-colored millinery" and "automobile veils" and many were carrying Japanese parasols of yellow, red, green, white, and blue. "The large number of women who witnessed the races made the events all the more interesting and attractive," said the paper. "The interest of the men was nothing compared to that of the women." A Mrs. Effie Shirley had driven all the way from Jamestown, New York, in a "double bucket, 30 horsepower" Overland with a party of women friends "unassisted by men." Women had been turning out in surprisingly large numbers for the practice sessions all week, "bedecked in veils" said the *Star*, and shouting things like "Look, he's slowing up already" and "Isn't that a bum getaway!" and generally "distracting attention from the drivers, oil, machinery and records"—but in a good way, the paper emphasized. Strong female interest in "the death-inviting sport" was no doubt one reason why the opening day crowd numbered about 16,500—impressive for a workday, not to mention an era in which five thousand was considered a good turnout for a major-league baseball game (the total, lest we forget, was also more than four times as many as had attended the balloon or motorcycle races). Fisher and his partners would have been delighted to have had 7,500.

Everyone paid at least $1.00, still a day's pay for a lot of people; a reserved box seat cost $1.50. Spectators entered mostly through the Crawfordsville Pike gate, which had been festooned for the occasion with hundreds of decorative flags, and which fed into an avenue lined with large tents housing temporary automobile showrooms. If you stepped inside, though, you saw that permanence and stability were what the manufacturers were attempting to project: besides the latest-model cars, set on risers or pedestals, each tent featured tree-sized potted ferns and palms, as well as rugs, armchairs, and couches (complete with the then obligatory antimacassars) for customers to sit in as they flipped through a catalogue or listened to a salesman's spiel about reliability (the customer's primary concern in those days of constant breakdowns), and how their company was in the auto business for the long haul—though in retrospect it's clear that at least 98 percent of them were destined to capsize in the wake of Henry Ford. One company that did endure in some form, Overland, displayed a "gold-plated car" that it proposed to award at year-end to the racing driver who had the best mile time of 1909. "Kodak fiends," said the *News*, gathered around to have their picture taken with the vehicle, which, as far as I can tell, was merely trimmed and flecked with gold paint and gilt here and there and in any case was never actually given away. If anyone was having a true golden age in 1909 it was the advertising managers and agencies, which were still unchecked by laws requiring at least a semblance of honesty.

Everyone seemed happy that morning, even those who couldn't afford a $1,250 Overland, and why shouldn't they be? It had been a summer full of good news (the first airplane flew across the English Channel), good music ("Shine On, Harvest Moon," ranked as number one in sheet music sales), and Manifest Destiny (in a few days, workers would start pouring the concrete for the Panama Canal). The wee-hours death of Littrell and the serious injury to Mrs. Trevesian both had made the morning papers, but only as discrete parts of the always entertaining there-but-for-fortune-fest that played out daily across the front page; their sorry tales had not been linked to each other, or blamed on the Speedway, by the boosterish local press—at least not yet. At the moment all seemed right with a world in which, for a roll of just introduced Lincoln pennies, you could experience what felt like a bonus state fair. Before the races started, there was but one blip that affected the general euphoria.

Realizing they had a large, captive audience on a day of possibly record heat, opportunistic concessionaires—independents who rented space from the Speedway founders—raised the price of soda pop from 5 to 10 cents. The increase began with one rogue vendor, and quickly swept through both grandstands, moving as fast as the drink sellers could alter their signs. In his office, Ernie Moross, that well-known pundit of the public temper, stopped what he was doing and cocked an ear as the crowd noise lowered ominously from cheerful din to all but inaudible murmur: hell hath no fury, he knew, like Hoosier passive-aggression. A moment later Moross materialized at the start/finish wire and through his megaphone was ordering the vendors to immediately drop the price of pop back down to a nickel or suffer the unstipulated consequences. The crowd cheered, and then, perversely, cheered more when, at the insistence of head engineer Park Taliaferro Andrew, three steamrollers rumbled onto the track to make one last desperate attempt to stabilize the surface. While this was a signal that competition was about to commence, and thus encouraging, the more fundamental message—that the track maintenance people *still* weren't satisfied—should have been troubling. The three hundred men still working on the track leaned on their tools and caught a breather as the machines—which if all had gone smoothly would have been locked in their garages a week before—made one more futile circuit.

Schwitzer neglects to pass along any of this (perhaps because he was too busy in the pits to register what was happening) but he does supply a couple of nuggets worth noting. One is that the drivers, riding mechanics, and company reps all realized from the laps being run in the practice sessions that morning that no last-minute miracles had occurred, and the surface had still not been beaten and steamrolled into submission. "Rocks and gravel were picked up by the tires which flew in the drivers' faces," Schwitzer writes of those morning runs. "It was not safe." But people were in their seats, the band was playing: there was simply no stopping the meeting now. As start time approached, some of the drivers rigged crude wire mesh "windshields" in an attempt to protect themselves and their co-pilots from the flying grit, pebbles, and tar chunks they knew they would likely encounter.

If it seems incredible that the drivers would not simply refuse to race under such conditions, the way, say, thoroughbred racing jockeys today decline to ride during a sleety or especially blustery day at Aqueduct, remember that auto racing was still inventing itself as it went along. No one was quite sure how to define "adversity"; the sport had not yet evolved enough to establish its own code of ethics or etiquette. Indeed, there was not even a consensus in 1909 on the best way to start a car race. Fred "Pop" Wagner, the sport's premier official at the time, had at first declared that each event at the Speedway would have a "flying start," with the field assembling 200 yards north of the main grandstand, then moving as a unit, maintaining position order as it roared down the homestretch toward the starting line, where, with the waving of a red flag, they would be given the command to go. This was the most impressive and most exciting sort of send-off, but in practice it often didn't work, owing to the drivers' well-known inability to rein in their aggression.

Sure enough, as the field of five approached the starting point of the Speedway's first race—a 5-mile sprint for stock cars with engines measured at 161 CID (cubic inch displacement)—drivers kept maneuvering to get ahead of the pole car, and the hoped-for "formation" became a ragged scramble. After trying a few more times, Wagner waved his yellow flag in frustration and ordered the field back to the line. If they couldn't control themselves, then fine—they would have a much less stylish standing start.

Ready ... set ... with a wave of Wagner's red flag, a roar of engines, and a Great Wall of smoke, the cars lurched forward, and the Speedway, for all meaningful purposes, began its history. The two-lap skirmish would consume 5 minutes and 18.4 seconds and prove largely uneventful—dull but incident-free. Schwitzer, driving the same white No. 19 Stoddard-Dayton that Littrell had fallen off the day before, grabbed the lead and held it the whole way, averaging 57.42 miles per hour. He knew his car well, having designed and built its engine in his capacity as chief engineer of the Atlas Engine Works, an Indianapolis firm that had gone into receivership two years before. Since then

Schwitzer had also designed for Marmon and several other automotive companies, and before he started his own firm a few years later he would work at perhaps a half dozen more. If you were talented in those highly competitive times, someone was always tugging at the sleeve of your coveralls and walking you away from your garage to make you an offer, and you could play the situation to your advantage. Less than four years after he had reached Ellis Island with that $18 stake, Schwitzer was living in Indianapolis and doing all right for himself. He tells us in his memoir that late in the afternoon of opening day, after he had won his race, claimed his trophy, and washed off most of the gunk, he could be found "sitting on the rear of the pit wall in a white silk shirt and white flannel pants," coolly taking in the remaining races. God bless America—and God help anyone who had to drive more than a couple of laps on that racetrack.

6

I want to die in my sleep like my grandfather. Not
screaming and yelling like the passengers in his car.

        —WIL SHRINER

ALWAYS THE SHOWMAN, Lewis Strang would not be outdone by the women
with pastel parasols. The rare driver who was not a mortal frontrun-
ner, he nonetheless gunned to the lead in the second race of the day,
a 10-mile event for cars with medium-size engines (231–300 CID),
while debuting a gray leather helmet affixed with a three-foot-long
red cloth streamer that stretched out straight behind him when he
reached 30 miles per hour and snapped loudly in the breeze. Beneath
his goggles, Strang also wore a wide, somewhat maniacal grin, for a few
moments at least, until the dust that was not supposed to be present
under the system devised by track engineer Andrew began caking in the
corners of his mouth.

The hat, the smile: it was definitely a look, and it seemed to ratify
the idea, periodically advanced in the press, that drivers were "speed
maniacs" who craved velocity the way vampires need blood. Earlier
that same year the *Cedar Rapids Evening Gazette* went so far as to beg
scientists to work at eradicating the "speed microbe" from the brains of
American youth so that they did not "scorch" on the highways or pursue careers as race car men. What Strang thought of this theory, whether
he actually felt somehow set apart from the general run of humanity, we
will never know, but in any case he played into the myth. "Gambling is

the greatest sport in the world, but I wouldn't take a minute's interest in a money stake," he had said earlier that year. "I like to gamble for something else. The sensation when you come close to a bad accident and yet don't 'get it' can never be put into words." Such feelings may indeed have been beyond Strang's descriptive powers, but some sixty-four years later, the English writer J. G. Ballard would publish *Crash*, a weirdly gripping novel whose principal characters derive a sexual thrill from participating in car wrecks—from being banged up a bit, in their case, but not so badly as to negate the accident's erotic effect. (The book was made into a movie by David Cronenberg in 1996.) The medical establishment has never recognized this particular fetish—the desire to be nearly killed in an automobile, or to watch someone hurt that way, has, as they say in the insurance business, no diagnosis code. Yet the more one learns about the early race car drivers, and peruses accounts of male and female fans responding to an accident by bolting from their seats, pouring onto the course, and pushing aside policemen so they could feast their eyes on the mangled bodies strewn about the track and infield—the less *Crash* reads like some perverted personal fantasy.

STRANG'S LEAD IN that opening day 10-miler would not last long. Louis Chevrolet caught him at the end of the first lap, zoomed right on by in the casual, almost insolent way he had of displaying previously withheld horsepower, and wound up beating the New Yorker to the wire by more than a mile. Bob Burman, meanwhile, got up for third, completing the all-Buick trifecta.

Two races, two lopsided victories: the many neophytes in the crowd could be forgiven for wondering why something that sounded like Gettysburg and smelled like the Chicago Fire could be as dull as *The Golden Bowl*. Was there something on the agenda to quicken their hearts? The answer would soon be apparent.

In the 10-mile event for the most powerful cars (301–450 CID), which began about twenty minutes later, Burman did his Wild Bob thing, exploding to the front at a barely controllable clip—only to find himself wheel to wheel with Billy Bourque, a man known for his success in backcountry hill climbs and grind-it-out marathon road races, but not racetrack sprints. As they headed into the second lap—both cars swerving deftly to avoid a depression in the track that was forming at the same spot just in front of the grandstand where Jake DeRosier had flipped his motorcycle—Burman's white Buick gained half a car length on Bourque's coffee-colored Knox. Burman owned the inside position, meaning Bourque had to go considerably faster than him just to stay even—but the quiet man from Springfield, Massachusetts, wasn't backing off. As he hunched his shoulders and squinted into the wind, his riding mechanic, Holcomb, kept his eyes locked on Burman, and shouted in Bourque's left ear (most cars in 1909, including Bourque's, had their steering wheels on the right) every time the Buick appeared to be inching to a greater advantage. (The wheel migrated to the left when it was discovered that the torque of the drive shaft tended to put extra pressure on the right-side springs, which could cause the car to sag slightly in that direction. Moving the driver's weight to the left side helped offset that effect.) This was exactly the scenario Bourque's boss back in Springfield had dreaded: his best driver getting caught up in the new-Speedway hoopla and taking too many risks on a track whose reputation for being, at best, "unsettled" was well known. But Bourque couldn't help himself; the lead by now had become less a tactical position in an automobile race than a point of honor. Heading into the homestretch the final time, the Knox and the Buick were traveling in perfect tandem, and the fans stood and cheered. Holcomb, though it was only the third race of his career, knew enough to crouch down behind the dashboard to lessen wind resistance, and that may have made the difference. At the finish line, which both cars reached in 4:45.50, Bourque's Knox was about three inches ahead.

So *this* was auto racing!

The crowd—once the modest Billy Bourque had accepted his trophy with a slight nod, a tight smile, and a quick wave—settled into a sustained roar that combined with the noise from the pits to create a din easily discernible at Monument Circle, five miles away. There couldn't have been a more propitious moment to bring out the field for the feature, the 250-mile Prest-O-Lite race, open to cars with the kind of powerful engines with which Americans were already deeply in love.

But dramatic pacing wasn't one of Carl Fisher's strong points. He had as usual overdone things, packing the program with enough events for several days. Before the long race, everyone would need to sit through another short one, a 10-mile "handicap" that mixed cars of various engine sizes and allowed the smaller ones to start first. Gimmick races like this were often part of the program in those days, one common example being a "courtship relay" in which drivers circled the track five or six times, picking up (and discharging) on each lap women passengers chosen by lottery from among the spectators. The Speedway's "special handicap" was really a test of the man who decided what the handicaps should be: if his calculations were spot-on there would be an eleven-car dead heat, and that would demonstrate beyond dispute that . . . well, that his calculations were spot-on. Not surprisingly, they weren't.

Ray Harroun, driving a lightweight Marmon, took advantage of a huge head start and won easily in 8:22.50, though a savvy observer could see that the most impressive performance had come from Charlie Merz, who finished a fast-closing third with his National despite having to hang back for 1 minute and 25 seconds after Harroun got going. The crowd reserved its warmest applause for Merz, though probably not because it understood the complexities of what it had just witnessed: twenty-one-year-old Charlie was a local boy whose father was also named Charles, and as many in attendance knew was an Indianapolis policeman stationed in the main grandstand.

So now, finally, the feature race.

Well, not quite. First, a gaggle of drivers with their eyes on the gold-flecked Overland prize would tour the track one at a time, trying to lower the mile record of 48.20, set in 1905 by Webb Jay in his "Whistling Billy," a steam-powered racer made by the White Sewing Machine Company of Cleveland, yet another established nineteenth-century firm trying to branch into the auto game. These "time trials" proved to be an exercise in tedium, as one by one the teams came out, warmed up their cars for a spell, tried to get a feel for the track, then took their best shot, passing over a trip wire stretched across the track at the starting line and another placed just beyond turn two, only to fall short of a mark which didn't mean much to anyone beyond the most gung ho gearheads. Even when Barney Oldfield at last appeared in his monstrous new Benz, and promptly shredded the record like a man attacking a dandelion with one of those newfangled International Harvester combines, taking it all the way down to 43.10 with apparent ease, few cheered. Why should they? The machine deserved most of the credit, after all, and it wasn't clear to the spectators, most of them born into rural circumstances in the horse-drawn age, how they should feel about a contest between a gasoline engine and a clock. Most folks figured it was none of their business, and used the interval to smoke the free cigar that came with every fried chicken box lunch.

FISHER WOULD EVENTUALLY see that less could be more, that the traditional horse racing model of sprints and routes and contests defined by various conditions didn't work for his Speedway, and that one long easy-to-grasp race like the 500 was all that the average visitor needed — and wanted — on a given afternoon. The mystery is why he didn't learn that lesson on the very first day of auto racing, by virtue of the abundantly eventful 100-lap Prest-O-Lite trophy race.

Everyone knew it was going to be a memorable contest when, after a longish opening interval during which the drivers seemed to be feeling each other out and testing moves like veteran prizefighters, Strang's Buick burst into flames on lap 36. He had just "hove in sight" coming around turn four, said the *News*, when "it was noticed above the cloud of dust that an unusual amount of fire was shooting from his red-hot machine." Some fans were put in mind of the time when Foxhall Keane drove in a race with his mustache aflame.

Strang, who had been running third behind Chevrolet and Burman in the field of nine, immediately pulled into the pits, where, obviously not realizing how dire his situation seemed, he superfluously employed, said the paper, "one of the special hand signals peculiar to each team to indicate he needed a fire extinguisher." His own crew, as well as members of other racing outfits, rushed to his aid and in a few minutes doused the conflagration. Although he had almost certainly lost all chance of winning by then, Strang began climbing back in the cockpit, only to be told by an AAA official stationed in the service area that he had been disqualified for receiving assistance from nonteammates. "This aggravated the eager and excited driver," said the *News*, "and he protested in a frantic manner to be permitted to get back into the fray."

Finally Carl Fisher, who had been worriedly pacing the pits, anticipating disaster of a different sort, weighed in, telling the AAA man that he thought Strang ought be allowed back in. After some additional begging from the driver, the official relented. Said the *News*: "With a cry of delight Strang leaped into the seat behind the wheel and soon had his swift car's wheels spinning, and his long red cap banner floating in the wind."

The man to beat that day—or so it had seemed in the early going—was Louis Chevrolet. The swarthy Swiss-born driver—one of the many known by the default nickname of "Smiling" this or that—had led for the first 49 laps. And even though he was starting to have a problem with grit and taroid creeping in around the edges of his goggles, and had as a result allowed his Buick teammate Burman to get by him on the 50th lap, Chevrolet was, as always, a threat to pull off the rail at any moment and—*There goes Smiling Louie!*—reclaim the lead. One of three racing brothers, Chevrolet was on the large side for a driver—he stood six feet and weighed 210 pounds—but it was his dreams that made him truly unique. Instead of wanting just to win a lot of races, bed a lot of women, and get out of the game alive, like most of his cohorts, he longed to be a car maker, a craftsman in the tradition of his father, a master clockmaker who had moved the family to France in the mid-1890s, just as motor car madness was sweeping that land. Though he lacked formal education, Chevrolet had worked up a detailed plan for a small, inexpensive six-cylinder car that he thought could compete with Henry Ford's wildly successful Model T, and about six weeks before the Speedway's opening, William Crapo Durant, then the head of Buick, had agreed to finance its development. Chevrolet planned to branch into the design and manufacturing ends of the business as soon as he could, but not caring so much about racing only seemed to make him better at it. He drove like a man whose destiny was elsewhere, maneuvering around the track with a palpably French nonchalance that caused one journalist to call him "the most audacious driver in the world." Which is not to say he never wrecked—he lost at least four riding mechanics to fatal accidents between 1908 and 1911—but that wrecks were something he did not let ruin his day.

The Prest-O-Lite race, though, would put his casual attitude to the test. As he began lap 58, Chevrolet, already nearly blind from the insidious track matter, took a walnut-size stone in his left goggle lens; besides grit in that eye, he now had glass. When he reached up instinctively to adjust his all but useless goggles, they broke apart and fell into his lap— whereupon he was immediately hit with a shower of taroid churned up by Burman's tires. No Longer Smiling Louis was at this point halfway down the backstretch, a full mile and a quarter from the pits. He couldn't see anything, but he could hear Burman's engine ahead of him, and he pressed on, trying to follow its roar. This, however, was too much even for his riding mechanic, whose name was neither registered with the Speedway nor reported in the press, and who grabbed the steering wheel, kicked Chevrolet's foot off the accelerator, squashed the brake pedal with his own right foot, and gradually brought the car to a stop in the weeds on the far side of the infield.

What happened in the next few minutes was for years a matter of dispute, and since the race was not filmed, and no photographs of this portion were taken, one is left to piece together the contemporary reporting. Most eyes at the time were on the distant figure of Chevrolet, who, having been helped out of his car, was being held at the elbow and led by his mechanic at a slow trot toward the hospital tent on the other side of the infield. Meanwhile Bourque and Holcomb, in the same No. 3 Knox they had ridden to victory in the earlier 10-miler, were coming around turn four, running in second place and nearing what might be called the "DeRosier Fault," though it had, in the course of the last 20 or 30 laps, eroded into a ditch two and a half feet deep and eight to ten inches across, at the bottom of which could now be seen a lead drainpipe. Everyone in the field had been studiously avoiding this spot since the race began, but for reasons that will never be understood, Bourque and Holcomb, on their 58th approach to it, both turned to look behind them—"as if they'd heard some kind of noise," one witness said—and the Knox's right front tire dipped into the crevasse, causing Bourque to lose control of the car (some said he had inexplicably taken his hands off the wheel when he spun his head around) at about 75 miles per hour. "We're gone," Bourque said, according to someone standing close to the scene, who, given the noise, must have been a lip-reader. Coming up from the ditch with its front axle broken, the Knox skidded a bit, then flipped twice end over end. Both men were thrown from the car and flew a considerable distance. Holcomb's head struck a fence running between the track and the grandstand and, said the *Star*, "his brains were scattered on the post and the grass." Coroner Blackwell would later determine by "field autopsy" that the mechanic "had three holes in his head and both arms broken."

Bourque was thrown further from the vehicle, which for a moment seemed consistent with his almost mysterious good luck. Back in Massachusetts, he had earned a reputation as a natural acrobat who could survive anything because he knew how to take a tumble. At the Lenox hill climb the previous year, Bourque's car had tipped over midway through his run, but he had scrambled out from under the machine, helped right it, then hopped back in and recorded the fastest time of the day. At practice for an event at Dead Horse Hill in Worcester in the spring of '09, he had been catapulted from his car after blowing a tire and hitting a boulder, but he bounced immediately to his feet. At Indy, though, Bourque's magic went missing. He landed near, but not against, the same wooden fence that Holcomb had struck. He was alive and for a split second seemed safe. But his car hadn't finished cartwheeling. First its shadow, then the vehicle itself came down across his upper body. Some papers described Bourque's injuries as a "smashed skull" and two broken arms; others said nothing about arms but claimed both his legs had been "pulverized." What almost all the dailies did agree on, and report with relish, was that Bourque's ribs had pierced his lungs and that he had, in the words of Blackwell, "drowned in his own blood, being unable to breathe as a result of blood pouring down his own throat."

Knowing the reporters' gluttony for ghoulish detail, the Speedway kept a press car standing by—it was sponsored by Overland—to deliver the reporters to the scene of an accident as soon as it occurred. A corps of newspapermen reached the bodies of Bourque and Holcomb before even the ambulance staff, but since the race was not halted, drivers found themselves having to steer around people with notepads and cameras who were wandering about on the track. A few minutes later the situation grew even more chaotic as medical workers and hundreds of morbidly curious spectators joined the journalists. "While the track was alive with terrific racing machines," said the *Star*, "the physicians carried the dead and dying across the track, dodging the huge steel creations that whizzed by, enveloping all in a cloud of smoke." Not only did management not stop the race, the Speedway declined to make any announcements about the condition of the injured or, for that matter, to even acknowledge that an accident had occurred. As the *Chicago Tribune* said, "Strang, Merz, Tom Kincaid and the other drivers kept up the race, the band played, and death was thrust into the background."

But the scene unfolding directly in front of the grandstand was impossible to overlook. As the bodies were being carried off, and workers were wiping red and gray matter off the fence post and grass, another Knox driver named Al Denison vaulted the fence and ran toward the ambulance screaming, "That's Billy! My God, Billy's been killed!" Denison, according to the *Star*, was Bourque's "life-long chum" as well as his roommate back in Springfield. "We taught each other everything we know about racing!" he wailed before falling to the ground and "groaning in anguish" until a doctor led him away.

Bourque did not die until about fifteen minutes later, by which time he had been taken to the hospital tent. As a sheet was being drawn over his large, handsome features, Chevrolet, still barely able to see, shuffled by his pallet muttering, "Too bad, too bad."

About fifteen minutes later the hospital was bustling again as twenty-year-old Fred Ellis, driver of the No. 53 Jackson, was carried in on a stretcher. Ellis had wrestled the lead from Burman, then suddenly pulled his car into the pits at the end of lap 88, and he and his riding mechanic, A. J. House, had hopped out to work on their engine. Whatever was wrong with it, it couldn't have looked worse than they did after negotiating 220 miles of bad road under a blistering sun. They fixed the problem, but when the Jackson, an unexciting but usually dependable car, stalled on its way out of pit row and Ellis got out again and started to crank it, he was overwhelmed by heat and exhaustion and passed out. House, stepping over him, grabbed the crank, gave it a couple of hard turns, and then he, too, keeled over in a faint. In accordance with his inferior status, the mechanic was taken not to the hospital tent but to the Jackson garage, where, though his course of treatment—ice packs and whiskey—was cruder than Ellis's, he bounced back quicker, and later that afternoon visited his still prone boss and told him he was "the best little driver that there ever was."

There was drama behind the scenes as well. After Bourque's accident, officials from the AAA, which had been closely following the news about the track surfacing troubles all summer long and had sanctioned the meeting with trepidation, wanted to halt the race and meet with Fisher in his office to discuss canceling the Friday and Saturday events, too. This action, though perfectly reasonable, might have been disastrous for the Speedway's future; if the racing was ended abruptly after one bloody day the place might never recover from the ignominy. Fisher, however, could not be found, and while Moross searched for him with painstaking slowness in various unlikely places, the race continued. It wasn't until around 7:00 P.M. that the Prest-O-Lite marathon finally ended, with Burman still ahead, when Fisher at last surfaced and was questioned by the AAA men.

In his 1961 book, *500 Miles to Go: The History of the Indianapolis Speedway*, a corny and artificial account that many Indy history buffs nonetheless venerate, author Al Bloemker quotes Fisher as saying "Hell, no!" when the mean old spoilsports from the automobile association ordered him to call off the remainder of the meet. Bloemker, a former PR man at the Speedway, paints Fisher as a lovably gruff iconoclast who forged his own path and boldly pushed aside those who stood in his always admirable way (his book is dedicated to Fisher). Yet other sources, as well as a cursory understanding of pre-1910 auto industry politics, suggest that the AAA had all the leverage in this situation. Rather than shouting down the representatives of that regulatory body, Fisher was obliged by a lack of palatable alternatives to humbly implore them for another chance. By working all night, he assured them, his tireless (and, as the newspapers rarely missed the chance to remind us, shirtless) grounds crew could have the track in reasonable shape by noon the next day. And perhaps because there are few things less entrancing to behold than a desperate man in patent leather strap-on shoes, the AAA officials said okay, all right, but please, just no more dead bodies, promise.

■ ■ ■

THE REPRIEVE FROM the auto association men didn't mean that everything was suddenly, to use a then current expression, the bee's knees. A screaming front-page headline in the next day's *Fort Wayne Journal-Gazette* said "Indianapolis Motor Track is Dedicated with the Blood of Two Victims," and there was plenty more ink of that ilk. The Knox Motor Company also announced that, out of respect to the memory and families of Bourque and Holcomb, it was pulling its cars from the rest of the meeting, and considering a retreat from the entire sport. "We will probably enter no more cars in automobile races," George Crane, a Knox salesman, said. "It is simply suicide; that's all it is." But despite all the outrage and the breast-beating, the Speedway saw a 25 percent surge in attendance on Day Two, to 22,000. "There were more women in the crowd than on Thursday and they appeared to be the most interested spectators," observed the *Indianapolis News.* "The killing of the two men, it seemed, only served to increase the excitement."

It is curious how sports evolve: early in its history, horse racing adopted betting as a way to make a potentially monotonous game more interesting to a mass audience; car racing had, as I have noted, not death, exactly, as a way of promoting audience participation, but the *possibility* of death—though that possibility did need to be stoked, like the affection of a primitive deity, with an occasional human sacrifice. This made it unique among sports. For though a fair number of prizefighters died with their gloves on each year, and football—despite a flurry of rule changes to make it safer, and the legalization in 1906 of the more finesse-oriented and less brutal forward pass—produced a steady drumbeat of early-twentieth-century fatalities, it was only in auto racing that death was simultaneously the worst and best thing that could possibly happen from a promoter's point of view.

THE SECOND DAY of the 1909 meeting at the Indianapolis Motor Speedway was like the middle of the three fights between Muhammad Ali and Joe Frazier: it was the one in which the participants seemed uninspired or overly conservative, the one that did not yield great lessons about sport and life and how those things are the same and how they are different, the one you are most likely to forget. The fields were small on Friday,

August 20—four cars in one instance—the margins of victory yawn-
ingly wide and the hero of the day before, Burman, too exhausted by his
efforts in the 250-miler to show up for work, able only to sit in the cool
darkness of his garage, petting Lizzie, his beloved "mascot goat." The
big news of Friday, if you read the *Austin* (Minnesota) *Daily Herald* or
any of a number of other papers, was "No Accidents in Auto Races,"
and this lack of incident forced the Indianapolis dailies to promote the
minor stories that on a bloodier afternoon might not have run. The
Star, for example, recounted in considerable detail the nontragedy of
Carl Kopanka, an eighteen-year-old Speedway spectator from Newcas-
tle, Indiana—home of the largest automobile plant in the nation, which
turned out the Maxwell car, "The Aristocrat of Runabouts"—who had
passed out from the heat in the paddock in front of the grandstand and
had been dragged into the shade where "restoratives were applied" until
he came to. Do tell. That paper also reported that "beyond treating
swollen eyes and bandaging burns, blisters and small cuts, the hospital
staff at the Speedway had nothing to do." Patrolman A. J. Bruce caught
"a negro and a white man, unknown to him, annoying women in the
grandstand and ejected them from the grounds." There was also this
scintillating subhead: "Track Oiling Watched with Interest."

The absence of catastrophe put people on edge. "More field glasses
were in evidence in the grandstand, the crowd was expectant of a rep-
etition of the accidents and every time a racer appeared to be in trouble
the people in the grandstand jumped to their feet and craned their
necks to see what the outcome might be," said the *Star*. Only once did
the paying customers come close to witnessing something scary. The
near disaster involved Barney Oldfield, and some people couldn't have
been more pleased. A coterie of patriots had been hounding the driver
all that spring and summer, objecting to his having the image of the
American flag painted on the hood of his National, which he promoted
as "The Old Glory." The plaintiffs claimed Oldfield was violating the
law that bans using the flag for commercial purposes, and in the days
before the Speedway meeting they had petitioned Indiana attorney
general James Bingham for its removal. On the evening of Day One,
Bingham ruled in Oldfield's favor, saying that because the car was his
personal property the merchandising statute did not apply. The flag

protectors got a measure of revenge, though, when, in the fourth race of the day, a 10-miler for stock chassis with engines of less than 600 CID, the engine of Oldfield's National caught fire, and the flames burned through the leather straps holding the controversial hood in place. With a thunderous clash, it flew up and back toward Barney, hitting him in the right arm, which he had raised to protect his face. Bloody and in pain, he was forced to retire from his first race at the Speedway, which was won by Johnny Aitken in another National automobile.

Underscoring the initially disappointing lack of death that day, romance—or something roughly like it: the volatile relationship between Strang and his wife, Louise Alexander—was briefly sucked into the vacuum at center stage. Arriving from New York about an hour before the Friday races began, Mrs. Strang came straight to the Speedway from the train station, striding swiftly ahead of her several baggage handlers, as if she had something on her mind. She found her husband in the pits, leaning over his Buick to make final adjustments, a task he did not like to delegate. As a circle of reporters gathered round, the actress smoothed her skirt and cleared her throat, allowing time for the dimmer and more distant journalists to become aware of her presence. Then, projecting her lines and wagging her finger extravagantly, she said, in her chirpy, high-pitched voice, "Why did you not win yesterday, Lewis? Now show your mettle today!"

Strang would do as instructed, taking the first race of the day, a 5-mile sprint for smaller cars, as well as the last, the featured 100-mile G&J trophy race. In the latter event, also for lighter machines, he led every lap and came home nearly nine minutes ahead of the second-place finisher, Buick teammate George DeWitt. Louise rushed into the winner's circle during the trophy presentation and, after waiting for newspaper photographers to set up, gave Lewis an extravagant kiss.

The odd thing about the second day of the meeting was that while nothing spectacular happened it changed everything by siphoning excess electricity from the atmosphere. People may have come to what they thought was the Little Charnel House on the Crawfordsville Pike, with their Kodaks loaded for crashes, but they left (at the more reasonable hour of 5:30) in a mellower mood, with the feeling that Thursday's gruesome wrecks had been an unfortunate aberration, and that the Speedway was merely, and perhaps thankfully, a respectable place to have an afternoon's fun. They had traded titillation for edification, guilt for hope, and that was okay; they would feel better about themselves in the morning. The next day's *News* would say, on page one, "The first automobile race meet on the Indianapolis motor speedway, which will end this evening with the completion of the Wheeler & Schebler $10,000 trophy race, is expected firmly to establish the fact that the $650,000 speedway venture is to be a success."

NOT EVERYONE WAS taking the success of the meeting for granted, though. After the Friday crowds had left, but before the drivers and mechanics could scatter for the evening, Arthur Newby, by far the most thoughtful of the Speedway founders, called them to an impromptu meeting beneath the grandstand. As the grimy troupers, including Newby's own National team, stood, sat on ticket takers' tables, or leaned wearily against the walls, he thanked them for their participation, and for whatever part they played in creating a safe day of racing at the Speedway. "But I have to remind you of something," he said. "The track is rough. And though we had a good day on Friday we had a bad day Thursday, with serious accidents. I just want you to know that you are free to stay out, to withdraw from tomorrow's competition with no recriminations, no financial penalties, no suspensions from the AAA, and I would hope no damage to your reputation." He paused, then added, "For some of you, depending on your circumstances, this may be the prudent choice."

After Newby had thanked them again and left, the autoists hung around for a few minutes, discussing their options. Later, Johnny Aitken would remember that he turned to the man standing next to him, a riding mechanic on the National team named Claude Kellum, and said, "Newby's right. We got lucky today but I don't like the way that track is cutting up."

Kellum offered no reply. Later, lawyers representing his family's interests would contend that the earflaps on his cloth helmet were down during the entire meeting, and he never heard a thing.

One of the last people to leave the grounds that night, several hours after his wife had retired to their rooms in the Claypool, was Lewis Strang. Like a lot of people up from the streets he was a fastidious man, and he had helped his crew of twenty hose and rub down the white No. 33 Buick that he had driven to victory in both the short and the long races that day, and then, in the drivers' shower room, set to work on himself, washing grit, tar, and oil from his sandy-colored hair, his face, his arms, every crevice of his body. He mustn't have known whether to laugh, because he'd managed to get so thoroughly grimed up despite his driving coveralls—or cry, because the black stuff he saw spinning around the drain was the surface of the racetrack.

7

Violence horrifies us, transfixes us, draws the eye and ignites the passions; overpowered by desire, we have no choice but to look.

—MARK DANNER, *Stripping Bare the Body: Politics Violence War*

A SERIOUSLY LARGE and ivy-covered school of thought back then held that 100 miles was the limit beyond which no human being could safely drive an automobile in a single outing. Just to be clear: we're talking here about 100 miles on a racetrack; making that daily distance on the highway was a question more or less moot. So bad were American roads in 1909, still, that even if you were able to reach a speed that would put you on a pace to get 100 miles before sundown, bumps, chuckholes, roots, and ruts—not to mention irate farmers throwing rocks at you and cursing your "devil wagon" (for its kinship to vehicles that continually ran over his chickens)—would wreak havoc on your power train, suspension, and tires (especially your tires, which in those days before carbon black was added to strengthen the rubber might last only a few hundred miles). Soon you would be sitting in the Queen Anne's lace, awaiting assistance—if you were lucky.

In his 1916 account of a cross-country car trip, *A Hoosier Holiday*, Theodore Dreiser wrote:

The best machine, as anyone knows who has traveled much by automobiles, is a delicate organism. Given good roads it can seemingly roll on forever at top speed. Enter on a poor one and all the ills that flesh or machinery is heir to seem at once to manifest themselves. A little mud and water and you are in danger of skidding into kingdom come. A few ruts and you feel momentarily as though you were going to be thrown into high heaven. A bad patch of rocks and holes and you soon discover where all the weak places in your bones and muscles are. Punctures eventuate from nowhere. Blowouts arrive one after another with sickening frequency. The best of engines snort and growl on sharp grades. Going down a steep hill a three-thousand-pound car makes you think always— "My God! What if something should break!" Then a spring may snap, a screw work loose somewhere.

For more information on this topic, consult Al Jolson's "He'd Have to Get Under—Get Out and Get Under (To Fix Up His Automobile)," a jaunty hit tune of 1912.

On a racetrack, even one built for horses, 100 miles was, for the driver and his trusty riding mechanic, a different kind of bad trip: there, the men tended to split their seams before the machines did. It all came down to vibrations, which would do you in on days when the track dust didn't. These excruciating excitations followed an upward trajectory, from the racetrack through the vehicles into the men. If humans could conduct vibrations the way an experienced yogi conducts unhelpful thoughts—that is, allowing them to enter the holy temple of his body if they must, but then promptly ushering the nasty little buggers right on out through the top of his skull—the early drivers of race cars might have emerged from a marathon contest (they called anything longer than 50 miles a "grind") rejuvenated and refreshed. But alas, reality is otherwise. Writing in *Collier's* in 1908, the journalist Julian Street noted:

> The constant pressure of the wind and the vibration of the steering wheel are very wearing, and the reason jockeys have never made successful drivers. The direct effect of the jar upon the driver's hands is the raising of great blisters, and when these break the surface the palm is left absolutely raw. After his Vanderbilt Cup victory [in 1908] George Robertson's hands looked like pieces of raw meat. Herbert Lytle, who finished second, told me that his hands and arms became so tired he could hardly

hold his car. [Arthur] Duray's right hand was in a sling for a week after the Savannah race.

NUMBNESS, BROUGHT ON by vibrations, ranked as the most common problem in races of longer distances. "Given the suspension systems of that day your butt would get so darn numb that you'd be in severe discomfort," three-time Indy winner Johnny Rutherford (1974, '76, and '80), an amateur historian who has driven the No. 32 Marmon Wasp credited with winning the first Indianapolis 500-mile race, told me not long ago. "It may sound funny but I can assure you that it's not."

Nor was it just the posterior region in which a lack of normal circulation, and hence a deadening of feeling and an uncomfortable and potentially dangerous stiffness, often occurred. Halfway through what would be Billy Bourque's last lap on earth, at least one witness said he saw Harry Holcomb vigorously massaging the driver's right arm "as if it had gone dead" after 220 miles of racing (yes, riding mechanics were masseurs, too). Others speculated that a first-rate driver like Bourque, in the homestretch moments later, did not really make the rookie mistake of turning around to look behind him—backward glances were supposed to be left to the riding mechanic—just before his Knox went into the ditch, but that, suffering from a weakened neck (due to 88 laps' worth of vibrations), his head was twisted in that direction by the onrushing wind. "Wind resistance" was a new concept back then in the pre-windshield era, regarded at times with a bit too much awe. "The wind resistance is the most notable change," Felice Nazzaro once said, describing to normal humans what it felt like to drive at more than 60 miles per hour. "At 70 miles per hour one feels one's body flattening out against the back of the seat, and the least movement in the direction in which the car is going must be made with conscious effort."

Yet another camp, meanwhile, believed that the pains of a grind were primarily mental—that the ceaseless vibrations, the idiot wind, and the nonstop whirl of scenery combined to cause temporary insanity. A veteran Lozier riding mechanic named Tom Lynch liked to tell about the time he was assisting the well-known driver Harry Michener during a long race at the Brighton Beach track in Brooklyn circa 1907. As they neared the 100th lap, Michener turned to him and asked, "What's that house? I never saw it before." When Lynch asked what house he could possibly be talking about, Michener pointed to the grandstand and said, "That house right there."

"Uh, I think you better go in, Mich," the mechanic said. "Your front tire's down."

As soon as they reached the pits said Lynch, Michener "dropped over the wheel in a dead faint."

But these are merely the colorful particulars of what can happen in a distance race; that the likelihood of problems, and even fatalities, increases the longer you stay on the track, pushing yourself and your machine, is a truism worth bringing up only because Fisher had scheduled races of 250, 100, and 300 miles over the course of his three-day meet. Why would he do this? For two reasons. The first and more obvious one was that grinds were grander, simply for being more time-consuming and more difficult to win; only some third-rate county fair would make a feature out of a 5-mile sprint, which is finished before a fan can find the weenie vendor. Secondly, and more significantly, the longer events played into that seldom spoken-of but vital part of the game that is about tempting fate. A savvy promoter could use long races to turn up the danger level, ideally to a point where the drivers had blood on their hands, but merely from broken blisters. If things started to get out of control, and men were dying, one could dampen the dangerousness, too, by adjusting distances downward. So it was that on Thursday evening, after two men had lost their lives in pursuit of the Prest-O-Lite trophy, Fisher and his colleagues had considered shortening Saturday's Wheeler-Schebler event from 300 miles to 100 or even 50 miles, and thus scaling back the chances of disaster. But then came Friday's bracing dose of boredom and the surge of optimism it engendered—quickly followed by the founders' own second thoughts about the legal and public relations ramifications of appearing worried about their own show—and they stuck with their original plan for a 300-mile grand finale.

ON SATURDAY, 37,200 came to the Speedway, many once again arriving more than four hours before the scheduled high-noon start of the first race. A high percentage of women was yet again noted by the local press. After all of the 6,500 seats in the main grandstand were taken, people continued to pour in and clog the aisles and walkways, causing some to yell "Down in front!" and "Keep moving!" Organized sports were still relatively new to America then, and the populace had not thoroughly worked out the protocols. When the police began to address the increasingly ugly situation they met resistance, though not so much from the spectators as from the state militiamen, who had been asked by Moross to provide security—he thought they lent a certain je ne sais quoi to the proceedings—but whose role vis-à-vis the Indy cops had never been established. Both agencies believed they had the superior authority, and for almost a half-hour, while tension built in the grandstand, and a couple of minor scuffles between seat holders and standees erupted, Sgt. Walter Barmfuhrer of the Indianapolis police department stood on the track apron and argued with Indiana militiaman Sgt. Thomas Strong, saying that the latter's troops were not on military duty, and thus had no official function—only to hear Strong state over and over that Barmfuhrer's men were powerless at the Speedway, because it sat outside the Indianapolis city limits. While they debated, an unidentified spectator ardently but vainly beseeched both sergeants to arrest a man who had told his wife to "shut the hell up and sit the hell down." At length the police sergeant petulantly stalked off and ordered his troops back to their temporary Speedway stationhouse, leaving the militia to, as the *Star* said, "handle the big brawny fellows who were inclined to do as they pleased."

When that sideshow ended, at around 11:45, the formal one began with a succession of cars trying, one at a time, to lower the world record for the kilometer. Even in Europe, the cradle of automobile racing (and the kilometer), this would have engendered ennui; in Indiana, where instead of ennui they had winter, and they didn't have kilometers at all, it meant only that the endless practice runs were over, the monstrous horse-drawn track-oiling trucks had been put away, and the real racing would soon begin.

The preliminary races were dispensed with crisply that day: the 15-mile handicap went to Tom Kincaid in a National; Eddie Hearne took the 10-mile amateur event in a Fiat; and Oldfield, in his big bully of a Benz, beat two challengers by over a mile in the 25-mile Remy

Grand Brassard, winning a silver arm shield (the *brassard*) and the promise, from magneto magnate Frank Remy of Anderson, Indiana, of $75 a week until the prize was raced for again. (A magneto is the electrical spark-generating device employed in early cars and still used on smaller gas-powered engines.) For anyone with an interest in a certain 500-mile race, two years down the road, the early part of the day was made notable by the first appearance on the Indianapolis Motor Speedway of one Arthur Greiner, a rich kid who finished third in the amateur race driving an expensive ($4,000) Thomas car similar to the "Flyer" that had won the renowned New York–to–Paris race of 1908. Apart from leading for two laps, he attracted little notice that afternoon, but he would become one of the starters in the first 500. Even in the community of race car drivers, a group distinguished, as we have seen, by physical recklessness, a dangerously romantic view of the world, and poor impulse control, Greiner stood out as nutso.

AFTER A GUNSHOT got the Wheeler-Schebler 300 off from a standing start at 1:25 P.M., all nineteen drivers put up an especially mad scramble for the lead, as well they might have. The race just *felt* important. Maybe the months of hype, or the undeniable magnificence of the silver Tiffany trophy (modestly billed by Moross as "the most important trophy in the world"), had worked their magic, but winning the Wheeler-Schebler suddenly loomed as a historic achievement. Though it was the longest race ever conducted on a track (except for the 24-hour marathons held at Brighton Beach and a few other places), getting good early position seemed crucial. One can't say "when the dust settled" because it never did—the one or two extant photographs of the early going show what looks like a portrait of a single, low-scudding cloud—but *if* the dust had settled after a mile or so, the crowd would have seen an Indianapolis boy, "Happy" Johnny Aitken, in front with his Indiana-made National. Although Aitken had expressed displeasure with the condition of the track earlier in the day, before the preliminaries had chewed it up all the more, he set an extremely aggressive pace, leaving the large field strung out behind him. Once or twice each lap, his riding mechanic, Claude Kellum, would swivel his head and flash Herb Lytle, racing in second place, a kind of gloating, unsportsmanlike smile. Though the thunder of the engines overwhelmed their cheers, and the dust and smoke obscured their vision, the spectators nevertheless roared.

Just after the 50-mile mark, Lytle's steering gear broke and his Apperson Jack Rabbit emerged from the dust cloud and slid toward the outside of the track. But it didn't stop; after the entire field had passed it on the left, the car somehow slid *back* across the width of the track and rammed itself radiator-first into a mound of topsoil piled near the inside of turn one. The impact threw riding mechanic Joe Betts from his seat; he was not seriously injured, just stunned, but by the time he'd regained his wits he found Lytle digging the Apperson out of the loose dirt with a shovel he had yanked from the hands of a nearby groundskeeper. Lytle and Betts actually managed to rejoin the race for a while before further mechanical difficulties put them out for good.

Aitken stayed in front for 150 miles, at which point he cracked a cylinder and limped in, also done for the day. Usually an even-tempered sort, he seemed severely downcast at his poor luck, and, despite being a good friend of Carl Fisher's, predicted to reporters milling about the pits that "Someone is going to get killed out there today the way that track is breaking up! There's so much dust I couldn't tell who was in front of me or who was behind me!"

That last remark could be interpreted as a slap at Kellum, whose job it was to keep him apprised of traffic. For his part, though, Kellum wanted only to get back into the fray, and when he realized the Jack Rabbit was permanently out, said the weekly *Motor World*, "he wept at being unable to continue."

Kellum's is a pathetic tale, a fable on the familiar theme of being careful what you wish for. Consider: while he was still bawling, Charlie Merz's National had battery troubles and rolled to a stop on the backstretch, the driver skillfully managing to get his vehicle out of harm's way and onto the grass. Merz then ordered his riding mechanic, Robert Lyne, to run the breadth of the infield, a distance of nearly a mile, and bring back a fresh battery. Lyne took off "like Heidippides of Marathon fame" said *Motor World*, but unlike the legendary Greek, collapsed from exhaustion, "a mad look in his eyes," when he reached the pits. Seeing a chance to rejoin the race, Kellum picked up a spare battery and ran it back to Merz, a fellow member of the National team. Together they installed it, then hopped in Merz's No. 10 car and took off. Kellum, who had not long before lived the unexciting life of a Kokomo, Indiana, mailman, was so delighted by the turn of events that he "waved a salute" to the crowd as he and Merz came around in front of the grandstand. Fate had granted him a second shot at glory, and a realistic one to boot: as Merz bore down on the leader, and cars continued to drop out due to dust-blinded drivers or miscellaneous mechanical woes, the National began to overtake the field.

At 175 miles (or maybe it was "just after 200 miles," as another source says; the distance in this case isn't important, but the confusion about the distance is worth noting in light of what would happen in the first Indy 500), Merz and Kellum were racing in fourth place. The leader was Leigh Lynch, in the No. 52 Jackson—or, if you go by that equally reliable alternate source, Burman, in the No. 35 Buick. What is beyond dispute is that as they rounded turn two, near the more economical ($1.00 as opposed to $1.50), roofless "balloon bleachers," Merz asked Kellum to lean over and take the wheel for a moment while he wiped the track dust out of his eyes—and that as the mechanic was doing as instructed, their right front tire blew. The explosion, like many tire failures in those days, was violent and loud, and it caused Kellum to lose control of the vehicle, which crossed the racecourse and plowed through the outer fence (as well as several signs advising people to stand back for their own safety) and into the crowd, striking a number of spectators, some harder than others. Kellum flew out and landed in a ditch twenty feet distant, but the National, still moving at race speed, went up a graded embankment and soared, some reports said, fifty feet into the air—with a soon-to-be-dead farmhand from Trafalgar, Indiana, named Homer Jolliff flattened against its steaming radiator. Jolliff's final words, according to his employer, Lora Vandiver, who had been tugging on his sleeve and urging him to leave so they could beat the traffic, were, "Just let me look at this one last car."

Merz's National next struck a fifty-year-old furniture factory foreman named Herman Tapking a glancing blow, crushed another man at first believed to be Indianapolis railroad engineer Benjamin F. Logan against a fence, then turned turtle. Within moments, the Overland press car was on the scene, followed not long after by the track ambulance and the inevitable crush of spectators. At one point so many nonessential people crowded onto the track and hovered around the injured bodies (Kellum was "bleeding from innumerable places" and, like Bourque, "drowning in blood") that the militiamen, said the *Star*, "charged the crowd with their bayonets" and might have killed someone if the police had not been drawn out of their self-imposed banishment by the mayhem, noticed the part-time soldiers losing their composure, and promptly intervened. While all this happened, Merz, who had been given up for dead, crawled out from under his car, reached back in to turn off the ignition, and dusted himself off. "I think I am about finished with racing automobiles," he was quoted as saying. (He wasn't really.)

But the race wasn't over. Although three men were dead or dying, and only six cars were still running, it continued without pause, at least for a while. About 10 laps later, the No. 75 Marmon driven by Bruce Keen hit a hole in the track as it was coming off turn four, spun around backward and smashed into the right side of the pedestrian bridge that spanned the homestretch. A few people told the newspapers that they had seen Keen "nod off" just before the accident, although that bizarre accusation may have been part of a campaign to shift blame away from the Speedway and onto the drivers, in order to fend off lawsuits. Keen in any case was rendered groggy from a hard knock to the skull; his riding mechanic, James Schiller, either jumped or was thrown from the spinning vehicle and suffered scalp and head injuries. Eager to gawk at these latest crash victims, about 150 people crammed onto the bridge that was built to accommodate only about a dozen, causing the structure to sag scarily. "Get those people the hell off there!" Carl Fisher screamed at the militiamen as he roared toward the scene down an infield service road in his open-top Stoddard-Dayton. The bridge was emptied without further incident, and Fisher, his face ashen, slumped back into his vehicle. When the crowd noise suddenly lowered he looked up toward the finish line and saw Pop Wagner standing in the official's box, waving the checkered and yellow flags, halting the race abruptly at 235 miles, with, for whatever it was worth, Leigh Lynch, in the No. 52 Jackson, officially ahead.

One local paper, the *News*, reported that the crowd grew solemn and quiet, seemed sad and embarrassed for the Speedway founders, and simply dispersed. That sounds believable. But so does the rival *Star*'s starkly contrasting coverage, which portrays thrill-drunk fans "loathe [*sic*] to leave when the last race was called off," and describes a scene of mayhem at the hospital tent, where people pushed forward to see what they could of Kellum and the three injured spectators (Tapking would survive), and where, "strange to say, the women gave the most trouble." When people managed to get close to a body, they often tried to tear off a button or an epaulette, or pluck away a driving glove, to take home as a souvenir. "I watched Carl's face grow white from my box in the stands," wife Jane Fisher's ghostwriter wrote in *Fabulous Hoosier*. "The glorious day he had planned had turned into a carnival of death."

In the hours after the fatal accident, Indianapolis police dutifully made their rounds, informing various local families that they unwittingly had, as one paper put it, "sacrificed a loved one on the altar of speed." When they reached the home of the thirty-five-year-old Kellum, however, they found that a couple who had been at the races and who knew Claude and Floy Kellum and their three young sons had already been there and delivered the bad news. As soon as Floy—who didn't go to the Speedway that day because she'd had a premonition of disaster—had seen her friends coming up her front steps on Bellefontaine Street with a solemn look on their faces, she had broken down sobbing, correctly intuiting what their visit meant. Kellum's mother, Louisa, who ran a millinery shop on Indiana Avenue, also had foreseen trouble for her son at the Speedway, and a few days before had told him, "Claude, if you will only stay away from those races I will give you anything I have."

"Now, mother, don't you worry, because I'll get back all right," he had told her, according to the *Indianapolis News*.

Still, Louisa Kellum's first reaction, when the police found her at her shop and told her that her son had been killed at the Speedway, was to vigorously deny the possibility. She had seen the afternoon papers, she said, and they had reported that a Claude *Kellog* had died, and had said nothing, to her great relief, about a Claude *Kellum*, and so this horrible thing that they were telling her couldn't possibly be true. "Look!" she said, sobbing as she thrust the newspaper in the officers' faces. "It says *Kellog* — Claude *Kellog*!"

Then, added the *News*, she "did not wait to put on her street clothes, but ran from the millinery shop, frantic with grief."

For at least one other Indianapolis resident, hastiness with the facts added a cruel, confusing twist to an already awful afternoon. Emma Logan, the wife of Benjamin F. Logan, burst into tears when told by policemen that her husband had been slain by a race car at the Speedway. It had been barely two years, after all, since she had received word that Benjamin had lost both hands and feet in an industrial accident at the Indianapolis Traction and Terminal Company, where he worked at the time. While that had turned out to be a case of mistaken identity, and horrible news for another Benjamin F. Logan who worked at ITTC and his family, the experience, she told the officers, left her "permanently nervous," and "dreadful of everyday existence." But as the police were consoling her, who should walk in but her supposedly dead husband, wondering what had brought the authorities to his home. Told that his name and address had been found in the pants pocket of a corpse, he gasped and said, "Oh, that must be Jimmy West!" an acquaintance who at the Speedway that day had invited him to join the fraternal society known as the Improved Order of Redmen, and to whom, in response, Logan had given his calling card. The police left immediately for the home of West, where they woke up his wife, delivered what one paper called "their dark news," then stood by helplessly as "her cries aroused the entire neighborhood." The next day Logan told the *Star* that he had also once received a love letter from a woman he had never met, and, though he himself found the idea of so many Benjamin F. Logans somewhat amusing, all these false alarms were definitely starting to wear on the missus.

Progress requires sacrifice, and sometimes results in human tragedy, yet could the three days of auto racing at the Indianapolis Motor Speedway in the summer of 1909 be said, by any stretch of the term, to be worth the misery that they caused? The Speedway had drawn a total of some 72,000 spectators for the meeting, received worldwide publicity, and, thanks to the suffocating heat, sold a Great Lake of lemonade — but if you counted Littrell and little Elmer Grampton, as many of the newspapers did ("Speed Saturnalia!" "Deadly Speed Carnival!" "Throng Sees Necks and Marks Broken!"), seven people had died on account of the races. The spectators had arrived in ever-larger numbers each day, jazzed by the possibilities—but how many dreamed on that Saturday morning, as they slipped their admission ticket into the band of their straw boater, put on their seersucker suit jacket, and headed out the door that they would end the day thrill-drunk and staggering backward from a flashing bayonet, while holding a dead man's glove? Such a breakdown of decorum—of common decency—surely must have left people, even those not directly involved in the ugliness, brimming with self-disgust and shame. Plato, in Book IV of *The Republic*, says of people's inability to turn away from the sight of dead bodies that "there are not many other cases that when a man's desire violently prevails over his reason he reviles himself and is angry at the violence within him." No, the only person who might have said "It's all good" about the Indianapolis Motor Speedway just then was the Marion County coroner.

John J. Blackwell did not skulk into the shadows when the newspapers questioned his autopsy-first-ask-questions-later approach to his position. Rather, he brazenly declared himself "The Official Undertaker of the Indianapolis Motor Speedway," inventing a locution that ought to qualify him for the marketing hall of fame (there is one, run by the New York–based American Marketing Association). As the meet wore on, Blackwell moved forthrightly, gathering his racing car victims while he may because who could say if such deadly doings would ever transpire within his jurisdiction again. Indeed, one outraged out-of-town newspaper, the *Syracuse Herald*, had in response to the first day's deaths already run an editorial urging the city of Indianapolis to "close up the Speedway and make a skating rink out of it."

Although relatives of Billy Bourque and Harry Holcomb had made arrangements with the Indianapolis funeral directors A. M. Ragsdale and Flanner & Buchanan, respectively, to prepare their loved ones' bodies for shipment back to Massachusetts, Blackwell, said the *News*, "came around to the Speedway in his black wagon" and "seized" both corpses, on which he had already conducted $25 autopsies. He then brought them back to his office, where billable embalming procedures were begun. It was not until the two rival undertakers showed up with letters from their lawyers that Blackwell surrendered the half-processed cadavers.

Blackwell's embalming room looked for a while like a wax museum memorializing the three days of mayhem. When the meet ended on Saturday poor Cliff Littrell's corpse was still there, lying alongside Kellum, Jolliff, West, and Grampton, all of whom, Blackwell's autopsies revealed, were indeed killed by automobiles, just as eyewitnesses (in some cases, tens of thousands of eyewitnesses) could have testified, at no expense to taxpayers and with no further disturbance of the corpses. The only body in the city morgue that had not been pulled into Blackwell's autopsy orgy, said the *News*, was that of "the penniless Negro" Gibson Hayes, who had been found dead on the street a week earlier and who, being indigent, excited no curiosity in the coroner. While Blackwell attended to his sudden rush of business, Hayes's body decayed so badly that the morgue's custodian asked the police to take it for burial to the potter's field on Cossell Road.

Blackwell by then had managed to wring yet another $25 out of a sad situation. His lawyer, G. R. Estabrook, had noticed, while perusing his client's official job description in the course of helping Blackwell defend himself from critics, that Blackwell got paid extra fees not just for autopsies but also for conducting such death-related "inquests" as he deemed necessary. And so it was that about an hour after the race meet came to its abortive ending, Blackwell tracked down Fisher and officially informed him that his presence was required at the coroner's office that very evening at 6:15.

8

OUR STORY SO far: a series of pratfalls, preceded by stumbles, resulting in gruesome deaths. To quote a well-known Midwestern bard, everything is broken, no direction known. How does it feel to be Carl Graham Fisher, making his way through the remnants of the Speedway traffic to the new courthouse? He can only hope, as he chugs by the cornerstone in his Stoddard-Dayton, that he is in fact the resident of no mean city, for Indianapolis, if it wants to, has plenty to be mean about. Fisher has reinforced his hometown's most intimate fear: that it is overmatched by the brutally fast and harshly competitive twentieth century.

The two preliminaries and the main event meant to establish the Speedway as the Churchill Downs or Polo Grounds of automobile racing had melted down into three distinct flavors of disaster. The motorcycle and the car meet could not even be completed. Auto manufacturers and other industry leaders would soon be calling for an end to long races (meaning more than 25 miles), the equivalent of saying there should be no boxing matches longer than three rounds, a restriction that would effectively end big-time prizefighting in America. That could have been a moot development, though, because the lieutenant governor of Indiana, Frank J. Hall, appalled by the carnage at Day One of the Speedway meet, had already started a movement to abolish automobile racing of any sort. "They talk about bull fights in Mexico," Hall said. "But did you ever hear of *several people* being killed in a bull fight?" Instead of putting the sport on a pedestal, the Speedway had jeopardized its existence.

MERELY STARTING ONCE again under the same circumstances would not be enough to save Carl Fisher's blood-splattered Speedway. With Moross's help he had already done that twice, saying in effect after the balloons and the motorcycles, No, never mind *that*, focus on *this*. He needed to make fundamental changes and—because Fisher was an eccentric and sometimes smart man but hardly the combination of Einstein and P. T. Barnum that his hagiographers would depict in many simpleminded magazine articles and in books called *Pacesetter* and *Castles in the Sand*—he needed help. Whether he ever realized that he was beyond rescuing himself, and that he could only be saved by a deus ex machina, we will never know. But a deus ex machina is what he got, and when it came along he embraced it eagerly.

The machina in this case had a name, or actually several. It was sometimes called the Warner Electrical Timing Device, sometimes the Warner Timing System, and on other occasions the Horograph. As Fisher was running his automobile meeting in late August of 1909, its inventor, Charles H. Warner, a thirty-six-year-old engineer, was perfecting it in his lab in Beloit, Wisconsin. The WETD looked like a sewing machine attached by wire to a vintage Victrola. Its purpose was to time automobile races and—here was its real breakthrough potential—*to allow the officials at such events to establish a reliable running order of cars*, no matter how big the field or how long the race. In terms of our story, the WETD or Horograph resembles the machina warned against by the Roman poet Horace in his work *Ars Poetica* in that it will unsatisfyingly swipe from the shoulders of our protagonist (Fisher) much of the burden that Fate had lavished upon him, and which we perhaps had anticipated watching him escape solely by means of his wits and wiles. At the same time it is unlike the original machina—a primitive "special effect" used to lower theatrical gods into hopeless plot developments— in that it didn't work. Ever. Not in August of '09, as Warner fine-tuned it, and not long after it had allowed the Indianapolis 500-mile race to grow into what we know it as today: a holy moment in American sport, the Greatest Spectacle in Racing. But that was okay: the fact that it did not work did not matter. Only the fact that it existed did.

Welcome to the twentieth century.

THE OBVIOUS QUESTION is, how could a timing device, of all things, help Fisher out of his present fix? It may seem at this point that his problems revolved around matters of human safety and moral responsibility—and, of course, taroid—and that the nerdy issue of precision clockings and the related matter of running order would be far from the forefront of his beleaguered brain. But in fact, as he made his way to the coroner's office, the issue of how to effect safer and saner racing was already settled, more or less, as far as Fisher was concerned. He had come to the conclusion, probably even before the auto meet began, that his young engineer, Andrew, had made a terrible miscalculation, that the situation was untenable, and that, if they all could just get through the three days of racing without too much mayhem, he, Fisher, could solve that problem relatively easily by throwing money at it. He would repave the surface with concrete (as at Brooklands), wood, or something else that *worked.* Fisher felt that any of those options, though no doubt expensive, would instantly and dramatically lower the number of accidents, quiet the critics, and allow him to conduct races that were titillatingly dangerous but not so frequently deadly. His restless mind was already on to the *next* problem, and if he seemed distracted and grim as he plopped into the chair across the desk from Blackwell that long-ago Saturday evening, it was because this looming issue was even more daunting than the one that had brought him to the coroner's inquest.

What concerned him was . . . let's call it graspability. The problem hadn't yet hit home with the general public because the spectacular wrecks and overstimulated spectators at the auto meet had served as a diversion, obscuring what for Fisher was the disappointing discovery that the Speedway had not proven to be a congenial place to watch race cars compete. It was, in fact, no more congenial than a road course, displaying one basic flaw that, if left unaddressed, could be fatal to the sport's marketability. To say it succinctly, almost as soon as a race started, you couldn't tell what the hell was going on.

Road courses had been problematic from the start. It had been clear to most astute observers after the first edition of the Vanderbilt Cup in 1904, for instance, that it would be all but impossible to turn that spectacle, as popular as it was in its first few runnings, into a viable business. Like virtually all road races, the Cup, conducted that first year on 30.24 miles of country lanes and more properly constructed highways in Nassau County, New York, was, to use a promoter's term, "ungateable," meaning that as spread out as it was, you couldn't restrict admission and charge people for access. It was also, for the same reason, spectator-unfriendly; race goers found a spot somewhere along the course and squatted there in a bemused state as the cars whizzed by in a blurred scrum. The fun, if any, was in just being there, seeing your friends, swigging some champagne, and having a picnic while begoggled speed addicts raced and wrecked.

Track racing, in which all the cars were constantly visible from a $1 seat in the grandstand, was supposed to make the event more graspable, and thus more exciting and enjoyable. This would be especially the case, most followers of auto sport assumed, on a purpose-built, two-and-a-half-mile circuit like the Indianapolis Speedway, a huge improvement, in theory at least, over any tight, poorly banked country fair track designed for harness and thoroughbred horses. But the 250-mile Prest-O-Lite contest, the 100-mile G&J trophy, and the 300-mile Wheeler-Schebler trophy race had told a different tale. Those races had shown that while you could, especially with the help of binoculars, take in the whole field at the Speedway (assuming the smoke and the dust were not too thick), no one in the grandstand, the press box, or even the judges' booth could speak with any certainty about the running order, at least not after the cars began passing each other, making pit stops, and having spinouts and accidents. Was No. 24 in the lead by a length? A lap? Or was he in fact a lap behind the leaders? Was No. 8 pulling away from, or just starting to catch up to, everyone else? And this No. 18, suddenly looming up on the outside—what lap was *he* on? Some officials shouted things from megaphones and others hung numbers on a scoreboard, but even when the shouters and hangers agreed, which was not always the case, how did *they* know what was really the truth?

The timing and placement system the Speedway had adopted for its inaugural auto meet, designed by one W. C. Baker, involved trip wires placed at intervals around the track (what the wires were connected to is unclear) and two stopwatch-holding operators, "one of whom," said the motor magazine *The Club Journal*, "was obliged to make rapid interpretations from the chronograph record and subtract one set of figures from another in order to secure the elapsed time. So much depended on eye, ear, voice and mathematical skill that the device was far from automatic." It was even further from accurate, and it appears that though it supposedly cost an astounding $10,000 to install (Moross's figure), it was largely ignored by officials and newspapermen in favor of their own simple observations and pencil jottings, which as we have seen in the case of the newspaper accounts of the Wheeler-Schebler race resulted in conflicting versions of who was ahead, and how much distance had been covered, at any given moment. In an age when so many sports were competing for attention, it was advantageous for auto racing to be unique. But to be the only game that was utterly incomprehensible—*Come on out and catch the chaos!*—seemed like a dubious selling point.

THE FUNDAMENTAL, AND closely related, problems of timing and placement had dogged the sport from the start. In its January 28, 1905, issue, *Scientific American* noted, "It is not strange that the inexperienced men usually called upon to time automobile races should record variations of an entire second or more. The need for an errorless automatic timing system is thus plainly apparent." Timing, in those very early days, was still being done by officials holding stopwatches, following the horse racing model then in use for several decades. In car races of any length or significance a committee of well-dressed clockers, each with his own watch, would do the timing and, if they came up with slightly different numbers, as they often did, they would hash things out among themselves before announcing an official result to the public. In such cases, the loudest shouter or the timer with the most social, political, or professional clout usually got his way, and accuracy took the hindmost. But what was good enough for horse racing, a suddenly quaint game in which people cared only about the time of the winner, if they cared at all, wasn't acceptable for the three-times-faster and more complicated business of motor sports. Yet what could be done? One early answer was to assign *teams* of timers to concentrate on *each car*, making sure it was clocked properly and on the same lap as the leader over the course of a race that might last as long as four or five hours. Yet even if human eyes could accurately track one car vis-à-vis all the others for such an extended period, the human thumb did not seem up to the new standards. Electrical chronometers could now measure time slices as thin as one one-hundredth of a second (mechanical stopwatches were mostly geared to quarter-second intervals), but to manually start and stop these precision devices seemed to defeat their purpose.

The Mors Company of Paris answered the need for an "errorless automatic" timer in 1904. Its device consisted, said the April 23, 1904, *Scientific American*, "of two instruments, one of which is placed at the start and the other at the finish, with a single wire running between them." One instrument was also attached to a "start wire" running across the width of the racecourse, the other to a similar "finish wire." When a car "stretched" the start wire, by running over it, an electrical impulse traveled to the finish line box, where a hammer fell and "a needle point is momentarily brought against a roll of paper to make a dot." As the car raced along, "a clockwork mechanism draws a band of paper from the drum by means of a set of rollers, the paper passing through a slot in the cubical brass piece." When the car "stretched" the finish wire, another lever made another dot on the paper. "The exact time from start to finish is obtained by counting the number of spaces and fractions which have been unrolled between the two punctures." The Mors Company did not say how its unwieldy system would handle races consisting of more than one car, or races on tracks, where the start and finish line are identical, or virtually so. Still, the *Scientific American* article does mention that when the lid on the starting line component is closed "it acts as a table," so the operator can at least have a sandwich and perhaps a glass of wine while he waxes nostalgic about the simpler days of the stopwatch.

While the Mors electrical chronograph failed to gain traction in the marketplace, it did set the ridiculously Rube Goldberg–esque standard for early-twentieth-century auto racing timers. A little less than four months after it profiled the French device, *Scientific American* was back on the case, describing an allegedly less complicated system developed by a Bostonian named Alden L. McMurtry that had been used recently at the Eagle Rock, Massachusetts, hill climb. McMurtry, like the Mors Company, believed in stretching wires across the course, in his case at intervals of a quarter-mile, but his wires (a mile long in some cases) were connected to a glittering carousel of conventional stopwatches (one for each quarter-mile interval), which were turned on in unison, apparently by hand, at the start of the race, and which subsequently clicked off one by one as the lead car passed over the wire. Could one determine the times of the cars following the leader? Well, no, not really. And how would you know the running order of the field? McMurtry did have an answer for that: "Each timing station is provided with a telephone, through which communication may be had with the main station." So, the judges at each quarter-mile were supposed to call one chief timer and tell him who was running 1st through, let's say, 20th? The reader will perhaps not be surprised to learn that following the Eagle Rock hill climb at least one rival timing device manufacturer issued a statement proclaiming that the system that caused such confusion there was definitely *not* his.

By the time that the Indianapolis Motor Speedway was shopping for a timing-and-scoring system in the spring of 1909, the W. C. Baker method was considered state-of-the-art. In publicity sent out in early August of the year, Moross promised that this system would include a sixty-foot steel tower "from the top of which large dials will record the first three cars, giving their time, the number of the car and the miles it has traveled." How Baker proposed to "record" and "give" this information via the tower, the Speedway did not say, and in any event no such tower seems ever to have materialized. Neither did the futuristic-sounding "team bulletin boards," also promised in Moross's press release, which were to stand "on the opposite side of the track from the main grandstand" and somehow "flash" messages from individual team managers to their respective drivers "as the pilots whirl by." Based on contemporary accounts of the races, it seems that these bulletin boards either didn't work or were never constructed; crews communicated with drivers in the usual way, through hand signals and blackboards.

Everyone in auto racing was learning as they went in those days, though, and the Baker system was at least a good teaching aid. By being so spectacularly inadequate it underscored the point that without reliable timing and scoring, a "championship distance" race became, after not too many laps, about as incomprehensible to the average motor sports aficionado as Balinese story-dance.

CARL FISHER WAS not yet aware of the Warner Electrical Timing Device when he arrived in Blackwell's office for questioning, but he would learn about it soon enough, when Charles Warner and his brother Arthur came to the Speedway to make a presentation a few weeks later, and Fisher would immediately recognize the system as heaven-sent for his needs. One thing he absolutely loved about the WETD was that it was so complicated, much more so than even the ridiculously convoluted and delicate devices that had come before it and on which it built. Frequently, "complicated" is a pejorative word, or a euphemism, but not to Fisher. He was not a less-is-more, keep-it-simple kind of guy, as his signing off on Andrew's parfait track, his overpacking of the Speedway programs, and his initial idea that his car showroom in downtown Indianapolis should "reproduce the annual auto exposition in Madison Square Garden" would indicate. Fisher liked the way Charles Warner thought.

To the elements employed by earlier timing companies—i.e., miles of wire, rolls of paper, inky ribbon, springs, automated hammers, telephones, and human links in the chain of supposedly flawless mechanical communication—Warner had added typewriter components, Dictaphones, bells, and . . . no, not whistles, but marbles—hundreds and hundreds of them that would be dropped into tubes to keep count of each car's laps. The one element his Horograph did not borrow from its predecessors was the stopwatch itself, rigged up in some newfangled way. Instead, Warner put in his "sewing machine" box, and at the heart of his system four roller-skate-size wheels "suggestive," Moross wrote, "of those used in the familiar recording telegraph or news ticker." Warner's wheels were embossed with numbers and capable of stamping on paper a time he claimed would be accurate down to a hundredth of a second. An ever-unspooling strip of paper, as well as a typewriter ribbon, rested along the tops of the ever-moving wheels (wheels that at any given moment might rip the paper and the ribbon to shreds). When a race car passed over one of two electrical wires that was stretched "a few inches" above the surface of the track (one at the start line, the other one mile further on), the current was interrupted and a hammer "actuated by an electro-magnet" thwacked down hard across the ribbons, pressing them into the wheels and recording a time. Warner said he could record each entrant's pass over the wire as long as one car was at least six inches behind another. When a race was in progress, especially a forty-car race like the inaugural Indianapolis 500, the hammer would *thwack-thwack* away madly, and all sorts of slightly askew time stamps would be produced. But which jittery row of numbers belonged to which car?

This is where the humans came in. The system required at least one main spotter for each car, with a backup man strongly suggested for longer races. As the racers whizzed by, the spotter assigned to, say, No. 27 would call out "27" when his man hit the wire. The head timer would then write this down on his scoring sheet, keeping an ear cocked for the exact order in which the numbers were being shouted. Of course, in a forty-car field such as competed in the 1911 Indy 500, several spotters were likely to be shouting at once, making the timer's job more than tricky. But no problem: three or four Columbia Dictaphones, each operated by a team of certified "recording specialists," were on hand to pick up the shouts, the theory being that these could be played back and sorted out later in case of confusion.

And confusion does seem possible, given that less than a minute after they hit the start/finish line, cars would strike the one-mile wire, where another team of spotters would record their running order by hand, then immediately telephone the head timer to give him *their* numbers . . . by which time the lead car was hitting the start/finish wire again, and other men were shouting more numbers. Also jammed into the crowded judges' stand—actually this was more like Rube Goldberg meets *A Night at the Opera*—were lap counters, one for every entrant in the race, who picked a marble out of a huge bowl and dropped it in a numbered tube each time the car they were watching passed the start/finish point. Additional teams of spotters counted laps from the pits (an intentional redundancy) and there were teams of runners constantly shuttling information to the teams of men who ran the Speedway's four far-flung scoreboards. Still more teams of technicians stood near the wires, watching that the cables didn't snap and attempting to repair them if and when they did. Teams of "timing guards" guarded the teams of technicians. And so on. In a 1911 puff piece about the Horograph, the *Chicago Tribune* estimated that approximately two thousand people were involved in its operation at any one time.

What Carl Fisher found most useful about a system this sprawling and serpentine is that it had the potential to impress. Today we revere Steve Jobs for putting a million ideas in a shiny black box no bigger than a cigarette pack, but in 1909 it was difficult to convince people that a more unobtrusive, simpler machine was an improvement over its predecessor. In a less ironic age, the bigger the better. When Fisher watched the Warner brothers pitch their device to him in his office in September of 1909, the Speedway president may have sensed that an "automatic system" that required an army to operate was unworkable if not downright insane. But as soon as he realized that the WETD was much more complicated than the failed Baker system, and in fact nearly impossible to understand, he knew that he could sell it to the public as something in which they could have unwavering faith.

THE RECORD SHOWS that Carl Fisher was at best a minor figure in almost all of the admittedly numerous fields—racing, automobile manufacturing, aviation, real estate, hotels, highway construction, finance—into which he ventured. A great many of the decisions he made concerning the Indianapolis Motor Speedway, before and after this point, proved to be bad. Nevertheless, Fisher remains worthy of our deeper consideration, if only because he understood as well as any member of his vertiginous generation this fundamental early-twentieth-century truth: that with a horse you could go only as far as your daddy and your mommy had gone—but with horseshit all things were possible.

PART TWO

CARL GRAHAM FISHER AND THE INVENTION OF THE INDIANAPOLIS 500

9

Now that automobiles are becoming so plentiful and are speeded so recklessly, breeders should use greater care than ever to mate their mares with good, sensible, brainy stallions such as get level-headed, fearless animals.

—*American Horse Breeder*, June 24, 1902

WHEN ELMER JESSUP left Carl Fisher's Prest-O-Lite factory shortly after 2:00 P.M. on December 20, 1907, he was many things—fairly tall; thirty-five years old; happily married to the former Mary Evrett; in a terrible hurry; a former hay baler who had only recently quit his nineteenth-century job and taken a twentieth-century one, as an assembler of gas-powered automobile headlights—but what Jessup was most immediately and most importantly that chill gray afternoon was on fire. To be clear: it was not his clothes that were burning; it was Jessup. His garments, inner and outer, had been consumed by flames before he exited the grimy old brick building on Indianapolis's East Street. Now, buck naked and transformed, as the *Star* would say, into "a human torch," he was running toward Washington Street amidst a shower of sauerkraut. Jessup had been polishing brass containers of acetylene on the first floor of the facility when, for reasons never determined, fire broke out near him, setting off explosions that ripped into the food processing factory next door, causing thunder and cabbage. He died thirteen hours later, knowing precisely but pointlessly how the well-grilled weenie feels: another victim of Progress in its myriad, foul-smelling forms.

Crazy things like this happened when you came within the gravitational field of the man they called Crazy Carl. Five years earlier, when

Fisher was still a barnstorming auto racer, he and the driver Earl Kiser, a pear-shaped Ohioan known as the Dayton Dumpling, brought their powerful Mohawk car to the Zanesville, Ohio, fair to put on a exhibition of speed over the half-mile horse racing track. This was thrilling merely in the abstract, since Fisher, born with a severe astigmatism, was by today's standards legally blind—but things would get more exciting still. As he and Kiser made a pass by the grandstand early in their performance, their right front tire blew, a spoke from the wheel caught in the track surface, and whoever was driving the car—some papers said it was Fisher; Fisher said it was Kiser; and Kiser at times claimed he wasn't even there—lost control; the Mohawk plunged into the crowd, injuring many, including an infant, and "crushing to a pulp," said the *Dayton Daily News*, the leg of John Goodwin, a sixty-four-year-old security guard. Goodwin, "a Civil War veteran and a prominent member of secret societies," according to the kind of obituary you just don't see anymore, died at the hospital the next day, the first of an uncertain number of people killed by the mad Mohawk. "I can't tell you how many there were [in total]," Fisher would say in later times, with a sigh, when asked about that day's fatalities. "They were dying for two years."

Fisher at least gets points—okay, maybe *a* point—for being regretful—okay, *wistful*—about the tragedy. You can perhaps give him another for saying shortly afterward that he and Kiser were so troubled by what had happened at Zanesville that they might never race again—though he goes on in the same *Indianapolis News* interview to whine about the sprained ankle he sustained in the wreck (he and the Dumpling, who broke a leg at wherever he in fact was that day, would return to the racetrack as soon as their injuries healed). Fisher is a tough guy to figure, and he would no doubt delight in knowing that he had thoroughly defeated the two welterweight biographers who have tried to reconcile his almost lifelong devotion to fun with his often grumpy manner and smallish, semi-hard heart. One shouldn't overstate his callousness. He was not, for example, as cold as Barney Oldfield, whose car blew a rear tire and killed a spectator in Detroit on the very same bright September day that Goodwin was crushed, and who, when such things happened, had nothing to say except "What do you want from me? That idiot shouldn't have been standing so close to the track!"

But though Fisher's face might turn ashen in times of stress, a tear was never known to trickle from behind his thick lenses. He tried hard to put sad subjects—like his father, his son, and the deaths of his employees—out of his mind. His default reaction, even in his bitter later years, was to make a joke, often a crude or dumb one, about everything. One report said that in early 1908 he and the owner of the damaged food processing plant in downtown Indianapolis jovially shook hands on a "settlement" after Fisher paid him $3 for his ruined barrel of kraut. Mary Jessup, it should be remembered, received nothing for her Elmer.

And yet if Fisher had allowed his own and others' sentiments to rule his thoughts, he could never have gotten out of bed; like military commanders, the unfettered industrialists of the early 1900s—meaning not just Fisher but much bigger kahunas like Rockefeller, Harriman, Carnegie, and Morgan—had to choose between a life of conquest or continuous mourning. What could one do? The gears ground, as they supposedly must, and every so often they caught a necktie or a shoelace. Some men are lucky and some are lubrication. To quote another fellow from Indianapolis: so it goes.

THE EXPLOSION AT the East Street plant in December of 1907 was the second of three Prest-O-Lite disasters that would damage as many different facilities during a twelve-month span, but those were hardly the only accidents the company experienced. Fisher and his friend James Allison had bought the basic concept of what became Prest-O-Lite in 1904 from an undercapitalized Purdue professor named Fred Avery, who held a French patent on a process that used compressed acetylene gas to solve the then nagging problem of how to produce illumination for nighttime motoring (batteries were undependable and short-lived, even after Thomas Edison took a crack at increasing their storage capacity). They paid Avery $2,000 for the rights to his patent. Fisher during his career hatched and backed many revolutionary schemes, some worthwhile (the Indianapolis 500-mile race; the development of Miami Beach as a winter playground), others flagrantly not (Zoline, about which more lies ahead; the Lincoln Highway). "I have a new hen coming off!" he would say by way of announcing yet another idea. But his impulse to acquire Prest-O-Lite, no doubt the least glitzy and glamorous of his many ventures, is what made him rich. As hundreds of manufacturers and individual car owners clamored for the gas lamps, which Avery had not had sufficient funds to bring to market, Fisher and Allison quickly became major players in the burgeoning automobile business. By 1908 the company was worth perhaps $20 million.

The downside was that an unfortunate number of the factories and canister refilling stations that Prest-O-Lite established around the country routinely exploded, resulting in injury and death. An Indianapolis blast in 1908 hurt several employees and blew patients at the nearby St. Francis hospital from their beds, resulting in at least one fatality, not to mention an editorial cartoon on the front page of the *News* that showed little men in high-top shoes and derbies flying out the windows of a quaking Prest-O-Lite plant. Dealing with these messes, managing the ensuing lawsuits and local police investigations, taking the newsmen assigned to the latest Prest-O-Lite story out for drinks—all this became the cost of doing business for Fisher and Allison, but never for a moment a reason to sell or close down such an immensely profitable venture. The money made them more than a bit giddy, and the partners, pals since their days as professional bike racers, eventually developed a blackly humorous code for communicating the latest news about explosions at one of their facilities, saying in telegrams, or when they stuck their heads into each other's offices, that "Omaha left at 4:30" or "Boston departed at 6:45." It wasn't that they didn't care about their employees, just that they cared more about other things. Always try to have fun: that was their philosophy. When life hands you a bloody industrial accident, they seemed to be saying to the world and to each other, make a Bloody Mary.

Men like Fisher, however they might enhance or diminish society by the way they do business, serve a useful function as human crash test dummies. By ceding to their impulses at virtually every turn they allow the rest of us good little boys and girls to see what happens when conventional attitudes toward moderation and self-denial get tossed aside. After the Prest-O-Lite money began to roll in, and for the first time in his life he had the means to do whatever he wanted, Fisher often ate steak and fried potatoes three times a day, chain-smoked foul-smelling cigars (he could afford Havanas, but preferred "the cheap ones that are half cabbage, half turnip"), drank scotch and water as if scotch *were* water, and stayed out very late making merry with practically every secretary he ever hired. He had, in other words, little imagination when it came to vices, but a greater than average willingness, when he woke up dry-mouthed and stogie-scented in some working girl's apartment, to dust himself off and stagger back into the fray, starting with, say, a nice beefsteak breakfast at Pop Haynes's restaurant down on North Pennsylvania Street.

"Living with Carl Fisher was like living in a circus," observed ex-wife Jane. (And, indeed, Fisher kept a pet elephant named Rosie while living in Miami.) "There was something exciting going on every minute of the day. Some of it was very good; sometimes it was very bad. Still, it was living. It was excitement that I never found again." (Not that she didn't try: Jane married six times after divorcing Fisher.) Certainly, a purer example of the sybaritic lifestyle would be hard to find, and those harboring a scientific interest in the effects of sin on the human nose might want to seek out photos of Crazy Carl taken shortly before he died in 1939 at the age of sixty-five.

One peculiar aspect of Fisher's pleasure seeking surfaced after the time frame of our story yet is worth noting. Several who knew him intimately during this period swore his drinking intensified markedly on a single, historic day: January 16, 1919, which was when the U.S. Senate ratified the Eighteenth Amendment to the Constitution, auguring the official start, one year later, of Prohibition. Once it was clear that he would be forbidden by law from acquiring alcohol, he switched, his friends said, from enthusiastic recreational drinking to defiant, self-destructive ossification. It was purely a matter of principle, his supporters insisted: if the Woodrow Wilson administration had outlawed asparagus instead of alcohol, Fisher would have eaten asparagus for breakfast; he was just that kind of pigheaded, populist guy. "Not even the United States Government could tell Carl Fisher what he should or should not eat or drink!" wrote Jane Fisher in her deranged and occasionally entertaining 1947 memoir *Fabulous Hoosier.* Said Cloyd Hewes, a worker on one of Fisher's Florida yachts: "Prohibition made a rummy outta him." From being as absentminded about liquor as he was about money—he and Jane previously had not paid much mind to current household levels of either, in the manner of the aristocratic WASPs they aspired to be, and they often briefly ran out of both—he became a hoarder of booze, scotch especially, storing a huge cache in his Florida basement, then ordering his groundskeepers to bury it in the backyard, only to have it moved again, to a boat, when he felt (incorrectly) that the feds were preparing to raid his Miami mansion, the Shadows, in search of the stuff. Of course, these could be seen as the actions of a paranoid addict, panicky at the thought of losing his stash. But his friends insisted that Fisher went to pieces, fatally injuring his liver, in the process of making a point.

The truth is, he always did have a Huck Finn–ish disdain for rules, a cocky, lower-class querulousness that may have been his single most endearing trait, making him, at times, agreeable to be around despite an array of off-putting personal habits that included (in addition to smoking thirty-five stinky cigars each day) constant spitting, swearing ("Christ on a bicycle!" was one of his favorites), and chewing on a cud of salted peanuts, which he replenished by snatching goobers from large jars placed strategically in his homes and offices, often near the requisite spittoons, and popping them into his mouth at all hours. (In *Pacesetter*, his biography of Fisher, Jerry M. Fisher, a distant relation, writes, "The entire household shared in shelling, roasting and salting the 100-pound bags of peanuts he brought home so that jars of salted peanuts could be available throughout the house.")

The overall impression he gave was that of a babe too soon denied the breast: orally needy and cranky about authority. Fisher couldn't help playing the bad boy. When he worked as a teenage "news butcher," selling papers, magazines, and cheaply bound books on the narrow-gauge trains making short runs out of Indianapolis, he hid a picture of a naked woman beneath his change apron: if you tipped him a nickel he would, after swiveling his head to see if any conductors were watching, flip it up and give you a peek. (He was fired many times for this but always rehired because "I was the best salesman out of the Union News Company at the time" and receipts dipped dramatically when he was in the doghouse.) In later years, when he sold bicycles, then cars, in Indianapolis, his numerous publicity stunts were usually pulled off to the dismay of the police, whose Keystone Kops outrage only underscored Fisher's devilish appeal.

To know Crazy Carl was to sooner or later receive unsolicited from him a plainly wrapped parcel that turned out to be *The Sexual Life of Savages in North-western Melanesia* by Bronislaw Malinowski, a scholarly but explicit work that Fisher found hilarious. Never mind that he wouldn't be there to see the man or lady of the house, or perhaps better yet their primly dressed maid, ripping off the brown paper and blushing. Fisher's philosophy was to stir the pot first and figure out exactly what he was cooking up later. That was certainly one reason that in the summer of 1910, with scientists, civic leaders, and auto industry spokesmen all agreeing and decreeing that ultra-long auto races of 250 or 300 miles were dangerous to human life, and a cruel and savage custom that ought to be swept into the dustbin of America's sometimes barbaric past, he announced that his Speedway would present the grandest grind ever—a 500-mile sweepstakes—and how do you like them apples?

CARL FISHER WAS born fifty miles southeast of Indianapolis on January 12, 1874, and grew up with the automobile—or more precisely, in a world where motorized vehicles were morphing rapidly from rumor to reality. The standard joke—alas, the only joke—in standard books of automotive history is that the first car race took place shortly after the second car was constructed. But while this may be almost funny because it is almost true, we can say with reasonable surety that the first *formal* auto contest ever staged in America (or likely anywhere) occurred four years after Fisher's birth, in Wisconsin. This was a 200-mile road race, from Green Bay to Madison, that attracted just two experimental steam-powered wagons, weird-looking conveyances (think of buckboards with boilers), which had been christened the "Oshkosh" and the "Green Bay." The latter broke down in midcourse and the only slightly less hideous former achieved an average speed of 6 mph as it strained and grunted toward the finish wire in Madison. So much excitement was aroused by this event that the second car race in America did not take place for another seventeen years.

A lot about cars needed to be worked out before ordinary folk like the Fisher family of Greensburg, Indiana, could get behind them in any meaningful way. Motorized vehicles had to be made practical—no twelve-foot-high black iron smokestacks, like the steamers in Wisconsin, please—and cheap, though their price never came down quite far enough for Carl's ne'er-do-well father, Albert, who died in the mid-1920s without ever having owned an automobile. Albert Fisher, a lawyer and drunk, was booted out of the house by his wife, Ida, in 1886. Carl would never completely lose touch with his derelict dad, though the letters the successful son included with small checks in later years often said "This is not for booze" and were never signed more warmly than "Yours truly." Carl's coolness was understandable, given that due to Albert's absence he had to work full-time at age twelve, news butchering and shoeshining to help support his mother and siblings. Not that he minded abandoning the classroom; because of his (undiagnosed) astigmatism he was considered, he often said in later years, processing the put-down into a kind of wistful boast, "the stupidest boy in school."

Carl's other claim to fame as a child was that he could run backward faster than many of his friends could run the regular way. The trick itself is less interesting than the fact that Fisher, in his neighborhood, was *defined* by a trick, an impulse to entertain and do things the irregular way, even then. Because accidents are an intrinsic part of the backward-running life even when you're not half-blind, and young Fisher so often sported a limp or a bump or a bandage, the other kids took to calling him Crip, short for Cripple. And precisely because it was not the sort of nickname one flashed in polite society—it was not Skip or Biff or Chip or Boomer—he wore the moniker with pride. In case it's not already apparent, Carl Fisher was the Bart Simpson of the Belle Epoque.

Instead of a skateboard, though, Fisher had a bicycle, always and everywhere. He started out with one of those high-wheel models, which were all you could get at the time, and then bought himself what was retroactively called a "safety" bike—in contrast to its predecessor, it had relatively low wheels of equal size and (thanks to a Scottish engineer named Dunlop) shock-absorbing pneumatic tires—not long after they hit the market in 1890 (or as soon as he got over the notion that they were something for sissies). Partly because they *were* women-friendly, safety bicycles sold by the millions to a global audience ready, after a century of revolutions and other struggles toward individual liberty, to see chains as a means of freedom and fun. But the bicycle boom didn't just catch Fisher's eye; it walloped him in the labonza. To someone like the teenage Carl, an impressionable youth casting about for a way to combine business and pleasure, a machine that could be used for transportation *and* recreation *and* racing *and* daredevilry touched him too personally to be merely a part of his life. This wasn't the chick you fooled around with; this was the girl you married. And so a full-on commitment it was: over the course of several months in 1891, the bike-besotted eighteen-year-old opened up a bicycle shop at 76 Pennsylvania Street, joined the Zig-Zag Club, a merry band of Indianapolis bachelor bikers who had a clubhouse adjoining the Empire Burlesque theater, and he began training for a career as a professional bike racer, happily discovering at the outset that all that backward running he'd been doing had given him quads of steel.

THE BICYCLE ACTUALLY constituted Fisher's second encounter with kismet. The first time he felt that he had stumbled upon something so ideally suited to him, and destined to be an important part of his life, had come in his news-butchering days, when he became intrigued by the writings of Robert G. Ingersoll, a freethinker whose speeches and essays, said a pamphlet from the Ingersoll League, "enable you to live ruggedly, comfortably, sanely. . . . So infectious is [Ingersoll's] gay, humorous viewpoint that you will adopt it before you have read a hundred pages of his singing, buoyant, fighting prose! His attitude is so sensible, so rewarding—so certain of *victory*!" Fisher sold Ingersoll's books in paperback editions on the trains, and rare was the customer who bought a copy not perceptibly pre-thumbed by its vendor. Plopping down at the end of a half-empty coach car after his papers had been peddled, and absorbing the positive aphorisms put forward by the former Civil War colonel, Fisher felt at once inspired and affirmed.

In some ways it was an unlikely attraction: Ingersoll, a pal of Walt Whitman's and the featured eulogizer at the poet's funeral in 1892, was an open-minded life-lover unburdened by the racial, religious, and ethnic prejudices that would become so pronounced in the mature Crazy

Carl. But at the center of his philosophy, "The Great Agnostic" had a four-point plan that harmonized perfectly with the daemon inside Fisher that was always nudging him toward the comic. To wit: "1. Happiness is the only good. 2. The way to be happy is to make others so. 3. The place to be happy is here. 4. The time to be happy is now." Toward the end of his life, long after he had abandoned Indianapolis and was devoting himself to the development of Miami and Montauk, Long Island, as posh resorts, Fisher still occasionally sent the twelve-volume complete works of Ingersoll, bound in maroon and gold leather, to cronies he had met nearly fifty years before in his hometown bike shop.

For Fisher, the bicycle world was what the university was to some of his better-bred peers: a place to forge relationships that would remain useful in one way or another for decades to come. At the Zig-Zag he met Howard Marmon, who would manufacture the car that would be officially credited with winning the first Indy 500. He also grew close to club founder Art Newby as well as Jim Allison, both of whom became fellow Speedway founders, partners in other business ventures, and valuable sobering influences on Fisher's life. On the rough-and-tumble racing circuit, where he had a decent amount of success once he learned to fall off a bicycle traveling 30 miles per hour, Fisher competed against—and occasionally as part of—a team called the Speed Kings, with a part-time elevator operator named Barney Oldfield, described by his biographer William F. Nolan as a master of the "dangerous wheel-tangling, handlebar-hooking tactics employed to eliminate stubborn novices." Fisher's fellow racers also included a host of slightly less wild wheelmen who would wind up driving automobiles in Speedway races. Meanwhile, back at the bicycle shop, he got to know *tout* Indianapolis, if only because that city had a raging case of bike fever running across all demographic lines, and, to paraphrase Montaigne's immortal line about defecation, even kings, philosophers, and ladies had to get their flats fixed—at two bits per puncture.

Which is not to say that the bike shop in the early days left him all that many extra quarters to fool around with, once he had given his brothers Rolla and Earl their weekly paychecks, and put aside a little something for Ida, and maybe sent a few bucks to papa Albert, too.

The depression of 1893 hit Indianapolis particularly hard; the city was a railroad junction and the financial panic had been caused largely by the overextension and eventual collapse of major rail lines like the Atchison, Topeka & Santa Fe. That and a steamy, virtually rainless summer that all but ruined a slew of Hoosier farmers combined to put the kibosh on bike sales. Times were so tough that as he reached his twenties Fisher was still living at home, sleeping in the same room that as a child he had exited many times by walking on a slack "high wire" that went from his window ledge to a backyard tree, stairs being more convenient but of little use in eliciting gasps of astonishment and anxiety from the neighbors. If the young shop owner hadn't been stirring up some excitement now by flogging the virtues of the newly invented tandem bike, as well as his own homemade variation, the "triplet," or bicycle built for three, Fisher's Cycles might not have survived those lean times.

IN RETROSPECT, THE financial adversity of the gray '90s was grit that produced pearls of publicity, or free advertising, the only kind Fisher could then afford. Fisher's interest in the newfangled art of publicity went back to at least the age of nine, when one snowy morning he got the idea of attaching a banner bearing the name of the grocery store where he was already working part-time to the back of his sled. He liked, as a child, to imagine life as an elaborate but well-oiled machine: he coasted downhill, the flag unfurled, the public took note, and comestibles flew from the shelves. A businessman himself now, he had, to use his homely expression, all kinds of hens coming off with regard to promotional ideas, but because of poor cash flow, little stock to sell to those who found their way to his doorstep. He set about remedying that situation by hopping a train to Toledo, where he had somehow wangled a Monday-morning meeting with Albert A. Pope, the elaborately mustachioed fifty-year-old Boston Brahmin who owned the Pope-Toledo Company, maker of the Columbia, the most popular bicycle in America.

Why would Pope agree to see him? Pope seemed to be wondering that himself when Fisher arrived. The magnate kept him waiting all day Monday and Tuesday, and then nearly two and a half days more, finally granting his twenty-year-old petitioner a grudging and grumpy audience just before closing on Friday. Rolling with the slight, Fisher strode in smiling ("Carl's smile was his greatest asset," Jane Fisher said) and told Pope that while his fellow bike racers thought the Columbia was the bee's knees, distribution in Indiana was scandalously scanty. Pope grumbled sarcastically that he supposed his visitor wanted to go home with a few pieces at a good price, eh? Fisher said no: he preferred an entire *boxcar* full of bikes—350, to be exact—on consignment. "You've got more nerve than a government mule!" Pope responded, but a week later the Columbias rolled into Indianapolis, and in another month Fisher had sold every last one.

Soon after—or maybe it was just before; Fisher didn't like talking about his hardscrabble early years, and he was sloppy with details on the few occasions when he did—he paid a similar call to another bicycle bigwig named George Erland, in Columbus, Ohio. "I want to build a showroom for bicycles in Indianapolis, Mr. Erland," he said, "a place where we can show every make of wheel." He came away from that meeting with only a dozen bikes, but he proved such a skillful mover of merchandise that Erland wound up extending him a $50,000 line of credit. This even more than the deal with Pope was what initially made Fisher as a businessman—and he never forgot it; decades later, just before the stock market crash of 1929 suddenly reversed his long, steep rise, he tried to press a Miami mansion on his old benefactor Erland, saying, "Take it—I want to finally say 'thank you.'" Erland refused the gift, insisting that he had already reaped sufficient profit from all the bicycles Fisher had sold. "You owe me nothing, Carl," he said.

Through his publicity stunts, Fisher made bicycles seem exciting, even to people who had no idea that they were in the market for one. As soon as he had acquired some inventory, he announced that he would ride one of Pope's Columbias across a wire strung two stories high, from the roof of his shop to the building facing it on Pennsylvania Street. This wasn't quite as daring as it sounded, since he had arranged to be attached to two "safety ropes" held by teams of helpers on either side, and he would wear a padded suit meant to cushion him in case he plunged, despite the ropes, to the pavement. As things turned out, falling would have been more like tumbling into a mosh pit: the street outside Fisher's Cycles that day was a sea of gawkers and horse-drawn carts. The entire city of some 190,000, in fact, was at a standstill because of one shopkeeper's circus trick. A cheer went up when Fisher made it across without incident—or almost without incident: the police, whom he got along with individually but not as a whole, sent over a sergeant to deliver a stern lecture about never trying anything of that sort again.

This was the beginning of a classic cat-and-mouse game. A couple of weeks later, Fisher stepped out of a second-floor window and climbed aboard a twenty-foot high-wheeler that he and his brothers had made, then took off on what he would later tell the press was "the world's largest bicycle" with a good portion of the Indianapolis police force in hot pursuit. A month after that, he announced that he was throwing a top-of-the-line $25 bike off his roof and would give a free replacement to the person who retrieved it, if in fact such a premium machine needed replacing. Fearing that this might set off a stampede, police surrounded the shop on the appointed day to prevent the proprietor from entering. But Fisher, anticipating such a maneuver, had spent the night on his roof, and at a moment in late morning, just as the cops were thinking that they might have stymied his plan, a shiny new Grande bicycle crashed down on the concrete, and was set upon by the mob. Fisher scampered away down the back stairs, and when the police got in they found a note saying that they could find him at the station house, surrendering. After spending a few hours in a holding pen, he was sent home.

And so it went. A few years later, in 1898, Fisher and his comrade-in-helium George Bumbaugh pulled one of the former's most fondly remembered stunts, releasing a thousand toy balloons filled with "illuminating gas" into a clear morning sky. It looked, someone said, "like a slow-motion fireworks display." Fifty of the balloons had "lucky number tags" that could be redeemed at the shop for a free bike. In his 2000 biography of Fisher, *Castles in the Sand*, Mark S. Foster quotes an unnamed someone as saying, "Every hill-billy who could steal the time off on the appointed day was out waiting for the release of the balloons." Some followed them on horseback; others tried to shoot them down. In the end, the sales promotion made for a fun-filled four- or five-day scavenger hunt that amused the citizens of Indianapolis, for once without rankling the authorities. Fisher by that point was one of the top five bicycle salesmen in the U.S., though the distinction didn't matter to him as much as it once might have. He had by then moved on—emotionally if not yet professionally—to a new love: the automobile. Many Americans would make this same journey as the bicycle craze gave way to the auto age—but not for a few years yet. Fisher, more restless than most, was ahead of the general population, purchasing, for $650, the second motorized vehicle ever uncrated in Indianapolis: a strange-looking three-wheeled conveyance that had come all the way from France.

Don't look for gasoline leaks with a candle or a match.
—FORREST R. JONES, *The Automobile Catechism*, 1906

THE NUMBER OF Americans who owned automobiles when Carl Fisher took the plunge in 1898 was tiny—probably no more than two thousand—but the sources for cars in those days were becoming mind-bogglingly numerous and varied. Some autos were homemade, others came from companies that turned out fewer than a dozen specimens a year, and still others were produced by relatively large manufacturing outfits in Indiana, Michigan, upstate New York—or (just as likely) Europe. Once a turn-of-the-century consumer got down to serious car shopping he faced a whole other layer of options: did he want to go bespoke or off-the-rack, so to speak, or try somewhere in between, with a roadster assembled Frankenstein-style, from various suppliers' parts and systems, according to the buyer's specifications? The bewildering American car bazaar was no doubt bad for business overall, because it confused consumers and caused them to hold back until the young industry organized itself, but it was inevitable given the machine's ambiguous and chaotic origins.

Henry Ford did not invent the car—alas, no one person did. Ford was the man who showed the auto business what it was destined to be: a font of reliable and relatively cheap vehicles, as opposed to the bizarre but once universally accepted notion that cars were luxuries intended for the elite few who could afford not only a $4,500 vehicle (in, say, 1903), but the chauffeur thought necessary to drive, maintain, and repair one—that is, when he was not taking joyrides with the French maid. (Joyriding chauffeurs were a major topic in the car magazines of the day.) Ford, however, was a seriously flawed man, an idiot savant when he was not being a plain old idiot, a hick brimming with racial theory as ignorant as it was cliché. He would be a poor protagonist for the automobile's creation myth, and yet he is, on the whole, probably preferable, from a reader's perspective, to what the myth, such as it is, actually has, which is no leading man or, for that matter, woman whatsoever. Thumb through the various automotive histories and you'll see why Hollywood has never come a-courtin'. Instead of an Alexander Graham Bell, a Thomas Alva Edison, or even a Les Paul—a central and preferably charismatic someone to say the equivalent of "Watson, come here, I need you!" or sing "Vaya con Dios" while his suddenly electrified guitar gently weeps—all we have is minor figures having eureka moments about gear ratios, cooling systems, and brakes. Timelines in the most popular published accounts fail to cross-reference or conform to a standard span. How far would you like to go back?

The Old Testament prophet Nahum, writing about 615 B.C., predicted that "the chariots shall rage in the streets, they shall jostle one against another in the broad ways; they shall seem like torches, they shall run like lightnings." Other scholars trace self-propelled vehicles to certain remarks recorded by Roger Bacon in the thirteenth century, an allegedly intriguing sketch made by Leonardo da Vinci in the fifteenth, or the so-called Orukter Amphibolos of Oliver Evans, a homely steam-driven dredge that was the first American-made vehicle to move under its own power, jerking around Philadelphia, at about 4 miles per hour, in 1805. A would-be scholar could easily see each of these contrivances—as well as any number of clockwork, coal-powered, sail-sporting, or electric monstrosities that once bumped briefly down a road called hope—as a notable evolutionary step. Or she could just as easily throw out the whole lot and do what the automotive engineers tend to do when discussing history: namely, focus on Gottlieb (Daimler) and Karl (Benz) as the Orville and Wilbur of . . . well, if not of the car itself then the internal combustion engine.

Born in Germany ten years apart (Daimler first, in 1834), the two were accomplished mechanical engineers who stuck to their knitting, avoided scandal, and, as far as anyone can tell, got off no Will Rogers–esque quips, à la "I never met a manifold I didn't like." The most fascinating thing about the duo, apart from the precocious and prescient things they accomplished deep in the innards of automobiles that so impress today's engineers, is that although both as young men once worked in the same steam engine factory in Karlsruhe, and both spent their adult lives making breakthroughs in the same field, and dealing with many of the same European businessmen (their companies would merge in 1926, long after Daimler's death), they apparently never met.

When they came along in the 1880s, would-be car inventors were experimenting with electricity and steam as much as they were messing with soot-centric internal combustion. Each method of propulsion had its passionate proponents and detractors, its objective pluses and faults. The electric car, for example, was clean and quiet but needed constant recharging (not even Edison, who called the automobile "the coming wonder," could develop a battery that lasted more than about forty minutes); the steamer ran on water and a little kerosene to heat the water and keep it hot, but took twenty minutes to reach a boil—an unacceptable interval in a speeded-up age. Gasoline engines had what our great-grandfathers would call "pep," but it was no secret, and no small thing even then, that gasoline engines tended to unfreshen the atmosphere. "All the gasoline motors we have seen belch forth from their exhaust pipe a continuous stream of partially unconsumed hydrocarbons in the form of a thick smoke with a highly noxious odor," wrote Pedro Salmon, an engineer who had developed a battery-powered car called the Electrobat, in the early 1890s. "Imagine thousands of such vehicles on the streets, each offering up its column of smell!" Thanks to Daimler and Benz, of course, we don't have to.

Not everyone, however, shared Salmon's revulsion to petrol. Gasoline is one of those fragrances, like horse manure and boiling vinegar, about which the general populace is sharply divided. (Both Henry Ford and Ransom Eli Olds, who predated Ford as a mass producer of automobiles, said that they were revolted by the smell of horses.) In the fifth volume of *In Search of Lost Time, The Captive*, published in 1923,

Proust writes that gas fumes make him think happily of "cornflowers, poppies and red clover." They also reminded him, more predictably, of motion: "a scent before which the roads took flight, the sun's face changed, castles came hurrying to meet me, the sky turned pale, force was increased tenfold . . . a scent which . . . revived the desire I had felt at Balbec . . . to make love in new places with a woman unknown." If a gas engine could make Marcel Proust think of Madeleines instead of madeleines, it was clearly a force to be reckoned with.

In fact internal combustion engines had several significant benefits that, in the eyes of many, offset their dirty ways. They were cheaper to build and maintain than the two competing types, and, given that gasoline was a mere by-product of kerosene making in those days, fueling them cost pennies. Their power could be far superior, too, as the two-cylinder, 1.5 horsepower gas engine constructed by Daimler and his lifelong assistant Wilhelm Maybach in 1885 dramatically demonstrated. Although certain aspects of that original Daimler-Maybach power plant remained crude—its ignition system involved a red-hot platinum tube that would ignite gasoline that had been injected into the cylinder—the partners effectively ended the three-way debate and put the automobile on a course that would not be seriously questioned until recently. "In spite of [the gasoline engine's] clumsy and complicated mechanism, it does not get easily out of order," said an article in the June 1900 *American Monthly Review of Reviews*, as quoted in James J. Flink's landmark 1988 book, *The Automobile Age*. "It will climb all ordinary hills; it will run through sand, mud or snow; it makes good speed over long distances—say, an average of fifteen miles an hour. . . . It carries gasoline enough for a 70-mile journey, and nearly any country store can replenish the supply."

Yet as the reader can see from the fifteen-year gap between Daimler's breakthrough engine and that critical rave, it took a while for internal combustion to catch on. In 1900 there were still more steam cars (1,681) and electric cars (1,575) produced in the U.S. than gasoline-powered ones (936). A steamer called the Locomobile was by far America's most popular car that year despite a harsh review from the visiting English writer Rudyard Kipling, who was put off by its general unreliability and regrettable tendency to burst into flames. ("It's quite true she is noiseless," he wrote, "but so is a corpse.") The twin brothers Francis and Freelan Stanley were so awash in orders for their famous Steamers that they wouldn't sell you one if they did not like your attitude.

One reason those Steam Nazis lasted so long was that Daimler and Maybach were archetypal inside men—backroom engine builders, not automobile merchandisers who thought holistically, in terms of a complete vehicle that would catch the eye and stir the heart of the consumer. The first Daimlers, in fact, were travel-scarred old stagecoaches with power plants tucked below the passengers' feet; they lurched and swayed down the road looking wrong in a melancholy way, like the grave-bound warrior's riderless horse. It was not until a few years later, when the Daimler technology was installed in a Panhard et Levassor car—and the engine was mounted, significantly and probably for the first time ever, in the front of the chassis and not under the seats—that the modern auto was born and ready to rumble.

Benz's first cars were no babe magnets, either, being tricycles powered by a 0.8 horsepower, two-cycle one-cylinder engine. He exhibited them at the Paris Exposition of 1889, but, overshadowed as they were by the brand-new Eiffel Tower, the six-hundred-person "Negro Village," Buffalo Bill Cody's Wild West Show (featuring Annie Oakley), and a kind of beer-making Olympics (won by Heineken), they generated little discussion and few if any sales. Wisely, Benz soon began thinking in terms of four-wheeled vehicles that over time were to feature such innovations as electric-spark ignition (as opposed to Daimler's scary "open flame" technique) and a vastly improved throttle, radiator, and clutch. By 1900, he was selling more than six hundred cars a year worldwide, which made him an industry leader. One could buy a Benz in Germany, in England, and in New York City at Macy's, Gimbels, and other fine department stores for about $1,000. The majority, though, were sold in France, where—despite Barack Obama's well-publicized assertion in February of 2009 that America was "the country that invented the automobile"—the automobile first flourished.

THANKS TO NAPOLEON and several other military men obsessed with mobilizing troops and artillery, France in the late nineteenth century boasted probably the best roads in the world. But the country became the cradle

of the car business, author James Flink tells us, not because of its superior highway circuitry but due to "a unique network of social relationships" that extended from Daimler and Benz through various Belgian
intermediaries to certain Parisian industrialists. It was those obscure
moneymen who, by backing the German innovators and building car
factories where there might otherwise have been cheese shops, cafés,
or sunflower fields, probably altered the chemistry of France as much
as any cardinal or king. French auto magnates concluded that, besides
advertising, the most effective way to educate customers and move
product was through the sport of racing. The machines that proved
victorious in open competition could legitimately claim to be the best,
n'est-ce pas?

And so automobile racing was born—or rather reborn, though the
organizers of the July 1894 Paris-to-Rouen race can be forgiven for
being oblivious to the great Wisconsin steam wagon showdown of 1878
and considering their event a historic first. The 80-mile French contest,
however, was pointedly not a test of speed but rather a "reliability
demonstration" to determine whose conveyance was, according to the
rulebook, "without danger, easily handled and not too expensive to
run." The magazine that sponsored the event, *Le Petit Journal*, received
102 entries, some listing as their means of locomotion such mysterious methods as "a system of pendulums" and "weight of passengers."
Twenty-one contestants made it to the starting mark, and the first to
reach Rouen, about eight hours later, was the thirty-eight-year-old
Comte Jules-Albert de Dion in a steam-driven car of his own devising.
It hadn't been an easy trip; at one point a blown tire caused de Dion
to run off the road and plow into a potato field, where after making a
quick fix he had to enlist a half-dozen peasants to push him back onto
the highway. Still, that momentary setback only made de Dion's apparent victory all the sweeter. So did the feeling, as he rolled over the finish
line in Rouen, that he was sticking it to the aristocratic relatives who
had tried to steer him into a hospital for the insane a few years earlier,
when he announced his intention of becoming a full-time professional
autoist.

But de Dion didn't win the Paris-to-Rouen race. Upon finishing he
was immediately disqualified for the previously unmentioned offense of

needing two operators—one driver and one fireman to stoke the boiler (the concept of the riding mechanic had not yet been introduced). The prize was thus taken from a man who did not (yet) manufacture cars commercially and instead awarded jointly to the two biggest players in the budding French auto biz: Panhard et Levassor and Peugeot. It is amazing how these things work out sometimes.

In 1895, a longer race, from Paris to Bordeaux and back, a distance of 210 miles, was won by Emile Levassor, driving the gasoline car that bore his and Panhard's name (and Daimler's engine). Levassor reached Bordeaux so far ahead of the other twenty-one cars in the field, and so much faster than expected (in just 22 hours and 34 minutes), that the relief driver who was waiting there to drive the car back to Paris was still asleep—although in what hotel no one could say. After searching for his teammate for an hour or so, Levassor decided to drive back himself; despite stopping along the way for "an elaborate snack, which made me sleepy," he still finished in 48 hours, about 11 hours ahead of the next-fastest car. Although this was a frustrating race for spectators—strung out as it was over so many miles and ultimately decided by another technicality when Levassor was disqualified for having four seats in his car instead of the now required two (the trophy was awarded to a Peugeot)—it was a milestone event because it eliminated any lingering doubts about the internal combustion engine (all but one of the cars that made it back to Paris were gasoline-powered; de Dion would make the switch from steam himself in a year or two).

Despite the yawning margin of victory, the race excited the entire continent, and beyond, about the joys and possibilities of automobiles. Thanks in part to heavy coverage of the race in American newspapers and magazines, more than five hundred patents for engines, brakes, steering mechanisms, and other component parts would be filed in the United States over the next three months. In a way, things would never be better for the European auto industry than they were in the summer of 1895, when its influence seemed limitless and car making was less about steel and smoke than about the dream of better living through automobility. The heady times wouldn't last long, though. Two years later, the fifty-four-year-old Levassor died of an embolism that was likely the result of a racing accident he had been in a few months earlier, and the innocent joy of the early years began to dissipate. The 1903 Paris-to-Madrid race presaged 1909 Indianapolis in the grimmest sense: cars skidded off the road, struck trees, and exploded at the tempo of a modern-day movie trailer. At least eight drivers and an equal number of spectators—a baby, several women, and a few old backwoodsmen who had probably never seen a car until one ran them over—were killed before the race was halted in Bordeaux. It would be twenty-four years before city-to-city road racing would be attempted again in France.

THE AMERICAN AUTO scene in the early and mid-1890s was superficially not all that different from Europe's. The U.S. had city dwellers (like Fisher) excited by the prospect of acquiring their first vehicles and bumpkins who cursed and threw rocks at those same cars. It was on the point of the vehicles themselves where the new world veered off noticeably from the old. "Compared to the best contemporary French designs," Flink tells us, "these experimental American cars were primitive motorized horse buggies." The problem with U.S.-made autos was essentially . . . everything: lousy metallurgy, imprecisely machined parts, dumb design. Unscrew the nameplates and it was easy to tell a European from an American car: the latter was the one that oozed oil, crumpled in a stiff wind, and caught fire at the most inconvenient moments. Many a one-horsepower U.S.-made clunker weighed in at 1,000 pounds, or about as much as one horse.

Why did the U.S. lag so badly with a product that would later be seen as intrinsically American? Some automotive historians blame the Civil War. The problem, they say, was not that the conflict channeled energy away from nonessential industries, the way wars usually do, but that it fueled a boom in railroad building that tempered the urgency for the car, as well as for the construction of hard-packed, rock-free roads that manufacturers need to test cars and that cars need to function.

Nearly forty-five years after Appomattox, Carl Fisher would address that continuing shortage with the construction of the Indianapolis Motor Speedway, a kind of artificial highway whose primary purpose, he at times claimed, was to give Indiana car makers a rare stretch of decent roadway on which to test their vehicles. But just as in France, the condition of the roads in the U.S. was not the deciding factor in determining the automobile's initial level of success. Charles Duryea, a Springfield, Massachusetts, bicycle manufacturer who with his brother Frank marketed a vehicle they named after themselves and misleadingly promoted as "America's first car," believed that U.S. car makers were handicapped chiefly by the average nineteenth-century American's hidebound sensibility. In an alternately feisty and self-pitying memoir he wrote for *Motor Age* just before the first Indianapolis 500-mile race in May of 1911, Duryea argued that as late as American car makers were in bringing their vehicles to market, they were still "about five years too early" for the average American consumer. In 1893, "no safe, sound and conservative business man would consider such a thing as a horseless carriage," Duryea wrote. "It would damage his standing in the community to associate with a crazy inventor, particularly on such a hopeless subject. The man who believed in such a foolish thing was almost as badly cracked as he who thought that 'some day' men would fly."

Even those who acknowledged a self-propelled vehicle to be within the realm of possibility, he said, voiced two principal objections, both based on ignorance. "I have had men complain of the smoke the motor car emitted, when really their cigars had it beaten by 100 per cent," Duryea wrote, a bit disingenuously, since gasoline-powered cars did indeed leave voluminous off-white clouds in their wake. The Gilded Age consumer's second most common complaint about the car, according to Duryea, was its attendant noise. Some people *liked* the roar of a pre–World War I engine—or at any rate Vladimir Nabokov said he did. "The very essence of summer freedom—schoolless untownishness—remains connected in my mind with the motor's extravagant roar that the open muffler would release on the long, lone highway," Nabokov wrote in *Speak, Memory* of his childhood days in St. Petersburg. But most Americans felt that roar was obnoxious and nothing Duryea or his salesmen said seemed to matter. Said Duryea: "Calling [the customer's] attention to the fact that, with air tires and double muffler, the clatter of the horse and buggy trotting alongside was a bedlam by comparison brought the further sage remark, 'Oh, but it is a *different* kind of noise.' Truly, there is no accounting for tastes."

To give the Duryeas their due, strong anti-car prejudice did exist in the America of the 1890s and early 1900s, especially in rural areas, sometimes running to ridiculous extremes. In Vermont, every motor car was required by law to be preceded by a pedestrian "of mature age" carrying a red flag. Iowa required autoists to call ahead to the town toward which they were headed "so that owners of nervous horses may be warned in advance." The Farmers Anti-Automobile Association of Pennsylvania, auto historian Beverly Rae Kimes tells us, "wanted to re-quire automobiles to be equipped with a large canvas depicting a land-scape scene for display in front of the car until the horse had passed." If the animal wasn't tricked by such trompe l'oeil the automobile had to be "pulled to the side of the road, dismantled and its parts hidden in the bushes, to be reassembled only after the horse was safely on its way." In vast stretches of upstate New York, any motorist whom the locals could lay their hands on would be beaten senseless, just because. The *New York Times* for a while had a regular column headed "Auto-mobiles Stoned."

Cars were thought to be not just unnecessary and upsetting but downright evil in any number of ways. If they didn't kill or maim you, some people believed, they would leave you with "automobile face"—a supposed paralyzing of the cheek and forehead muscles as a result of riding in the windshield-less cockpits of the day at speeds of 30 to 40 miles per hour, the chief danger allegedly coming when the mouth is frozen in an open position, allowing for its violation by dirt, bad air, "bacteria, viruses and other microbes." The fledgling auto industry attempted to counter this myth by saying that wind forced into the mouth and pores during long car rides actually had a healthful, cleans-ing effect upon the autoist. What's more, car makers claimed, the bone-jarring jolts that rattled passengers in their nearly shock absorber–less vehicles were actually a superb way to lose—or gain—weight, depend-ing on the shortcomings of your particular frame.

TO HELP CLEAR up some of the myths and controversies about the car—and stimulate newspaper sales in the process—Herman Kohlsaat, the then brand-new publisher of the *Chicago Times-Herald*, announced in July of 1895 that he was sponsoring a race from his city to Milwaukee on November 2. "The first motor race in America," Kohlsaat called it, showing disregard for early Wisconsin steam car history. But then Kohlsaat, who had made his fortune with a chain of lunch counters, didn't pretend to know the slightest bit about the whole autoism thing. He even found it difficult, he admitted to his readers, to announce such a race because he didn't know what to properly call the self-propelled vehicles he was soliciting. There didn't seem to be any consensus on a name, he said, and he was right about that. Some of the precursors for "automobile" in play at the time were autokinet, molectros, ipsomotor, galone, and sineque. In hopes of improving upon those, and perhaps settling the matter for good, the *Times-Herald*, as part of their race promotion, invited readers to send in their suggestions, with the best in the opinion of the publisher to receive $500. According to Kimes, the ideas that poured in included autobain, petrocar, motorig, mocle, mobe, and viamote. Some people wrote merely to protest the term "automobile" because of its glaring Frenchness. The prize went to a New York City telephone repairman who submitted "motorcycle." (From the modern perspective, this does not seem like a terribly original term, though, since there was already a monthly magazine—about cars, not motorcycles—called *The Motorcycle.*)

But cars by any name were hard to come by in the America of 1895. Kohlsaat's initial call for race entrants, which came with the announcement of $5,000 in purse money, had brought in inquiries from a high percentage of the standing fleet, which then probably numbered about two hundred. By early October the "motorcycles" willing and able to start in his race, now just a month away, came to a mere six: two Duryeas, an Electrobat, a Benz that had been "adapted to the plumbing business" by a contractor named Hieronymous Mueller of Decatur, Illinois, and a pair of vehicles designed by Edward Joel Pennington, a tall, courtly Hoosier who would become known as one of the early auto age's boldest con men. Pennington developed a simple scam that he repeated with only slight variation: he would pop up in a small- to medium-size town, present to the local businessmen his elaborate and impressive-sounding plans for some kind of revolutionary means of motorized transportation, collect investment funds—then take their money and run. Only on rare occasions—as with his curious proposal for a motorized baby carriage—did he actually bring his inventions to market and legitimately lose his backers' funds. In the *Times-Herald* race Pennington proposed to run two "motor coaches" of his own devising that he claimed could use almost anything as fuel, an advantage he would demonstrate, he said, by eschewing petrol, steam, or electricity, and making the approximately 75-mile run from Chicago to Milwaukee on nothing but candle wax.

Proceeding with such a small, strange field of vehicles understandably worried Kohlsaat. Hoping to get more entries, he pushed the date of the race back to November 28, Thanksgiving Day, and then, worrying further about the weather that late in the year, shortened the distance, stipulating that the motorcycles would go from a spot on the Midway Plaisance near what is now the Museum of Science and Industry, to Evanston, Illinois, and back, a circuit, on the roads he had mapped out for the occasion, of 52.5 miles. Intent on trying to please everyone, Kohlsaat also promised a "consolation race" on November 2 for those who had worked hard to meet the original deadline. Alas, only two vehicles showed up for what the *Times-Herald* was now forced to describe as the race *before* the first American race ever. These were an extremely lightweight Duryea and the ponderous plumbing-shop Benz. It was Mutt versus Jeff for a consolation prize of $500. The Duryea, piloted by elder brother Frank (one of the few things the brothers agreed on was that Charles, though he had more than a dozen automobile-related patents to his name, did not yet know how to drive), grabbed the early advantage but promptly broke the drive chain and had to stop for repairs, allowing the Benz to open a commanding lead. Once back on the road, though, the Duryea was able to reach the impressive speed of 15 miles an hour and start closing the gap. But just when it looked like there might be a thrilling finish, a farmer pulled his horse-drawn hay wagon across the route. To avoid it, Duryea had to take his car into a ditch, and in doing so he broke the housing on his differential and put himself out of the race. The Benz, meanwhile, cruised on to an easy victory. Undaunted, the Duryea brothers said they would ship their car home to Springfield, Massachusetts, for repairs, and have it back in time for the third and perhaps final first American car race ever, twenty-six days hence.

This time three of the starters were Benzes: the plumber's, one that had been used to haul iceboxes in New York City, and another owned by R. H. Macy's department store. Two electric cars were also entered, although the drivers of the Electrobat and the Chicago-made Sturges Electric knew that they would be unable to complete the course due to a lack of battery-recharging stations along the route (a strange plan, theirs: to promote electric vehicles by running out of power in public). Rounding out the field was the patched-up but plucky little Duryea. Most observers gave Frank Duryea the best shot at winning—until the impartial "riding umpires" were randomly assigned to each car and the seat in the Duryea fell to Arthur W. Wright, a Toronto newspaperman fat even by the morbidly elephantine standards of late-nineteenth-century journalists. Sitting beside the easily three-hundred-pound Wright in his 729-pound car, the stocky Frank Duryea, said a witness, looked "slender and nervous."

Carl Fisher was in Indianapolis at the bicycle shop, which was open, even on Thanksgiving, to perform emergency repairs and fix flats. In all likelihood he, like the vast majority of Americans, did not know about the race until it was over, because other newspapers were stingy about giving advance publicity to a *Times-Herald*–sponsored event. "Some papers gave it serious comment," Frank Duryea wrote years later, "while others were quick to ridicule and had secretly hoped that it would turn out to be a fizzle." It almost was a fizzle. The gaggle who saw the motorcyclists off—they departed one at a time, a few minutes apart, sacrificing spectacle for safety's sake—numbered roughly 150.

Duryea had the luck of the draw when lots were pulled for the starting order and he got to leave first, though that meant cutting his own path through the six inches of snow that had fallen the night before. A few minutes later, the Macy's-owned Benz rolled from the starting line, followed, after a similar pause, by the Benz that had been refitted for the hauling of refrigeration equipment. The latter car skidded on the snow for a bit, gently spinning this way and that, and rolled to a stop. Nothing particularly dramatic seemed to be happening, but its driver, Frederick C. Haas, jumped out and announced to the press crew—which was following the competition on a horse-drawn sleigh—"I have decided not to race!" and then hopped into the media vehicle. The Macy's Benz was having trouble finding traction as well, but its driver,

Jerry O'Conner, got out and pushed the car until it reached a dry spot. Within twenty minutes or so, all five remaining "motorcycles" were on the road and racing.

At the corner of Rush and Erie streets, Duryea felt a change in the vibrations of his tiller handle—none of these cars had a steering wheel—and realized he had broken a steering gear. As he pulled to a stop, the Macy's Benz chugged by him at about 10 miles per hour. It took Duryea fifty-five minutes to make a repair, but because O'Conner got into what would have been called a fender-bender if his car, or the horse he had bumped into, had fenders, and the other contestants were making extremely slow progress on account of the snow, the delay did not cost Duryea all chance of winning. It did, however, seem to buoy the hopes of those backing the plumbing-shop Benz, who were moved, if one can believe the contemporary account in *The Motorcycle*, to spontaneously and in unison produce one of the strangest "cheers" ever cheered, in the direction of driver Oscar Mueller: "We're just one hour and sixteen minutes out from Jackson Park! We're just one hour and sixteen minutes out from Jackson Park!"

The Macy's machine was first to reach the "relay station," at Grace Street and Sheridan Drive, where O'Conner took on water and oil and spent several minutes, said *The Motorcycle*, "looking over his machinery and making a hitch or so in his running gear." He took off at 11:10:30. Duryea, still running second, pulled in twenty minutes later for similar servicing. He was closing the gap despite the handicap represented by Wright, who gratuitously assured a policeman standing nearby, "we'll overhaul O'Conner pretty soon."

In auto racing as in life, smugness often cometh before a fall, but not this time. As he reached the turnaround point in Evanston at 12:50 P.M., Duryea had a slight lead—a lead that only lengthened when the Macy's car collided with the press sleigh, which had overturned while crossing the railroad tracks near Calvary Cemetery, and then collided again, a few minutes later, with a stubborn horse-drawn hack driver who refused to give the right-of-way in Rogers Park. Duryea reached the second and last relay station, at North Clark Street and Devon Avenue, so far ahead that even though he proceeded to take a wrong turn and go two miles out of his way, his victory was all but certain. With the outcome now obvious, and the hour getting late, "the crowds waiting for the finish in Douglas Park," said the *New York Times*, "were entertained by about 200 small boys who snowballed and put to flight the city police guarding the approach of the racers."

Still, toward the end of a 10-hour race, it was hard to sustain much merriment. With only a few miles to go, the thoroughly exhausted Oscar Mueller "went to pieces," according to his riding umpire, and passed out at the tiller; his Benz rolled sadly to a stop. Duryea, maddeningly close to the finish line, was held up by a passing freight train for more than four minutes. "Wet and cold, darkness coming on and not a motorcycle in sight, the small boys and the little girls and the older folk went home," said *The Motorcycle*.

Consequently, when, a few minutes before 6 o'clock, the Duryea motor came through Douglas Park, laboring with ever bad roadway, there was no one to greet it on California Avenue but a representative of the *Times-Herald*. Lacking spectators, except here and there a solitary workman on his way home, or the belated watchman of one of the ill-smelling soap factories in the district, the men on the motor gave way to war-whoops, cheers and cat-calls and other manifestations of joy over the victory they were winning.

To Ashland Avenue but one sleigh was passed. The darkness was on and, hidden behind two horse-drawn rigs, the [Duryea] motorcycle was comparatively unnoticed. . . . Not fifty people saw the last stages of the finish or knew that the Duryea had established a world's record in the capacity of a motorcycle to conquer even King Winter himself. It was just 7:18 when Frank Duryea threw himself out of the seat of his motor and announced the end. His hand was grasped by the few who saw him cross the line.

IT IS SAFE to assume that Carl Fisher read reports of the *Times-Herald* race the following morning—no newsmen were injured in the upsetting of their sleigh, and, once it was over, other papers didn't seem to mind running their enthusiastic accounts, which often made the race sound a lot more exciting and competitive than it actually was. Indeed, Fisher may have sought out stories of the race in all four Indianapolis dailies.

Although still three years from buying his first car, he was by then inhaling and absorbing every bit of information on the horseless carriage that he could find. Just a month or two earlier, in fact, someone hanging around his bike shop had brought up the subject of automobiles and wondered if there were any yet in the state of Indiana.

Without missing a beat, Fisher, who was busy just then oiling a bike chain, said, "There are eleven."

The shop fell silent. A moment passed.

"Wouldn't it be something," Fisher went on, still not looking up from his work, "to see them all in a race?"

11

The motor car has been a gold mine for lawyers.

—*The Horseless Age*, 1911

THE STORY OF Carl Fisher between the mid-1890s and late August of 1909, when he was called in by Marion County coroner John J. Blackwell for an "official investigation" following the disastrous inaugural meet at the Indianapolis Motor Speedway, is a tale of innocence lost. The fresh-faced, backward-running bike shop owner (and part-time bicycle racer) who would beguile people with his squinty smile and dazzle them with his knowledge of all things automotive, and who had (according to one local girl who nurtured an unrequited crush) "the most kissable lips I've ever seen," had become, fourteen or so years later, a sallow, bespecta-cled, and jowly thirty-five-year-old paper millionaire, juggling a stable of litigious finances, and starting to lose his battle with booze. It was almost as if Fisher had in the interim put aside the robustly inspirational books of Robert Ingersoll and replaced them as his Bible with a manual called *On Becoming a Walking Cliché*. The striver from small-town Indiana now played croquet and polo and was shopping for a yacht. He went about with a black servant-sidekick, a man noticeably older than he, whom he referred to, in mock British-butler style, as Galloway.

But try as Fisher might to ape the upper-crust types he had encoun-tered in novels and the occasional stage play (or more likely burlesque sketch), his Crazy Carl uncouthness would always show through, in bizarre and memorable permutations. If he caught business associates or buddies looking cross-eyed at Galloway, he would point to his long-suffering lackey and declare, "This man just might take his shoes off and show you that his feet are cleaner than yours!" Talk about nouveau riche: Fisher, five years into his Prest-O-Lite period, carried a cash-wad so large that he sometimes had to take it out of his pocket to be comfortably seated. On such occasions he might study the roll at arm's length, tidy up its several rubber bands a bit, then remark matter-of-factly to those around him, as if the thing were a meteoroid that had one day plopped down before him on life's unpredictable path, that it contained "no bill smaller than a sawbuck." His desire to bring the greasy, noisy, country-fair sport of automobile racing to Indianapolis, and to put it on the kind of fancy pedestal that had once been reserved for the supposedly aristocratic sport of thoroughbred horse racing, was all of a piece with this classic parvenu-ness. Few people around Indianapolis were neutral on the subject of Carl Fisher. Either they dismissed him as unspeakably vulgar, or they delighted in watching an unspeakably vulgar man enjoying such an exhilarating trip.

Cue "The Ballad of Jed Clampett."

Actually, "enjoying" isn't the right word, after a point, for Fisher was to learn—needless to say, in keeping with his affection for cliché—the hard way, that money doesn't buy happiness. He hadn't reached outright disillusionment just yet, as he took a chair in Blackwell's office in the otherwise empty courthouse building on the evening of August 19, 1909, a blank expression on his pasty features, a cheap cigar between his no-longer-so-kissable lips, but he was already one of those little kings with both the Midas touch and blood on his hands, and, as they say on the playing fields of Eton and certain other places where they are exposed to more Aristotle than Fisher ever got, well begun is half-done.

The coroner's inquest of August 1909 is I think worth examining briefly, though it goes unmentioned by both of Fisher's biographers.

The official transcript has disappeared from the Marion County, Indiana, files, so all we have to go on are newspaper accounts of what transpired in John J. Blackwell's office on that long-ago Saturday evening. Still, it is possible to see in that brief encounter an interesting dynamic, and at times weird, disjointed energy. This could be in part because Fisher was, to put it in twenty-first-century terms, so *over* the problem that caused the investigation, and so on to other, more challenging concerns—his mind was only intermittently present in the coroner's office—and yet he found himself in something of a tight spot, facing off with a minor functionary who had the potential to do more than merely annoy. There was an outsized stinger on this bureaucratic gnat, who had the power to pass along any or all of the Speedway death cases for criminal prosecution, as well as to find Fisher civilly responsible for the fatalities, which would have left both the Speedway president and his corporation liable to lawsuits. And this was no small consideration in what was, despite what one might assume about the stoically Protestant Midwest of a hundred years ago, a fairly litigious milieu.

Blackwell's initial questions were for the record and presumably meant to allow the several scribblers present—an official stenographer and (it seems) a few newspaper reporters—to get their pencils in gear.

"Can you state your name, please?"

Fisher does, in full. But then the coroner feels obliged to dilate on the witness's identity.

"And are you the same Carl Fisher," he asks, "who owns and operates the Fisher Automobile Company?"

"Yes, sir."

". . . And you're the same Carl Fisher," Blackwell goes on, displaying an undertaker's penchant for overkill, "who for a time drove racing automobiles?"

"Yes, sir."

With enemies like this you don't need lawyers. The coroner no doubt saw these throat-clearing questions as the sort of thing that smart and important people say on such occasions, but this was a blatantly amateurish misstep, especially since the newspapers would open up this hearing to an audience of untold thousands. If Blackwell intended to tear down or cuff his witness, to either demonstrate that the Marion County coroner couldn't be intimidated, or to link Fisher to the shady, bloody game of auto racing in order to discredit him, he was already failing at his inquisitorial task. For what he had done in effect was to ask Fisher if he wasn't truly one of the most fascinating men in Indianapolis, a successful businessman who simultaneously drove race cars. And this of course presented his adversary with the chance to say, well, as long as you brought it up, as a matter fact, yes, I am.

Fisher's rise in the community was legend, the story of his show-room on North Capital Boulevard an oft-recounted local myth on the theme of America's bountiful, if at times thrillingly capricious, benevo-lence. His bicycle shop had done just fine for itself, once Indianapolis and the nation recovered from the depression of 1893. By the following year, in fact, Fisher had been able to travel to New York City for what the *New York Times* described as a "love feast" of bicycle industry big-wigs, meeting to discuss how to capitalize on the biggest nationwide fad since tomatoes had shed their reputation as a poisonous fruit and come into vogue in the mid-1880s. But prosperity of the sort that can bemuse and ultimately depress a man did not befall Fisher until he returned to Manhattan in January of 1900 to visit the weeklong auto show at Madi-son Square Garden, an event that can be seen as doing for the horseless carriage trade what the 1913 Armory Show did for modern art—that is, moving a kooky "outsider" activity into the cultural mainstream. Wandering among the thirty-one spindly, still mostly steam-driven vehicles in the cavernous exhibit hall (then in its second incarnation, on 26th Street and Madison Avenue), Fisher found himself impressed and excited by the Wintons, McKays, and Rikers—and, like many of his fel-low ten thousand attendees, enthralled by the prototype for a "curved dash" runabout designed by Ransom Olds, a daredevil best known for pushing experimental vehicles to speeds approaching 40 miles per hour on the sleek Florida beaches of Ormond and Daytona. Fisher, who had been increasingly obsessed with automobiles for at least five years at that point, decided on the spot to switch businesses—a decision not quite as momentous as it might initially seem, since the bicycle fad al-ready was fading fast—and to effectively re-create the Garden show in Indianapolis, by offering for sale a number of brands simultaneously. In a few months he had America's first auto dealership up and running— and the financial wherewithal to finally move out of his mother's house.

Although he was a prominent businessman in 1909 and no longer a precocious entrepreneur, silly stunts remained central to Fisher's style. He duplicated his Great Bicycle Fling on a larger but less rascal-ish scale by pushing a Stoddard-Dayton (a car he would soon be selling exclusively) off the roof of his new four-story building. The police had been alerted this time, and the street was cordoned off; after the car landed, right side up, Fisher got in and drove it away triumphantly, leaving a trail of shredded tires while the cops just shook their heads and smiled. On another occasion, apparently in a milder mood, he offered a free car to anyone who could guess the number of bees buzzing inside a large glass canister in the middle of the sales floor. And then, in 1908, he performed his *coup de gaz*, with another Stoddard-Dayton and George Bumbaugh's gigantic mustard-colored balloon. "People can't buy what they don't know exists!" he said at the time, explaining why he seemed to be such an attention junkie. The dealership made him rich, but just as important, it put him in a position, as a high-profile player in the auto business, to be approached by Fred Avery, the holder of the patent for what became Prest-O-Lite car lamps. Pretty soon people were dying so that Fisher could do . . . well, whatever the hell it was that he was doing with his runaway and seemingly limitless life. At that point, he didn't yet know himself.

Race car driving was never meant to be more than a temporary sideline but it was, in the meantime, a glamorous, girl-getting way of floundering about. Fisher in those days sometimes campaigned on his own, with his trusty one-cylinder, Cleveland-made Winton car. At other times he left the Prest-O-Lite business in the care of his partner Allison and toured as one of the Big Racing Four, a barnstorming act ("The World's Most Daring Automobile Racers") that included his old bike racing teammate Barney Oldfield, the almost as famous Webb Jay, and Al Webb. The experience was not always as glamorous as it perhaps sounded; the Big Racing Four made as much money from giving $10 car rides to rubes who wanted to go around the racetrack as from appearance fees—yet even that put him in a superior position—*Hang on tight now, my friend!*—and made him the object of envy, a car-and-parts dealer with dash.

After the bloody debacle in Zanesville, Ohio, in which his car killed the Civil War veteran, Fisher attempted to go legit as a racer, designing a car with the Premier company of Indianapolis that he intended to enter in the 1905 Vanderbilt Cup race on Long Island. Although neither he nor the Premier seemed the best advertisement for American ingenuity and auto racing prowess, he had hoped to win the prestigious international event as a way of showing that the U.S., and Indianapolis in particular, could produce drivers and vehicles as proficient as anything that came from Europe. Alas, in typical fashion, he grossly overdid the effort, showing up with a monstrous (923.4 CID) one-off machine that, although stripped of all cosmetic niceties, weighed 2,500 pounds, or some 300 more than the rules permitted. Now on permanent display at the Speedway museum, Fisher's 1904 Premier looks, in all its gray-grunge glory, like a paint-deprived radiator from a pre–World War I mental hospital. It never did race in that second edition of the Vander-bilt Cup; Fisher's desperate attempt to make weight by having holes cut in the chassis and engine frame, and replacing the drive shaft with drive chains to each of the rear wheels, fell short (as did his pleas with race officials to allow him into the event anyway, simply because he was, *goddammit*, an American).

In the end he seems to have raced his scary, Swiss-cheesy chariot only once, winning a 5-mile handicap with it on October 21, 1905, at the Indiana State Fairgrounds at an average speed of 59.21 miles per hour. That was not a bad time considering the length (one mile) and surface (cinder) of the track, but Fisher knew the clocking was impressive only by American standards. He had that very summer traveled to Clermont-Ferrand, France, where he watched in embarrassment as the U.S. team, driving cars turned out by his former bicycle supplier Albert Pope, got badly beaten in the James Gordon Bennett Cup. "The European cars still go faster uphill than ours go down," Fisher had said at the Indianapolis meet, where, with Allison, Newby, and Wheeler, he sat around a campfire in the infield in the wee hours of the morning, half-watching a twenty-four-hour race grinding on the old trotting horse oval, and first hatched the idea of a permanent speedway as a way of getting Indianapolis cars up to snuff.

Fisher had certainly never intended to be what is known in the world of sports as a front-office type—a suit who spent hours on the phone talking to gravel merchants and local politicians or dictating letters to the lawyers of peanut salesmen who had slipped in a puddle of soda pop and wrenched their sacroiliac. In other words, he did not really desire to be the president of an auto racing speedway. But just as being in the car business had put him in a position to acquire the Prest-O-Lite technology, the money from Prest-O-Lite gave him the opportunity to pursue his dreams, one of which, harbored since practically the first time he climbed into a race car and saw how hard it was to get around the tight, flat turns of a horse track, was to build a track strictly for automobiles. Quite a few people remembered him dreamily sketching ovals on the cloth napkins at Pop Haynes's restaurant. Originally he had thought in terms of a 3- to 5-mile-long circuit that could also serve as the site of the Vanderbilt Cup. Then he got busy with other things, and back-burnered the idea—until the day in October of 1908 that Fisher and his friend Lem Trotter traveled by car to Dayton on business. They had two flat tires and broke down three other times on the trip, arriving back in Indianapolis late, greasy, and cranky. "What this country needs," Fisher is quoted as saying that very night in *500 Miles to Go*, "is a big race track to give manufacturers a chance to test their cars and equipment." The next day Fisher and Trotter were out looking at the Pressley place, a conveniently flat plot of land nicely located near the intersection of several railroad lines. When it turned out that the dimensions of the farm allowed for a track no longer than two and a half miles, Fisher figured he could live with that, and he and Newby, Allison, and Wheeler promptly formed a corporation, closed on the land, and broke ground for what they were then calling a "motor park."

BUT BACK TO Blackwell's office, where things were starting to get weird.

After that opening exchange, in which the coroner had clumsily conjured up images of a more fresh-faced and admirable Fisher, Blackwell broached the central matter of the track surface. In the newspaper accounts, Fisher at times sounds predictably defensive as he attempts to shift blame from himself and Speedway employees who might be considered responsible for the track conditions onto the racing teams involved in the tragedies. Yet it is sometimes hard to follow his line of reasoning. He tells the coroner that he had personally examined the Knox car in which Billy Bourque and his riding mechanic, Harry Holcomb, were killed on the first day of the meet and found two of the "axle bed plates" broken. "One was badly shattered," he says, "and the other so broken that the axle was let down to the ground." One of the plates, he adds, was "crystallized"—a detail that seems to suggest that Fisher believed, or wanted Blackwell to believe, that the car broke down because it had not been properly lubricated, and not because it hit the fairly narrow but deep ditch that had opened in the track just in front of the grandstand. In a response that is quoted only indirectly in the *Indianapolis News*, Fisher acknowledges the presence of the rut but says that he is sure that it played no part in the fatal accident *as the car was going 70 miles per hour when the axle plate broke.* The italics (mine) indicate a statement that, in case you're wondering, makes no sense. Seventy miles an hour in 1909 was a pretty darn good clip.

Blackwell, understandably, is "apparently not satisfied with [Fisher's] answer," the *News* reports. He then asks Fisher if the Speedway management did not put on the races before the racing surface was ready, saying, "Is it a fact that you did not have time to complete the track?"

At this point, for some reason—a desire just to be done with this tedious Saturday-evening inquiry? A sudden attack of conscience? The fact that he was seldom entirely sober?—Fisher seems to sag and drop his defenses.

"Yes, that is true," he answers.

"You were expecting an accident of some kind, were you not?" the coroner continues.

"Yes, sir."

"And for that reason you had the hospital built there [on the Speedway grounds]?"

"Yes, sir."

Fisher's responses are startling, to be sure, but not exactly unprecedented. He sounds in this exchange like the same Carl Fisher who, feeling . . . what? frightened? defeated? exhausted? depressed? . . . rained on his own parade by telling the *Star* on the day before the meet began that he wished it were possible to postpone the automobile races. To make matters even more bewildering, Fisher, as the hearing wears on, halfheartedly returns to his own defense, grumbling, in response to a question about the motorcyclists, that they made a botch of things because they "didn't know how to run a meet," and claiming that the track would never be perfect because "a gang of men was constantly kept busy making repairs when the racers were not on the track." The latter remark could be read as a thick-tongued, cotton-brained way of saying that a racetrack by its very nature will always be a work in progress. Still, it's difficult to tell what was going on. Could it be that by mixing semi-inscrutability with moments of contrition Fisher was attempting to throw his interrogator off stride? Or are we overanalyzing the actions of an alcoholic who was never more than an arm's length from a few stiff belts?

As those who regularly spent time with him knew, Fisher was always prone to intemperate outbursts as well as impulsive—and seemingly inexplicable—actions. In *Fabulous Hoosier*, his wife, Jane sums him up at one point as simply "incomprehensible." Certainly, Fred B. Smith, the president of the Merchants' Distilling Company of Terre Haute, would agree. Once, in 1906, while giving Smith a gratuitous postsale "demonstration ride" in a fully loaded $5,000 Stoddard-Dayton that Smith had just bought from him, Fisher ran the car into a tree, completely wrecking the vehicle and sending Smith flying some twenty feet. Witnesses said that Fisher, without saying a word, had climbed from the cockpit, pulled Smith's check from his wallet, and ostentatiously kissed it goodbye. Then, stumbling over to where his customer lay, Fisher stuffed the check into Smith's coat pocket and staggered off into the sunset.

IF FISHER COULD not or would not mount a rousing and consistent defense of himself and the Speedway, others were more than willing to step into the breach. Over the next few days, as Blackwell considered the "evidence" he had unearthed in his odd little inquiry, some voices rose up to say that despite appearances all had actually gone as well as could have been expected. Mayor Bookwalter, reached at his summer home on Lake Maxinkuckee, said that while the loss of life was to be regretted, he "wished there were a hundred Fishers" bringing automobilists to the city "because it has been my observation that the man with the automobile is of all men, most generous when it comes to spending money." Henry Lawrence, an executive at the Claypool Hotel, told the *Star* that he heard a Chicago man say he would give a million dollars to have such a speedway in Chicago, and heard a New York man say there was nothing like it in New York. Former Indiana attorney general

W. L. Taylor said of Indianapolis, "We have no lakes and no rivers, but we have our railroads and our Speedway . . . what better advertising could be had?" A. N. Collins, the general manager of L. S. Ayres's department store, said that local merchants had noticed a surge in sales during the meeting, blamed Bourque's death on the driver's own "daredevilry," and said the spectators who were slaughtered on Saturday afternoon while watching the races "should not have been standing in the wrong place."

Still, the strongest and most detailed defense of Fisher and his Speedway came from Indianapolis auto manufacturer Howard Marmon. Fisher and the scion of the Nordyke and Marmon Company were friends who in many ways could not have been more different. The latter was the heir apparent to a small business empire that had been turning out milling machinery since 1851; he was also a graduate of the University of California at Berkeley. Fisher was a self-made sixth-grade dropout. But being close contemporaries—Marmon was about eighteen months younger—they had gone through the bike craze together in Indianapolis, and were now both making their bones as pioneers in the automobile business. They knew each other well; as members of the Zig-Zag and more recently the Columbia Club, they had discussed a few business ventures they might get into as partners. Marmon was also a close friend of Arthur Newby's, his father having given Fisher's Speedway co-founder his first big-city job, when Newby (who was born in Monrovia, Indiana) came to Indianapolis from California in 1881. These relationships, however, went unmentioned in a long letter written by Marmon that ran under the headline "In Defense of Speedway" in the weekly *The Horseless Age*, and that soon afterward was reproduced in several dozen newspapers.

Marmon's letter is wordy, windy, and frosty in regard to those who had lost their lives on and around Fisher's Speedway. In it, the thirty-three-year-old industrialist argues that track dust and driver fatigue as a result of trying to negotiate a scandalously rough surface on a broiling hot afternoon—the factors, in other words, that contributed to the death and injury of about a dozen racers and spectators in the opinion of participants and grandstand witnesses alike (not to mention the opinion of Carl Fisher as expressed at the coroner's inquiry)—all these things, Marmon maintains, had nothing to do with causing "the Roman holiday of destruction" currently being decried in newspapers from Bangor to Oakland. Heat, he says, was of no concern whatsoever. Why, "one of the best-organized racing teams wore sweaters while driving and commented afterward that they were glad they had them," Marmon wrote. As for dust, "driving a race car is a man's game," Marmon noted. And "though after a number of hours drivers' eyes began to smart from the dust, it was to no such extent to any way suggest blindness." Immediately after some of the longest races, Marmon contended, fresh-looking drivers fairly bounded through the pit area asking if there was anything they could do to help their crewmembers and apologizing for making them endure such lengthy contests when they all could have been out enjoying the sights of Indianapolis.

Then Marmon moved from the ridiculous to the self-serving. "It was not the track or the drivers that were not ready," he wrote, "but the majority of the cars," with "weak points in construction which had not yet revealed themselves." In other words, the blame for the deaths and injuries rightly belonged to his *competitors* and their second-rate Knoxes and Fiats and Buicks. If every man had driven a Marmon—a make of car that did indeed win one race, and avoided breakdowns in the other five in which it was entered—the world would be giving "the coterie of energetic and public spirited men back of the Indianapolis motor speedway all the success their daring and enterprise deserves," instead of blaming them for the destruction caused by dangerous, if not downright evil, non-Marmon racers.

How many opinions were influenced by Howard Marmon's letter can of course never be known. What is more important to auto racing history is that Marmon in 1909 did his friend Carl Fisher a sizable public favor—something that Fisher, the perennial parvenu always flattered to receive the approval of the Indianapolis establishment, was not likely to soon forget.

Anyone attempting to understand what would happen two years later, at the first Indianapolis 500-mile race, should not forget it, either.

12

IT IS TEMPTING to think of Carl Fisher as now standing at a crossroads. Certainly a more normal person after launching an auto racing speedway and then winding up in similar straits might have seen himself trembling before two large and conflicting arrows labeled Bail Out and Plunge Ahead. Ego and momentum would naturally incline the creator of a project toward the latter option, but those strong forces were counterbalanced in this case by the weight of conventional wisdom, or perhaps it would be better to say national outrage, which might easily have broken the spirit of a saner man. First the Indianapolis debacle, and then a pair of deaths during a 24-hour race at Brighton Beach a week later, had newspaper editorialists spewing indignation, spiced at times with sarcasm for added bite. "Seven killed in five days is a record any speedway can be proud of!" said the *La Crosse Tribune*. Suggesting that the Speedway had been greedy in taking so many lives so quickly, the *Fort Wayne Sentinel* said, "One or two dead and five injured ought to be regarded as a fair sprinkling of bones and blood in a short season!" The *Detroit News* wondered, "What is the significance of these seven deaths?" and said that "Spectators of these events have time and again demonstrated that it is the human lust for blood that calls them to the big track meets. This is the final straw. The blood of the Indianapolis

The Speedway still looked more like the old Pressley farm when the famous New York driver Lewis Strang dropped by on a dreary day in March 1909 to inspect a "scale model" of the first track in the United States built expressly for auto racing.

Because the track was not ready for automobiles, the very first event at the Speedway, in 1909, was a balloon race.

The high-living founders of the Indianapolis Motor Speedway (left to right): Arthur Newby, Frank Wheeler, Carl Fisher, and James Allison. Their invention of the 500-mile sweepstakes was a last-ditch attempt to reverse sagging attendance and create an event that would galvanize the city of Indianapolis. The idea worked—instantly and beyond their imagining.

Before the founders switched to bricks, they struggled with a track made of packed gravel and "taroid." The second event conducted at the Speedway, a motorcycle meeting, only underscored the inadequacies of the racing surface, as the rough stones ripped up tires and caused several accidents.

As this picture from 1910 shows, Speedway promoters were having trouble filling the grandstand. The solution, Carl Fisher and his partners decided, was to stage one big annual event—a 500-mile sweepstakes, the longest (and therefore the most dangerous) race ever conducted on a track.

Smoke was a detriment to visibility in the early days of auto racing, as this photo of the start of a 1910 Speedway race demonstrates. But once a race began, dust kicked up by wind and tires was an even bigger problem because it ripped through goggles and drove glass and grit into the drivers' eyes.

Barney Oldfield was the most famous racing driver of his day—and the most frequently sanctioned. The former boxer and bicycle racer set many legitimate records, but made most of his money barnstorming around the country. Because he was serving a suspension for having raced against Jack Johnson, the black heavyweight champ, Oldfield couldn't compete in the first Indy 500, but he covered the race as a syndicated columnist.

The forty-car field—the largest ever assembled to that time—waits for Speedway president Carl Fisher to lead them on the first "rolling start" in the history of auto racing.

David Bruce-Brown, an heir to the Lorillard tobacco fortune, behind the wheel of his Fiat with his steady riding mechanic, Anthony Scudalari, in the co-pilot's seat. Bruce-Brown, 23, probably led for most of the first 500 (timing and placement records were incomplete and inaccurate) and eventually finished third. He and Scudalari died a little over a year later while practicing for a race in Milwaukee.

"Smiling" Ralph Mulford, a Brooklyn-born choirmaster famous for his sunny disposition and his habit of eating gumdrops as he drove, wasn't so happy when he returned to the Indy winner's circle after taking a victory lap in his big white Lozier and found Ray Harroun being congratulated for winning the $25,000 sweepstakes. Until he died in 1973, Mulford maintained he was the true winner.

Although relief driver Cyrus Patschke took the wheel for at least 30 laps, Ray Harroun was so exhausted after finishing the 1911 Indy 500 that he could barely respond to those who congratulated him for being the official winner. After he got some food and water, Harroun announced that he would never drive in races again, saying it was simply too dangerous—and he kept his promise.

The Swiss-born Louis Chevrolet was one of the best and boldest drivers on the early racing scene, but he aspired to design his own line of reasonably-priced automobiles. A few months after the first Indy 500, he helped found Chevrolet Motor Company.

Motor Speedway has probably rung the knell on track racing in the United States."

The *Piqua* (Ohio) *Daily Call* noted that "One would think that such foolhardiness would become unpopular and be stopped by the common sense of people. But this country is going stark crazy about automobiles and we can expect almost any kind of demoralization amongst the people until the craze wears out." The *Lima Daily News* saw the careless attitude toward life at the Speedway as becoming contagious, infecting society as a whole. The paper said that cars came down Lima's Main Street as frequently as once every half-hour these days, many piloted by "Speed Maniacs" who occasionally "crushed a tot of the city" and then kept going, the local authorities being too lily-livered to track down the scorchers. "No good," said the paper, "can come from making a mile in 40 seconds." Even the *Indianapolis News* now turned on Fisher, publishing a front-page editorial cartoon that showed the pathetic scene of a dead driver's wife and children huddled before the hearth—never mind that it was late August—and waiting in vain for his arrival.

It wasn't just heartland journalists who were so irate. The *Los Angeles Times* said that "Auto racing to a moderate degree is considered a necessary escape for a certain flow of animal spirits and energy characteristic of the American people, which must have such a blow off or find their outlet in evil ways, possibly"—but wondered why this couldn't be accomplished with races at distances "within the bounds of reason." In an editorial headed "Slaughter as a Spectacle" the *New York Times* on August 30 said that "Automobile racing of the sort seen recently at Indianapolis and Brighton Beach is only attractive, so far as anybody has yet explained, because the spectators buy with their admission tickets something better than an even chance of seeing one or more men get killed. . . . [The races] bring out the very worst of human nature by providing a most barbarous form of excitement. . . . They are an amusement congenial only to savages and should be stopped. . . . There is abundant legal warrant for doing so."

The latter sentiment was most likely a reference to Blackwell's official findings, which the coroner delivered to the press just three working days after his brief inquest. Essentially, Blackwell came down as hard on Fisher as the newspapers did, recommending that a grand jury look into his culpability in the deaths, and declaring that the Speedway as a corporation should be held liable for civil damages. "It is clear that the Indianapolis Motor Speedway Company knew there was going to be a loss of life and limb," he said in his statement. "They were prepared with a hospital, ambulance forces and every convenience to take care of the dead and dying." Ultimately, the district attorney would ignore the recommendations of the man who, after all, was one of the "conveniences" Fisher was accused of having at the ready, and decline to pursue the matter in criminal court. The only successful personal injury lawsuit against the Speedway for the 1909 deaths seems to have been one pressed by the family of riding mechanic Claude Kellum, which resulted, six years later, in his widow, Floy, receiving $7,000.

Still, Fisher could be forgiven if, in the wake of the inaugural meet, he felt almost friendless. Stoddard-Dayton, the company he represented, and National, the company owned by his Speedway co-founder Arthur Newby, both announced that they were withdrawing from racing in the wake of the Indianapolis deaths. Apart from Howard Marmon and a few others in high places in his hometown, all of whom had some financial interest in the Speedway's success, virtually no one was coming to his defense, and many were eager to taroid-and-feather the man who just days before had been held up as the savior of both Indianapolis and automobile racing. "The lumpy going" was inexcusable, Charles Emise, a Manhattan man who was manager of the Lozier racing team, told the *New York Post.* "It was so rough that the National and Fiat cars broke spring clips, something that rarely occurs," Emise added. "Our car broke a set of thick recoil straps *every day.*"

What happened at the Speedway was "positive proof that endurance races should be abolished," said W. W. Sears, president of the Sears Auto Company of Des Moines, Iowa. The automobile men of Southern California were vowing that they would look to Indianapolis only as an example of how *not* to stage high-class auto racing. The Cincinnati Automobile Club wanted to simply ban all track racing, which in its opinion clearly took drivers beyond the limits of "mortal mind and frame." A Texas driver of Stoddard-Daytons, Tobin DeHymel, told his hometown paper, the *San Antonio Light,* that the Speedway was "a complete failure," complained of pebbles breaking his goggles and chunks of flying tar jamming his valves—and, most interestingly, claimed that the judges, and not just the reporters, had lost track of the running order in the climactic Wheeler-Schebler trophy event. Officially, that race ended 65 miles short of its scheduled 300 with the No. 52 Jackson, driven by Leigh Lynch, in the lead. In a bylined piece he wrote for the *Light* upon his return from Indianapolis, DeHymel, who is listed as finishing 7th in his No. 62 Stoddard-Dayton in that race, said the record book bore no relation to reality. "As a matter of fact, when the race was stopped the Jackson driver had succumbed to the heat," he wrote. "He was in the emergency hospital, dead to the world [figuratively speaking]. His wife just managed to reach his side when she, too, fainted."

Could the judges have confused Lynch's dark blue No. 52 Jackson with the dark blue No. 53 Jackson driven by Fred Ellis, which was officially cited as being in 10th place, 34 laps behind at the finish? Or was this a case of Indianapolis officials looking for a reason not to award their top prize to a car that happened to be made in (Jackson) Michigan, Indiana's main rival in the automobile business? Either of those possibilities seems more likely than the idea of DeHymel misremembering, or publicly lying about, what had happened just a few days earlier. DeHymel's contention, in any case, did not deter the Jackson company from immediately suing the Speedway, the Wheeler-Schebler Company, and the Fisher Automobile Company for what several newspapers called "the bloody $10,000 trophy"—and "damages" of $100,000. Jackson executives openly scoffed at the "certificates of participation" the Speedway was planning to issue the Wheeler-Schebler entrants in lieu of the well-advertised top prize. Its suit never came to trial, but by framing Fisher as a bane of car makers in court papers and its statements to the press, Jackson threatened his ability to pull together future races at the Speedway or anywhere else.

The AAA, meanwhile, had a more direct plan to limit Fisher, saying just after the meet that it would soon issue a "radical revision" of rules and would never sanction "races of extraordinary length" again. A week later, though, the AAA, perhaps bowing to pressure from Howard Marmon and other influential Indiana auto men, seemed to be backing down a bit, saying that if it ever *did* sanction 250- or 300-mile events (anything longer was beyond realistic consideration), drivers would have to be changed at 100-mile intervals, and physicians would need to be present to examine the drivers as they left the cockpit. The proposal neither assuaged the angry editorialists—"A.A.A. to Make Half-Hearted Examination of Drivers," said a front-page headline in the *Dunkirk* (New York) *Evening Observer*—nor pleased Fisher, who understood that automobile racing, like any sport, needed its heroes, and that no kid ever fell asleep clutching a picture of a relay team and its trusty physician.

IN GENERAL, THE criticism was too harsh, widespread, and accurate to ignore. So Fisher ignored it. Like Napoleon, who would let his mail sit for three weeks before opening it (and whose portrait Fisher hung above his bed), Fisher had the ability to resist engaging with the critics, beseechers, naysayers, toadies, and tattletales who were always trying to blunt and blur his agenda with their evanescent unease. Beyond issuing quick statements that "Loss of life must be prevented" at the Speedway and that he would follow whatever new rules the AAA finally settled on—statements that allowed the tidal wave of newspaper anguish to harmlessly wash over him—Fisher kept moving forward with his version of Plan B.

And because he was the kind of person who felt steadier leaning into a wind than having the wind at his back, Plan B was vastly superior to Plan A. Or it would be once he got his thoughts in order, and made and corrected a good number of further mistakes. Not caring what other people thought and ruling out any possibility of closing down the Speedway were not the same as having a clear vision of what the facility should be, as modern-day marketing people like to say, going forward. Fisher, for example, saw the necessity of canceling a 24-hour marathon race scheduled to happen at the track on Labor Day, but not the absurdity of saying that he would finish (or perhaps rerun; it's not clear) the Wheeler-Schebler trophy race in late October as part of an elaborate "motor and air carnival" that would include an appearance by the famous aviator Glenn Curtiss. He hadn't even settled on a replacement racing surface at that point.

Not that he wasn't thinking about what it might be. Fisher seriously considered concrete, which had not been working out especially well at Brooklands, and creosote-soaked wood as a successor to Andrew's never named parfait method. He even had a brief flirtation with another "compound" surface that involved gravel, tar, and intensive steamrolling. In a press release Moross confusingly described this topping, which was called "bitu-mineral," as "a cement substance" and promised it would be "smooth as a boulevard" when installed. What Fisher liked about bitu-mineral is hard to figure, but in late August, Moross wired key people in the Indianapolis press, saying he was in Paris, Kentucky, "with instructions to purchase at a cost of $5,000 an entire [bitu-mineral] manufacturing plant which will likely be moved to Indianapolis and located on the Speedway grounds."

Fortunately, a St. Louis man named Will P. Blair got to Fisher before this plan could be implemented. Blair, the secretary of the National Paving Brick Manufacturers Association, was known for his passionate belief in his product, and for his hard-sell techniques. He would not hesitate to tell the mayor of a town that he felt could benefit from bricked-over byways, "your streets right now are not worthy for dogs to walk on!" What he said to Fisher in his sales pitch is not known, but Blair's most persuasive argument could not have been price-based: it would take 3.2 million bricks to cover the Speedway, and the job would cost $180,000, almost double the estimate for bitu-mineral; bricks were by far Fisher's most expensive alternative. On the other hand, Blair could promise that if Fisher went with bricks the Speedway president would at last have a track that stayed where his workmen put it, instead of constantly breaking up and flying up in the drivers' faces. Fisher was intrigued enough by whatever it was that Blair said to install about two hundred yards of brick on the main straight and conduct tests.

On September 11, Johnny Aitken ran up and down the newly laid stretch in his National, then tethered the car to a pair of posts set in concrete and gunned the engine, to see if his madly spinning tires would shave off some of the ceramic. Fisher does not seem to have been present for the tests, but before the acrid-smelling smoke could clear, a half-dozen or so Speedway employees ran over and saw that the bricks beneath Aitken's hard-used back tires had retained their ruddy good looks. Six days later, trucks were covering the entire length of the track with three or four inches of sand as a bed for bricks. Moross told the press that the resurfacing would take a mere three weeks. He also said that the "motor and air carnival" scheduled for October 14 and 15 would now be strictly an aeronautical show, but that a program of auto races and time trials had been added for November 1. It will probably come as no surprise to the reader to learn that the bricking-over of the Speedway took about twice as long as Fisher had anticipated and that both of those promised events had to be canceled.

It took a while to cure Fisher of his belief that the general public adored airplane and balloon shows. ("Two factors in our civilization have been greatly overemphasized," E. B. White wrote in 1928. "One is aviation, the other is sex.") Although air travel was a major cause of both excitement and anxiety in the new age, and the phrase "air carnival" has a nice ring to it, airborne sport, a mixture of races and attempts to set records for altitude and flight duration, did not tend to make for compelling spectacle, at least not from a seat in a grandstand, where it was difficult to keep track of flying machines as they droned or floated around an often cramped and poorly defined course (one common event was "for the machine making the slowest lap of the course in the air"). Failing to register the message sent by the public during the poorly received June balloon meet, Fisher promised Curtiss, a New York–born aviation pioneer who had just won an air race in Rheims, France, a fee of $10,000 if he would appear at the October event. The amount was ridiculous, Enrico Caruso or Sarah Bernhardt bucks, but Curtiss responded by asking for even more money, something totaling closer to $20,000, for a package deal that would include himself, Henri Farman, whose many distinctions included being the first pilot to fly a woman passenger, and Louis Bleriot, who a month before had made the first powered flight over the English Channel. The situation got more complicated when Orville and Wilbur Wright heard about Fisher's air show and threatened to sue the Speedway if it presented any European aircraft (such as the ones flown by Farman and Bleriot), against whose makers the brothers had filed lawsuits for patent infringement. Undeterred, Fisher ordered that airplane hangars be constructed, and telephone poles be taken down, in preparation for the big sky show. He soon called it off, though, because it would have disrupted the track renovation work that was already running behind schedule.

Some people like living in the shadow of the eight ball. They feel more comfortable—or maybe it's that they feel more excited, more alive—when they take on too much and allow themselves too little time to deliver; they don't exactly invite the displeasure of their colleagues and patrons, but they seem to feed off a fear of it, and are sometimes unable to go forward until they have given themselves something extra to overcome. Think of the man who looked you in the eye and promised to have your kitchen finished by Christmas. Why this is so is the subject for another book, but Fisher (the kid who left his childhood room via a high wire) was as prone to sabotaging his serenity as any home improvement contractor or freelance writer. The moment that logic dictated that he must lay down at least part of his burden was the moment he would pile more on his back.

Thus with some two hundred bricklayers working frantically against the onset of winter, and his unrealistic deadline, Fisher ordered Moross to approach the National Amateur Athletic Union about the possibility of staging the 1912 Olympics (or as they were then known the Olympian Games) at the Speedway. He also during this interval founded Empire Automobiles, a company that would make a car called the Aristocrat from 1909 until 1912, and, with Howard Marmon and his three Speedway partners, started two aviation companies: one that proposed to build airplanes, and another that proposed to build airplane engines. Then, a few days after incorporation papers were filed for the latter projects, he suddenly decided to marry his young girlfriend, Jane Watts, and take off with her on a trip out West that was itself a complicated variation on the traditional honeymoon.

Jane was as surprised as anyone by his proposal, since, to hear her tell it, the thirty-five-year-old bachelor previously had never said anything more romantic to her over several months of courtship than, "Aw, shucks, honey, I love you better than two skunks." He even made a point of having practical reasons for popping the question. "I've got a Prest-O-Lite suit [in regard to another plant explosion] on in Los Angeles," she quotes Fisher as saying in *Fabulous Hoosier*. "If we marry now you can come on the trip. I'm tired of traveling alone. I've got to cut out this courting business and get back to work."

The next day—October 23, 1909—a German band hired by Fisher assembled at 6:00 A.M. beneath Jane's window in a driving rain and woke her by playing "Ach, du lieber Augustin," an interesting choice of song, since she may have been one of the few people then living in Indianapolis who could not claim German heritage. Fisher arrived a few hours later, accompanied by his mother and Galloway, and he and Jane were married in her parents' living room. In *Hoosier*, she depicts his behavior during the ceremony as that of a half-tamed wild man: he sweated profusely, couldn't stand still, and constantly worried his shirt collar. At what seemed like an arbitrary point in the proceedings, when he had grown tired of listening to the minister speak, she supposed, Fisher seized Jane's hand and, she writes, "shoved the ring at me wildly. 'Here, take it!' he said. 'Good God, we must be married by this time!'"
Not all of his semicivilized behavior was so innocuous; some of it was mean. Later that day, on the train West, he would take out his pocket-knife and begin cutting the ornamentation off her predominantly blue-and-black-striped wedding dress. "I wept," she writes, "but he kept on slashing. 'I just naturally can't stand gold braid,' he explained." (Her use of "explained" here seems unwitting, in contrast to Ring Lardner's immortal "'Shut up,' he explained.") Then he said, "Honey, I've got to see a man about a boat—I'll be back," and stormed out of their first-class compartment to see a boat salesman he had arranged to accompany them on their trip. On her wedding night, Jane wrote, she cried herself to sleep, alone, but she learned a central lesson about Fisher: "There would always be men, business, big money and big deals. They came first."

There would always be other women, too. For someone like Fisher, leading one life at a time was never challenging—or stressful—enough. When he proposed to Jane he was having at least one other affair: a lengthy and seemingly much more romantic relationship with a willowy blond professional singer named Gertrude Wakefield Hassler. Fisher had first encountered Hassler in 1902, when he saw her perform at a cabaret one evening while he was on a business trip to New York

City. He sent a note backstage saying he would like to see her for dinner at the Empire Hotel, where he was staying. Hassler, who happened to be an Indianapolis girl, knew who he was. She showed up at the Empire, and before long they were passionately involved, with him sending her notes almost daily—he called her "Dutch" and begged for one of her velvet slippers—and her lovingly preserving each missive, especially the ones in which he vowed that they would marry.

After he upped and married Jane he told Miss Hassler, now as crushed as a tot of the city, that he hoped they could stay friendly; he sent her $5,000 and promised to send $1,000 more each month, and to leave her at least $25,000 in his will. When the monthly payments ceased a short time later, she threatened to cause trouble. In 1912, after making angry noises for a few years, she would sue Fisher for breach of promise, asking for $500,000 in damages and pointing out that she had been "acting as his fiancée" until four nights before he married Watts. Ultimately a jury awarded her $50,000, and she settled for $25,000, but not before several of Fisher's love poems—horrible in a disappointingly conventional way ("I'll crush thy lips until nerve wire/Shall quiver in its mad desire/To reach the sea of liquid fire/That burns within")—were read before a crowded courtroom ("Most spectators brought their lunches," said the Indianapolis News) and published in the daily press. As for Jane, she wrote that she was just a kid of fifteen when all this happened, and thus too young to understand what was going on. "I did not know in those days," she wrote, "that such creatures as 'other women' existed." Poor Jane. Being a teenager has always been difficult, and, based on the ages she gave out during her lifetime, she was one for nearly two decades.

ON NOVEMBER 26, though the track was still not quite finished, Jim Jeffries, the recently un-retired heavyweight champion, became the first person not on the construction crew to get a ride around the new brick surface, taking the passenger seat in Jim Allison's Stoddard-Dayton beside his fawning chauffeur, Carl Fisher. The thirty-four-year-old Boilermaker had just reentered training for a bout the next summer with Jack Johnson, the first black heavyweight champ, famously saying, "I am going into this fight for the sole purpose of proving that a white man is better than a Negro." Jeffries was passing through town on a sort of theatrical training tour; in his twenty-five-minute shtick (interlarded in a program of well-choreographed pro wrestling bouts) he worked pulleys, shadowboxed, tossed a medicine ball, and talked up the Johnson fight. When Moross learned that Jeffries had a one-nighter booked at Indianapolis's Tomlinson Hall, he invited him to visit the Speedway for a ride and a tour of the grounds including the aviation hangars.

Meanwhile, when Johnson was in town just the week before, performing a similar training-themed turn at the Empire vaudeville theater, he found that his request to take what he called "a few hot laps" on the Speedway course could not for some reason be accommodated, and although the champ was known to be a car buff (he owned five) and a fan of auto racing (he spoke of possibly becoming a driver after he retired from the ring), Moross tendered no offer to do so much as come out and see the venue. Johnson is said to have reacted with a mirthless smile. Slights sometimes speak as loudly as felonies. Not that the Speedway tour went so well for Jeffries, who stumbled coming down the steps of an airplane and smacked his head on a steel beam, getting a taste of what Johnson would provide in torrents seven months later.

In late November, Moross announced that on Monday, December 7, a "celebrated personage," as yet to be determined, would lay a gold-plated brick at the finish line, symbolizing the end of the renovation, and that a program of auto races would immediately follow. As usual with Moross-ives, this was an approximation of the truth, and not a particularly close one. The celebrity turned out to be not (as many had hoped) Sophie Tucker, who was then appearing at the Colonial Theater on a bill headlined by Hardeen the Handcuff King, and singing her trademark tunes "Nobody Loves a Fat Girl, but Oh How a Fat Girl Can Love" and "The Older They Get, The Younger They Want Them" twice a day. Rather, it was Governor Thomas R. Marshall, an uncharismatic career politician who had gotten lost on his way to the balloon races in June and who today is known only as the coiner of the phrase "What this country needs is a good 5-cent cigar." The date of the ceremony-cum-races turned out to be Saturday, December 18. And the brick was not a gold-frosted loaf of solid silver, weighing 80 pounds, as the publicist had claimed. Rather, it was 53 pounds of bronze with a thin brass coating, something tossed off between carburetors by the boys at the Wheeler-Schebler machine shop. One advantage of its being worthless was that it wouldn't have mattered if someone had stolen it from the window of L. S. Ayres' department store, down on West Washington Street, where it sat for a week guarded by an implacable man with a shotgun.

The Ayres window showcasing the brass brick drew better than the December races. There were two reasons for this. The first was that the events planned for those two days didn't in a single case pit cars against each other; they pit cars against the clock, in an attempt to set records for different-size engines. Fisher had learned by now that fans didn't get worked up about such technical stuff, but he probably thought the excitement of the Speedway's reopening would compensate for the sterility of the competition, and that the car manufacturers would appreciate and flock to the kind of meeting where they could race nonstock vehicles and "hang" an impressively fast record on an experimental model that carried their brand name, without risking the ignominy of finishing behind anyone else. It was one of Fisher's chief worries following the August meet that car makers would not want to appear at his Speedway because of its association with death; he had been especially worried about a de facto boycott since the Vanderbilt Cup, which was run on Long Island on November 1, and a new two-mile speedway in Atlanta financed by Coca-Cola king Asa Candler that opened eight days later, gave the car manufacturers less controversial options. Fisher had even cut short his honeymoon trip, such as it was, to deal with the problem of what was turning out to be an apparent industry-wide hesitancy to enter his races.

To Fisher's relief, his friend Howard Marmon once again came to his aid, stepping forward and announcing that not only would he put two of his cars in the Indianapolis Speedway's December meeting, but he would drive one of them himself. After that, a decent number of entries had come in, and the manufacturers, he noted happily, were sending at least a few of their top drivers, notably Strang, Harroun, and Aitken. Still, it wasn't shaping up as a particularly crowd-pleasing card even before the second attendance-depressing factor—the extreme weather—kicked in. It was 9 degrees in Indianapolis as Marshall, with an assist from the armed guard, ceremoniously laid the brass brick. Although Fisher had cut the prices of admission by half, to 50 cents and a quarter, barely five hundred people stood—or, rather, as one of the dailies said, "continuously jumped up and down"—in the stands as the 3:00 P.M. post time neared. Not even all of the founders were there. Fisher was apparently away on a yacht cruise with Jane and two of his male cronies, and Arthur Newby, who had reconsidered his decision to pull his Nationals out of the racing game and had a couple of cars entered in the December meet, but who was also the most physically fragile of the founders, stayed out of the weather in his downtown office. Conditions were harsh for even the heartiest Hoosiers, and as if to acknowledge as much, Moross stalked out stiffly to the finish line with his trusty megaphone at about 2:55 and announced that ushers would soon be passing among the patrons with free ice cream cones.

That got a laugh from the diehards, but only a brief one; the day was becoming less about sport and diversion than about simple survival. "The judges' stand looked like a country grocery store," said the *Star*, "as the men huddled around the round coal stove." Everyone wore several sweaters beneath and above their overalls, and Strang wore all that plus his double-breasted, brass-buttoned, navy blue "street overcoat." His chief mechanic, Anthony Scudalari, improvised a few modifications on the 120 horsepower Fiat his boss was now driving, placing a sheet of leather in front of the radiator "to keep the cold wind out of the carburetor," said *Motor Age*, and attaching "a hot air pipe to the carburetor leading from the exhaust pipe to keep the big car from freezing."

The drivers demonstrated that they could be macho and decorous at the same time. Some wore no gloves, saying they weren't strictly necessary for real men and anyway made their hands slip on the steering wheel. A few apologized to reporters for not being clean-shaven, saying that it had been so cold in practice the last few days that they had decided to cultivate some natural protection. It was hard to see their faces, though, on account of the makeshift "chamois skin" masks, held on with their goggles and rubber bands, that most of them were wearing. Just before the timing runs began, Johnny Aitken turned up in the grandstand, looking to trade his thin cloth helmet for something more substantial. When he saw a twelve-year-old boy with a homemade balaclava ski mask he offered to make an even exchange, but the kid wouldn't part with his headgear until Aitken threw in a dollar. In the end, "all the brave men wore similar face covers," said the *Star.* "Only the eyes can be seen and the driver looks well the part of a Kuklux Klan."

The strange little things Scudalari had done to the big Fiat had a wonderful effect: Strang took an astounding 53 seconds off Barney Oldfield's record for 5 miles, lowering the mark, set by the Speed King in his Blitzen Benz at Indianapolis earlier that year, from 4:11.30 to 3:17.70. But almost nothing else good happened during those frostbitten days. All but one of the trials beyond 5 miles were canceled on account of the cold; a stiff wind nearly blew two record-minded motorcyclists off the course (they gave up on the spot); one of the wires on the Warner Horograph snapped, causing confusion and temporarily putting the stopwatch back in style. The quintessential moment probably came, however, when Tom Kincaid, exactly 12.5 miles into his attempt to lower the mark for 20 miles and traveling well ahead of the record pace in his spiffy blue National, ran out of gas. His crew had forgotten to fill his tank. Before, between, and during these minor disasters, men frozen into the shape of race car drivers were being pried out of their vehicles and set beside campfires to thaw.

Many of the participants wanted to cancel Day Two and simply hole up in their hotels until 7:00 that evening, when the Commercial Traveler's Association was presenting its seventeenth annual possum dinner at Frank's restaurant. But Strang and a few others favored pressing on with another day of time trials, and someone noted that the forecast for Friday called for a balmy 13 degrees, and so for once the Speedway finished out its advertised schedule. Moross announced free admission for Saturday, a kind of a fan appreciation day. Approximately 150 people showed up.

Fisher, had he been there, might have looked around and thought, "So, it has come to this." Yet pathetic scenes—of which he was rapidly becoming a connoisseur—seemed only to trigger his Crazy Carl energy. His only regret about the December meet, he would say later, was "slow times due to frigid weather." The possibilities of 1910 excited him, he said, adding that there would be at least four aviation meets and three automobile meets at the Speedway next season. There would even be some weird event combining the two—cars with airplane propellers—as well as cars taking on an obstacle course to be built in the infield. Motorboat races were a possibility as well, though obviously a lake would need to be dug or a venue built in some nearby river town like Broad Ripple. As the new year dawned, Fisher fairly bristled with bad ideas, and seemed long overdue for a good one.

13

Of the two jobs, driver and riding mechanic, I think the latter post is the less pleasant. Working on the car while it's moving in a race is sometimes dangerous. Going around curves can be especially bad. In some cases a driver can keep the mechanic from flying away by holding him with one hand, but not always.

— GLENN ETHRIDGE, riding mechanic for
George Robertson

AS HE BEGAN to enjoy major success and prestige as a driver of racing cars, Ray Harroun had but one wish: to get out of the race car driving game as quickly as possible. In general, 1909 had been a good year for the man they called (because of his careful, conservative dress and scholarly mien) "The Little Professor." Working sometimes for Buick and sometimes for Marmon, he had won the 190-mile Wheatley Hills Sweepstakes on Long Island, a 100-mile race in New Orleans, and a 10-mile handicap at the Indianapolis Speedway, among other relatively significant events. And he had managed to have some fun along the way: one day in July, while heading from Chicago to Los Angeles with a cadre of drivers who would compete against one another at Ascot Park, a swankily named dirt track built on the site of what had been the Gardena, California, city dump, his train, pushing high into the Sierra Nevada, passed through a sudden snow squall, and when the engineer stopped for a few minutes to wait out the weather, he and the other drivers, most of whom wouldn't think twice about putting a wheel under each other on the racecourse, hopped down from their Pullman cars and had themselves a rollicking snowball fight.

At the December meet in Indianapolis, Harroun had been happily impressed with Fisher's new brick racing surface—it was hard and bumpy enough to numb your butt and shake out your dental fillings, and slices of brick did at times still come flying up in your face—but he felt that overall it represented a giant step toward safer conditions for professional auto pilots. "Indianapolis is my favorite track—I can't wait to get back there," he told reporters wherever he went in early 1910, an endorsement that no doubt had an aphrodisiacal effect on the feelings already flowing between the Speedway and the Marmon camp.

Harroun's problem was that he would rather be watching the races than driving in them. He was not, at bottom, a Speed Maniac, as much as the papers liked to lump him with his crazier colleagues. Nor, for that matter, had he legitimately come by his most popular nickname, "The Flying Bedouin," a moniker bestowed upon him by Moross, who, thinking "Harroun" sounded vaguely Arab, and sensing that the driver could badly use a shot of charisma, had put out the myth that the quiet, sallow-complexioned Pennsylvanian traced back to Harun al-Rashid (763–809), the fifth Abbasid Caliph. Harroun did not go out of his way to deny the tale, even though he was as Scottish as Johnnie Walker, and in high school might have been voted Least Likely to Wage War Against Byzantium.

"I remember my dad as a very mild man," Dick Harroun told me. "On the street, in his own vehicle, Dad was very cautious, very sane—he actually drove kind of slowly." Perhaps Ray tacitly accepted the Bedouin billing because he thought it impolite to contradict all the reporters who had already run with Moross's useful fib.

"Ray was always nice and considerate of people's feelings, and he got along wonderfully with everyone, including his ex-wives," said Harry Hartz, a longtime driver for Duesenberg, who was the best man at all but two of Harroun's weddings. What made Harroun's behavior noteworthy in the drivers' community was that it was normal middle-class stuff: he'd rather get home for dinner than die. He considered himself an engineer, not some grease-streaked daredevil like Bob "I just stand on the gas pedal and turn left" Burman, or Hartz, who in 1932 would accept a gig that had him driving a DeSoto backward across the continental U.S. to publicize Chrysler's short-lived midpriced line. Though it was the depth of the Depression, and work was scarce, Harroun would have never taken an assignment like that, even if his association with the rearview mirror (about which more shortly) would have made him a cleverer choice. Unlike Hartz—and Carl Fisher—he was not the sort of person who could conceive of traveling backward if the forward gear still functioned; he was no hunter and gatherer of gratuitous stress. This was a man, after all, who had his first wife, Edith, standing by with what she called "a complete medical kit" wherever he raced. So, then, what was someone so sensible doing driving race cars? That was a question Harroun often asked himself.

But he knew the answer—which was that he was extraordinarily adept at his unloved occupation, and had been from the start.

RAY WAID HARROUN was born in 1879 in Spartansburg, Pennsylvania, not a one-horse town, to be sure, but probably not a twenty-five-horse one, either. His father, who may have been a bit flashier than Ray (he went by his middle name of Lafayette rather than his given name of Russell), worked in a mill and farmed a bit; his mother, Lucy, devoted herself to raising Ray and his three sisters. Ray was not particularly fond of cars as a kid—there weren't any in Spartansburg to be fond of—but he did have an interest in all things mechanical. The first mention of him in print is in the "Neighborhood News" column of the October 11, 1895, *Titusville Morning Herald*, which reports that the sixteen-year-old "Ray Harroun came over from Meadville Saturday on his wheel," meaning, most likely, an already old-fashioned high-wheeled bicycle. A year or so later he began apprenticing with his brother-in-law, a local dentist, with an eye toward becoming his assistant. Eventually, though, the prospect of a life in Dullsville changing drill bits and unclogging spit sinks gave pause even to Harroun, and when the Spanish-American War broke out in the early months of 1898, he joined the Navy. He did not see combat, or much beyond the gunwales of the coal-carrying cargo ship on which he served, yet he did develop a love of, or at least an interest in, the sea: after his discharge, he worked for a year on square-rigged ships that carried passengers and merchandise to ports in South America and Europe.

If our young mechanic crept up warily and even a bit comically on the machine age—in sailing vessels, on high-wheeled bikes—it may have been due to the early lessons he received in just how mindlessly cruel machinery, newfangled or otherwise, can be. While Ray was coming of age, his Uncle Frank had broken his back driving a runaway horse-drawn garbage wagon in Syracuse, New York—and Ray's cousin Frank Jr. had lost a hand messing around with an electric sausage grinder. So Harroun, in pursuing his machine age dreams, proceeded with caution. He still didn't know how to drive when he moved to Chicago in 1902—which is noteworthy because he came there to take a job as a chauffeur for William C. Thorne, the son of the co-founder of Montgomery Ward. Such moxie may seem out of character for Harroun, but it was not unusual in an age when people were constantly reinventing themselves in an effort to keep pace with a strange new fake-it-till-you-make-it world. Besides, those early chauffeurs tended to be hound dogs, always sneaking off for joyrides with the female help, and Harroun, the quiet but ardent ladies' man, may have felt his natural affinity for the breed counted for as much as a driver's license. Fortunately Thorne had nowhere to go during Harroun's first few days of employment, and his new hire spent the time teaching himself to operate the boss's Olds.

Like Fisher, indeed like a lot of young men (and women) in those days when tillers were as common as steering wheels, Harroun felt a sense of arrival when he first slipped behind the controls, a feeling that he had reached his personal Promised Land. For the rest of his life, cars would consume him. Within months, he had quit his chauffeur's job and joined the ranks of artisanal automakers, selling a lightweight, more or less homemade two-seater he called "The Harroun Special." Others, noticing that the thing most special about the Harroun car was the way it kept sputtering and backfiring, started calling it "The Sneezer," and as quickly as our man had gotten into the manufacturing end of the game he was out of it again, and looking for a way to make a living.

Patches of Harroun's life, especially his early years, are wrapped in what may be a permanent haze. One problem was that he was not, under normal circumstances, the most sought-out interview on the circuit—no man who says, as Harroun said after pulling up in the winner's circle at the 1911 Indianapolis 500 and gazing upon a sea of expectant reporters, "I'm tired—may I have some water, and perhaps a sandwich, please?" would be—and so large portions of his biography have gone unplumbed and now seem unplumbable. ("Ray Harroun comes as near to saying absolutely nothing as any man I ever met," a female reporter wrote in 1910. "But his smile is sweet.") After his 1902 Chicago interlude, we mostly lose track of him for several years—he may have found employment, if the May 1984 issue of *Petersen's Circle Track Magazine* can be believed, as a ribbon salesman—until he surfaces, in 1906, sans Sneezer, as a jack-of-all-trades for Buick in Lowell, Massachusetts, working simultaneously as a "test driver" on the factory grounds and a salesman in the showroom.

By the standards of the auto industry, Buick was an ancient company, having been founded seven years earlier, in Detroit, as Buick Auto-Vim and Power, by a fortysomething Scottish immigrant named David Dunbar Buick, about whom the pioneer adman Theodore McManus once said, "He sipped from the cup of greatness, and then spilled what it held." David Buick invented a popular lawn sprinkler, the still esteemed method for enameling cast-iron bathtubs, and the first car to use overhead valves, a breakthrough system that greatly increased the efficiency, and thus the power, of internal combustion engines. Buicks had a reputation for zipping up hills and muddling through mucky stretches at a time when such quotidian achievements could not be taken for granted.

It was on the management end where David Buick got mired. By the time Harroun joined the firm its founder was already deep into a series of bad decisions—mostly having to do with spending too much money on development and making unwise loans—that, by the end of 1906, would cause him to lose control of his company to William Crapo Durant, a former Flint, Michigan, carriage maker who would use Buick as a cornerstone of his General Motors company. (Michigan's bountiful forests helped make it a center of the horse carriage trade, and many carriage makers made a relatively easy transition to the automobile business.) Yet to most people Buick looked simply like a vital and prestigious brand, known for aesthetic and engineering excellence, and represented on the racetrack by the dream team of Lewis Strang, Bob Burman, and Louis Chevrolet. Like David Buick, Chevrolet would one day angrily stalk away from the firm that bore his name, and eventually die almost penniless.

The Buick racers were managed by William Hickman Pickens, a storied promoter who got his start posting broadsides for Moross, and were backed by an outrageously extravagant $100,000 annual budget. When the team needed a riding mechanic in the spring of 1906, Pickens offered the position to Harroun, whom he probably knew had some racing experience as part of a four-man relay that had set a record by driving a Columbia automobile from Chicago to New York in 58 hours and 35 minutes. Harroun might have been flattered by the invitation if the job being proffered wasn't, by many people's lights, the worst in racing. In exchange for low pay (usually $25 a week and a small percentage of the prize money) and less glory, the RM was entrusted with greater responsibility than any driver. He was the last person to check the engine before the leather hood straps were secured; he had to crank the ignition at the start, and, once the team was off and running, to make sure that gravity was keeping the fuel supply flowing and that the primitive "splash" oil system was functioning in its intended if inefficient fashion. He also had to inform the driver of who might be coming up on his left or right and pass along to him any signals or chalkboard instructions sent from the pits. RMs and drivers communicated with each other through hand signs—one finger meant "car coming"; two meant "car getting closer"; making an O with the thumb and forefinger meant "we need oil." Although they sat hip to hip, signals were required because as Joe Matson, a pilot for Chalmers-Detroit once explained, "the rush of the wind, the bark of the exhaust, the roaring of the other cars and other things make talking impossible in a race."

For the dedicated RM, maintaining one's dignity could be just as difficult as being heard. During a long race he might find himself obliged to act as a doting mama-bird, popping hot dog chunks and candy or pouring lemonade into a driver's yearning piehole. He might hold a cigarette to the other man's quivering lips, massage his arms and neck, or lean across his lap and take the wheel while the driver unbuttoned his fly and relieved himself into a container. There was no telling what a driver might want an RM to do. When changing gears, Ralph DePalma would signal his co-pilot as he was stepping on the clutch, at which time the mechanic would do the actual shifting; the pressure was intense on the RM because he and DePalma had to be perfectly in sync, but DePalma calculated that by keeping both hands on the wheel through the process he was able to save a fraction of a second on each lap. Barney Oldfield liked his RM to keep his eye on his ever-present unlit cigar, and replace it when it became too bitten down, lest Oldfield lose the cushion that kept his teeth from abrading and chipping as he negotiated the era's rough racing surfaces. In road races, Oldfield also wanted his RM to thump him solidly in certain spots on his back to indicate "downshift for a blind curve" and other specific developing situations. Louis Chevrolet liked his RM to pass him an open bottle of beer when they made pit stops.

But no driver was more demanding than Louis Disbrow, who, the reader will recall, had managed to avoid conviction in the 1902 murder trial of his girlfriend and her male companion. When he lost a pin from a front rod and found his steering compromised in the September 1909 Long Island Stock Car Derby, he refused to stop, and instead, via hand signals, ordered his riding mechanic, Herbert Bailey, to crawl out on the hood of their Rainier and attempt the necessary repair at 70-something miles per hour. Journalist William Nolan describes the incident in his book about Oldfield: "Here, with his feet braced, hanging to the radiator cap with one gloved hand, [Bailey] reached down and held the steering rod together" while Disbrow drove the remaining 20 miles of the rough 22.8-mile circuit. The Rainier finished in mid-pack, and afterward Disbrow seemed more concerned about not winning than about the contributions of his RM. Asked if he had been worried about Bailey, the driver shrugged, blew a smoke ring, and said, "I didn't even slow down on the turns."

The attitude is typical of the times. Riding mechanics came and went, often like rockets when their cars spun out or stopped abruptly, and their "last words" were frequently four fingers straight out, thumb down, racing sign-speak for "There's an idiot behind us who appears to be coming straight up our butts." ("All the skill in the world will not save a good driver when some dub who has crept into the race by virtue of a weak head and a two-dollar licensing card from the sanctioning-governing body shoves a machine across his road," Oldfield once said.)

Although Johnny Rutherford noted, when I interviewed him for this book, that the riding mechanic's seat might in some cases be the safer of the two for having no steering wheel or other obstacles to a hasty exit should an accident occur—this is the "you want to get thrown clear" theory—the anecdotal evidence suggests that most flights from the vehicle ended in eulogies and tear-salty ham sandwiches at the home of a grieving mom. By the time Harroun was asked to serve as a floating co-pilot for whichever of the Buick stars needed him, RMs were routinely extracting promises from car manufacturers to pay their funeral expenses in the not-so-unlikely event that "something happened."

As a native of Spartansburg, Harroun was quite content with nothing happening. He took the job that Pickens offered, but he didn't waste any time that summer migrating, like the flounder's eye, across the great divide that separated an anonymous co-pilot from an admired (and slightly less endangered) Buick wheelman. He never explained how he convinced Pickens to give him such a break, though it is not hard to see why the manager, once he saw Harroun in action, was happy to make him the first driver off the Buick bench. Harroun's secret was essentially the same as Louis Chevrolet's: he wanted to be a designer and builder of cars, an engineer, not a driver, and so he came to the game with a fresh perspective and a distinct style. But while having his own agenda put Chevrolet on autopilot, and made him relaxed and instinctive, the same circumstances turned Harroun into an especially keen and calculating competitor, the rare man willing to be patient and go easy on his tires and engine, the better to avoid spectacular breakdowns at high speed and live another day. Harroun was not *always* back in the pack in the early going, but he was off the lead much more often than he was on it, content to eat the daredevils' dust and wait for the right moment to surge on by.

The technique—if that's what we can call a method so naturally an extension of the man—worked wonderfully from the start. Harroun spent little time pumpkin-vining his way through the county and state fairs that were the auto racing minors. In 1907 he drove for Buick while also accepting assignments from smaller outfits like Marriott and sometimes dusting off his flyweight Sneezer (it weighed only 1,000 pounds) and racing that. He wasn't winning much yet, but he was making a living, and the occasional headline as when, in September of '07, the *Chicago Tribune* mentioned him in a preview piece as one of the few points of interest on what the paper saw as a particularly dull local program.

Still, even before he lost his rookie status as a driver Harroun was looking for a way out. In February of 1907 a *New York Times* reporter who was in Ormond Beach, Florida, to cover the races and time trials came upon him conducting experiments that he hoped would help him break into the aviation business. Harroun was strapped to a large kite that was tied by cables to an automobile so that, when it moved forward along the seashore, he was able to achieve altitude. The escapade sounds utterly un-Harroun-ish—until you read on and see that the kite lifted him just 20 feet on three brief tries, and each time, wrote the *Times* reporter, Harroun "looked glad to get back to earth." No Flying Bedouin he.

Harroun seems to have competed very little, if at all, in 1908, perhaps because the recession of that year subdued the racing scene, or more likely, because he took a job in July as an engineer with Marmon in Indianapolis. As we've seen, this was a fluid time in the auto industry, with engineers, drivers, and mechanics perpetually on the move from company to company. That same year, Pickens and Strang both quit Buick, the former to manage the aviatrix Katherine Stinson, who billed herself as "The Flying Schoolgirl," the latter to drive an Italian-made Isotta race car in the U.S. and abroad. But from the start the Harroun-Marmon matchup had the makings of more than just a brief fling. When it came to mechanics, Howard Marmon and Ray Harroun were both deep thinkers and inveterate tinkerers, men with the rare ability to see themselves on a continuum—to understand that the automobile, in the first decade of the twentieth century, was a mere prototype of what it would eventually be, and that anyone who designed and built cars was challenged to tease out their potential.

Marmon cars were almost always, in some sense, experimental. The very first one, built in 1902, was an overhead-valve, air-cooled twin V with pressure lubrication. This was followed by a V4, which in turn gave way to a V6 and then a V8 before Howard Marmon switched to in-line engines, and left the V design to his panting rivals. Even his advertisements were ahead of their time, always eloquently written, consistently designed, and often built around still fresh news of the car's racing accomplishments ("The Marmon Wins Again—This Time at Elgin!"). Marmon was also among the first car companies to use a celebrity spokesperson—and not just some arbitrary sports or screen star. Casting about for someone to bolster his company's claim that it manufactured "The Easiest Riding Car in the World," Howard Marmon hit upon Helen Keller.

"I am delighted with my Marmon," Keller said in full-page magazine ads that pictured her sitting serenely in the backseat of a sedan.

> To my touch the workmanship seems perfect. Borne along on deep, springy cushions, I find a long drive in it lulling and alluring. I do not have to hold on to keep my balance. In other cars I am keenly conscious of curves, but in my Marmon I hardly know when we turn a sharp corner. Recently we drove over Catskill roads, but I hardly felt any difference from pavements. I knew we were in the mountains by the atmosphere and the odors peculiar to high altitudes. Riding in a Marmon is just like sailing . . . same smooth, vibrationless motion. I can hardly say enough in praise of this wonderful automobile. It gives me so much enjoyment.

As part of his marketing plan, Marmon for a while employed a woman racing driver. The success, indeed the very presence, of Martha Foster in races and point-to-point endurance runs not only got his brand talked about—it also sent a positive message about Marmon to the 50 percent of the American population to whom other manufacturers weren't speaking. The conventional wisdom back then was that automobiles were too unreliable for women to take on trips of any distance (in her 1909 book, *The Woman and the Car: A Chatty Little Handbook for All Women Who Motor or Want to Motor*, Dorothy Levitt suggests that "If you are going to drive alone on the highways and byways, it might be advisable to carry a small revolver"), and too unwieldy for them to steer and crank-start. Maybe that was true of other makes, Martha Foster told the auto racing press wherever she went, but *she'd* never had any trouble with her Marmon.

Although they were not always warmly welcomed, women made some notable contributions to the early auto scene. The silent film actress Florence Lawrence, known in her day as "The Biograph Girl," is widely credited with developing the turn signal and the brake light, continuing a family tradition that started when her mother, vaudeville singer Charlotte Bridgewood, invented the windshield wiper. (Perhaps because they considered themselves artists, and not engineers, neither woman bothered to take out a patent, and both were beaten to the marketplace by rivals who borrowed heavily from their designs.)

The most accomplished female racer of the era was Joan Newton Cuneo, the Massachusetts-born wife of a wealthy New York banker. Her best year was probably 1906, when she turned twenty-six: driving an air-cooled Knox ("The Car That Never Drinks"), she won two races at the March Mardi Gras meet in New Orleans, both times beating fields of top male drivers, and a month later steered a lightweight Maxwell to victory in a fiercely contested one-mile sprint in Atlantic City. She also competed in all five of the grueling Glidden Tours that were staged between 1905 and '09. When Cuneo limped into Manhattan at the end of the 1,500-mile 1907 Glidden with a broken spring and a cracked axle, the judges awarded her a special silver loving cup for "skillful driving and pluck." But Cuneo didn't need such condescension. Although in other ways a typical Long Island matron, she had a reputation in racing for being as bold and fearless as Burman or Strang. When Cuneo was arrested in Yonkers for "scorching" at 43 miles per hour, she told the *New York Times* that she was perfectly comfortable at that rate, having reached 112 miles per hour in a race at Palm Beach not long after delivering her second child. Racing promoters were sometimes dismissive—or scared—of her, but the public wasn't. The *Albany Times* reported that when she passed through town in 1907 crowds greeted her with this allegedly spontaneous song:

> *O, Mrs. Cuneo, O, Mrs. Cuneo*
> *The greatest woman driver that we know*
> *She keeps a-going, she makes a showing,*
> *Does Mrs. Cuney-uney-uney-O!*

Still, she stopped racing in 1909, when the American Automobile Association, worried about the ramifications of a female fatality, banned women drivers from competition (the organization had already banned blacks). To the disappointment of many, Cuneo meekly accepted the ruling. "Would that I could cultivate some suffragette tendencies and fight for my rights," she said. "But I can't. I have instead always tried to keep the woman's end in automobiling sweet, clean and refined. I drive and race just for the love of it." She did not resurface until four years later—as a contributor of recipes for orange marmalade and piccalilli in a magazine called *Home Helper.*

Marmon driver Martha Foster also retreated into the domestic life—as the second wife of Howard Marmon. Her retirement from the racecourse, also on account of the AAA ban, opened up a slot for a driver on the company's team—a slot into which Ray Harroun went, not kicking and screaming but sighing existentially, in early 1909. He may have felt that he had finally put driving behind him when he took Marmon's offer of a job as an engineer, but even if he hadn't been such an agreeable sort, he couldn't say no to Marmon, who was revamping his racing team, and asked Harroun to come back for just one more season to drive his latest and greatest model ever, the Marmon 32. And when 1909 turned out successfully, and Howard Marmon again asked Harroun to stay on as head driver for just one more season with a new and improved 32, Harroun sighed again and said yes again. But this time he mustered the courage to tell the boss that when it came to race car driving, 1910 would definitely be his last rodeo.

NINETEEN TEN TURNED out to be the best year Harroun would ever have on the racetrack. In all, he won forty-one races, a total that earned him the title (albeit twelve years later, when the AAA finally got around to recognizing the stars of those early times) of national driving champ. There were three main reasons he did so well that season. The first was that he improved as a driver as he gained confidence and perfected his knack for nursing his equipment and staying out on the racetrack for as long as possible before pitting. On April 8, at the inaugural meeting of the Los Angeles Motordrome, he won a 100-mile race on the wooden boards of that track without ever coming in for servicing or fuel, and a week later he won an odd race there called the Two Hour Free-For-All, covering 148 miles in the prescribed time, again without making a stop.

The second reason for his success in 1910 was that the Indianapolis Motor Speedway held three automobile meets that year—three days of racing in May, three more in July, and two in September, the most it would ever offer—and since that was the track where he usually practiced, and he understood the nuances and eccentricities of its turns as well as anyone and better than most, Harroun enjoyed a long stretch of home-field advantage. He won six races at Indianapolis in 1910, including two designated as "special events": the 50-mile Remy Grand Brassard and the second edition of the Wheeler-Schebler—which had been shortened that year from 300 to 200 miles.

But the chief reason Harroun hit his professional peak that season had to do with his car. The Marmon 32 had made its racing debut at the inaugural 1909 meet, easily taking the August 19 10-mile handicap event with Harroun at the wheel. The 32 was "a relatively small, cleverly simple and consequently very light automobile with apparently conventional suspension masking remarkable ride and handling characteristics," according to George Hanley and Stacey Pankiw, authors of *The Marmon Heritage*. For a Marmon was in many ways an unusually conservative car: water-cooled instead of air-cooled, with in-line cylinders instead of a V configuration, and it employed, says automotive historian Dennis Horvath, "torque tube drive with a rear transaxle that was currently in vogue at the time." Rated at 32–40 horsepower, the Marmon 32 was, according to its own ad copy, "a sensible, logical car," a bit buttoned-down, perhaps, but designed impeccably and built as solidly as anything then on the road. Not surprisingly, given its characteristics, Harroun had a hand in its creation. Yet it was aimed at an entirely different market than his ultra-light, nearly disposable Harroun Special. While the industry as a whole would soon follow the lead of Henry Ford and build affordable cars for the common man, Howard Marmon (like the people behind the Packard, the Auburn, and the Lozier) stuck to his original vision of first-class machines for the well-to-do. Houdini himself used a Marmon in his stage act to demonstrate that he could escape from heavy chains binding him to the most durable chassis ever constructed. Such quality and glamour, of course, came with a price.

Depending on whether you wanted the two-door, four-door, or limousine model of the Marmon 32, prices ranged from $2,650 to $4,000 in 1909, a year when you could buy a Model T Ford for $650.

Howard Marmon believed success on the racecourse was key to selling the 32. And once that success started coming, he took pains to emphasize, in ads and interviews, that his company didn't and never would produce a special line of esoteric racing vehicles; what you saw on the track, he wanted everyone to know, is what you encountered in the showroom. But for their yellow and black racing colors (which first appeared in 1909), and their lack of fenders, the 32s that Ray Harroun and the other Marmon drivers (Joe Dawson, Harry Stillman, and Bruce Keen) steered around the Indianapolis Motor Speedway were identical to the 32s coming out of the company's factory on Kentucky Avenue.

Except that they weren't. Like a lot of manufacturers, Marmon had begun modifying the cars in its competitive fleet, and otherwise pushing the borders of what was allowable, as soon as the company started racing. Lightening his load considerably, Harroun drove the 32 in a race at Atlanta in November of 1909 with the riding mechanic's seat unoccupied—and the brazenness went on from there, limited only by what Marmon could get away with under a system of elastic AAA rules and less than strict inspections. Other companies were playing fast and loose with the definition of "stock," too. Said Benjamin Briscoe, president of the United States Motor Company: "An entrant in a stock car event who depends upon a stock car—the same car that is delivered to a purchaser—has as much chance of winning a race as the *Lusitania* has of crossing the Atlantic in 24 hours."

Howard Marmon took advantage of his position as an industry leader to stretch the rule book further than most: on May 5, 1910, Harroun showed up at the Atlanta Speedway with a radically streamlined 32 that had only one seat, a narrow body that, said *The Horseless Age*, "reminded one of a rowing shell," covered wheel discs, and an odd, pointy tail, features that were nowhere to be found on the Marmons for sale in downtown Indianapolis. Instead of four cylinders, this car had six, which made it more powerful than a stock 32 and put it in the next-biggest class in terms of cubic inch displacement, CID, the standard way, then and now, of measuring engine size for racing purposes.

Newspapermen had been referring to Marmon's fleet as the Yellow-jackets or the Yellow Peril (a racist term then in vogue for the perceived threat posed to American workers by the influx of Asian immigrants). Marmon christened this new, muscled-up model himself, however, telling people who watched Harroun take practice laps with it at the Speedway that they were looking at, and soon would be hearing more about, a little something he called the Wasp. After it won a 200-mile race on the Atlanta dirt track later that month, the nickname became part of the auto racing lexicon.

The way Harroun drove the Wasp in the May 28, 1910, Wheeler-Schebler race showed that he trusted the car implicitly. He started out as usual, hanging back and allowing someone else—in this case, Louis Chevrolet's younger brother Arthur—to grab the early lead. But after only about 12 miles he moved boldly to the front of the nineteen-car pack and held the spot for the next 75 laps as Barney Oldfield survived a violent tire explosion and Marmon teammate Joe Dawson, driving a conventional (non-Wasp) 32, spun out and smashed into the outer wall on the backstretch (wrecking the car but not seriously injuring himself). Stopping only once in the 200 miles to refuel and change a couple of tires, Harroun finished in the world-record time of 2:46.31.

And yet in the pictures taken immediately after the Wheeler-Schebler it is difficult to read Harroun's mood. He had every reason to be happy—thanks to the special arrangement he had with Howard Marmon, he got to keep the $1,000 check that came with the victory (most drivers had to pass these winnings on to their employers, and be content with their modest salaries)—but there is no particular joy radiating from his oil-and-dust-smeared features. ("Mr. Harroun is a quiet, dark man," a *Chicago Tribune* reporter who used the pen name Mae Tinee once wrote. "He has slender hands, the stillest you ever saw, and eyes that look at you, but don't seem to see you.") Harroun at that moment may have merely been registering the mixed emotions he openly expressed about his profession.

"My dad never got too carried away with himself or his success," Ray's son Dick told me. "He was humble because he knew that as a driver you were only one day away from a serious crash." In this case, make that two days. On the 30th of May, while running practice laps in the Wasp before the last afternoon of racing, Harroun's left front tire blew and he spun out and smacked into the same backstretch wall that had claimed Dawson's car. He was not badly hurt, but twenty-five years later, while he was letting Dick drive a lap around the Speedway in their street car, he made his son slow down so they could see the chinks in the concrete. "That right there," Ray said, proudly pointing to the spot. "That was *me.*"

IF 1910 WAS a good year for Ray Harroun it was an even better one for Marmon race cars. In the ninety-three races the company entered, its drivers won twenty-five, with twenty-four second-place finishes and thirteen thirds. Howard Marmon must have been pleased, even if—because he was bucking the trend toward cheaper and less deluxe automobiles and because the public couldn't help but notice the disconnect between the stock and racing Marmons—the success on the racetrack never translated into robust sales.

But, really, was it *just* Marmon's approach that was keeping his business from taking flight, à la that of Henry Ford? Was racing helping *any* manufacturer sell its cars? No one in those days did the kind of research that could yield reliable answers, but the best guesses were no and no. The harsh truth was that racing, for all that had happened over the last few years, was as much a semi-disreputable mess as it had ever been. Although the bricks had made a dramatic difference at the Speedway, the nation's premier auto track—there were no fatal accidents at the December 1909 time trials or the three-day May 1910 meet—the dangers of automobiling remained graphically on display. Wrecks marred several of the Speedway's May races. Tobin DeHymel, the driver who had contended that the judges gave the trophy to the wrong Jackson car in the 1909 Wheeler-Schebler race, was killed while driving his Stoddard-Dayton in a race in San Antonio. A Springfield lawyer and amateur driver named La Rue Vredenburg went to a fiery death before fifty thousand at the Illinois State Fair. And on July 6, Tom Kincaid—a typically aggressive twenty-six-year-old driver who once said "Speed is all that concerns me"—lost control of his National during a late-morning Speedway practice session and crashed through a heavy wooden wall, dying instantly. At the October Vanderbilt Cup on Long

Island, eight people—six spectators and two riding mechanics—were killed in a series of spectacular wrecks that also injured about eighteen others. Even the drivers were starting to get sick of the carnage; a group led by Oldfield threatened to boycott the Vanderbilt Cup if conditions there were not made safer for both the racers and their fans.

But if outraged newspaper editorialists and community leaders were correct about deadly accidents boosting attendance at the races—and no sane person doubted that they were—such bloodlust wasn't helping quite enough. The Atlanta Speedway was struggling to sell seats and a proposed Detroit auto track was put on hold as its backers noticed how the crowds at the Vanderbilt Cup were dwindling. In Indianapolis, too, the numbers were taking a steep downward curve, though what the numbers were exactly was hard to say.

On the first day of racing at the Speedway in 1910, Friday, May 27, Ernie Moross told the press that more than fifteen thousand people had paid their way in, but pictures in the next morning's papers showed a mostly empty grandstand and a sparsely populated track apron, making it look like the actual attendance was half the announced amount. (*The Horseless Age* in fact put the number at six thousand.) The next day Moross reported a suspiciously high—and round—25,000. Monday, May 30, Memorial Day, definitely brought out the biggest crowd of the meet (blue laws barred Sunday racing)—but surely nothing like the "over 60,000" that the director of racing announced (*The Horseless Age* guessed twenty thousand).

Moross may have felt he could exaggerate so flagrantly because he was halfway out the door. As soon as the May meeting ended, he resigned from his Speedway post to become what today would be called a freelance publicist. (His initial clients were the Fiat racing team and a group investigating the possibility of building a speedway in New York City. A year earlier Moross had quit to help start a track in Detroit, but returned to the Indianapolis Speedway a month later. Like several other speedways then being proposed, including the Detroit one, the New York City track was never built.) Moross's departure had a dramatic effect on the attendance figures, not because anyone had been paying to catch a glimpse of him, but because without him to provide an official tally, newspapermen were forced to estimate the house themselves.

And so it was that two weeks after the spring auto meet the Speedway presented an aviation show that, despite Moross's claim in late May that it would "be bigger than the meet in Rheims, France," on the first of its three days drew fewer than five hundred souls, according to the Indianapolis dailies. By the second day of the air show, Carl Fisher had assumed the role of official spokesman and announced an attendance of nineteen thousand, a number not quite as ridiculous as it may at first seem, since the grounds in fact were flooded that day with visitors who had been shuttled over from a big downtown trade show (and admitted for free). On the third day, Fisher issued the oddly vague claim that there were "even more people than the day before," but the reporters noted that while a respectable-sized crowd had been present at the start of the events, only a few hundred were still hanging around by the time the last plane landed.

At the second auto meet, in early July, the attendances for the three days were given by the Speedway's new publicist, C. E. Shuart (a former member of the *Star* staff), as five thousand, five thousand, and (on July 4) twenty thousand. Even if they were accurate, which they probably weren't, these figures paint a picture of a business in something like a free fall. With demand so soft, Fisher canceled the twenty-four-hour race that had been scheduled for mid-August, and announced that the three-day Labor Day auto meet would be shortened to two. Attendance for the first of those programs, on Saturday, September 3, was never officially announced, but in D. Bruce Scott's book *Indy: Racing Before the 500*, the author says that "several thousand people" showed up. On Labor Day itself the crowd was given at a probably inflated eighteen thousand, down from an obviously fake sixty thousand on Memorial Day.

Some extreme weather had cropped up over the course of the meets, keeping the crowds down on certain days, but weather wasn't the Speedway's problem. The problem was the product. While there had been some genuinely exciting moments—Oldfield's steering his Knox around the circuit on three tires in the second edition of the Wheeler-Schebler; the second lap of a 5-mile race on Labor Day, when four different cars claimed the lead before Johnny Aitken inched ahead of Joe Dawson, Arthur Greiner, and Harroun at the wire—eight programs of racing felt excessive and dull. On May 28, the overly long card had included a ho-hum 5-mile race followed, two events later, by a ho-hum 10-mile race for the very same set of five 231–300 CID cars. (Dawson edged out Harroun in the first; Harroun edged out Dawson in the second.)

Sorting the cars in terms of cubic inch displacement may have been necessary for the sake of fairness, and may have pleased the gearheads in the gallery, but for the average fan, who wanted a simple storyline to go with his "Bread Ham Sandwich" (10 cents on the concession menu) and buttermilk (a nickel), such technical slicings and dicings only dissipated the drama. It was as if the competitors were looking inward, to criteria and records that interested only people in the auto industry, and not outward to something that might capture the imagination of the masses—all the while inviting the masses to pay to watch them settle their arcane scores. Cutting back the Wheeler-Schebler from 300 to 200 miles made it a saner, safer race, to be sure, but winning it then became a less heroic achievement. As for all those gimmicky handicap races, with cars starting at different times, depending on their engine sizes, this was a format that had even industry insiders scratching their heads over who was ahead, and wondering what it all proved in the end. All the general public wanted, when you came right down to it, was simply to see daring young men risk their lives to win something. When they got instead hours of dust and noise and long waits between races so that drivers would be fully rested (a new AAA-imposed stricture), they found other things to do. On the final day of racing in 1910, more than three times as many people (65,000) watched the Labor Day parade in downtown Indianapolis than came to the races (18,000).

WHO OR WHAT would save auto racing?

Well, there was always Barney Oldfield. "The Daredevil Dean of the Roaring Road," as he was sometimes billed, didn't have an altruistic bone in his body, but he had a very low threshold for boredom, and plain-vanilla racing excited him as much as it did the average citizen. In finding ways to stay interested—by racing his cars against planes, trains, horses, and human track stars, and engaging in other odd bits of business and publicity stunts—he managed to keep himself and his sport in the news. In 1906 Oldfield had appeared on Broadway for ten weeks in a musical called *The Vanderbilt Cup*, which featured a climactic race between him and his friend and fellow driver Tom Cooper, both pretending to steer real Peerless cars set on treadmills. In late 1909 Oldfield had made headlines by picking a fight in the press with heavyweight champion Jack Johnson on the seemingly not-worth-discussing subject of which man was the better race car driver. Johnson eagerly took up the gauntlet, though he didn't have much of a case beyond his generally high opinion of himself, and correspondingly poor opinion of Oldfield. The fighter probably felt that the banter helped promote his July 4 bout with the driver's old fishing buddy Jim Jeffries. But the public dares and disparagements continued beyond that date, as Johnson and Oldfield hatched a plan to "settle the matter" with a match race that they would film for distribution to the nation's movie theaters.

Competition between a black man and a white man was not a simple thing to sell in the America of 1910, and the fact that Johnson recently had caused a great white hopelessness by punishing Jeffries for fifteen rounds did not make matters easier. The AAA let it be known that it would consider a showdown between Oldfield and Johnson to be "an outlaw race," owing to its policy banning black people from driving race cars at its sanctioned tracks, and that if Oldfield continued to pursue the venture he would face a lengthy if not permanent suspension. Oldfield was no humanitarian, but he didn't like the AAA telling him what to do, so instead of backing down he raised what he knew would be the highly annoying possibility of the match race happening at the Indianapolis Speedway. For his part, Fisher was open to the idea, but in a lukewarm way, proudly noting in a statement to the press that he had "banned" the heavyweight champion the year before (when in fact he had simply failed to invite him) but saying that Johnson would "probably" be allowed to drive in an exhibition race at the September meeting. With business so bad, Fisher couldn't afford to turn away attractions that might make his turnstiles spin.

But others in the sport were not so open to the prospect of a black-versus-white showdown. The *Washington Post* reported that "Protests have arisen from all parts of the country, and more than one famous auto pilot will refuse to ride over the brick track at Indianapolis in September if Johnson is allowed to appear on the course in his machine." The two most loudly opposed were Louis Chevrolet and Bob Burman. "There are no negro automobile-race drivers at the present time," Chevrolet said, "and if I understand correctly there is a ban against it. I am not willing to allow my name to be used in the same race program as that of Jack Johnson, and if the Indianapolis Motor Speedway management cannot confine itself to automobile racing without bringing in a negro barn-storming pugilist, I believe it is time for the white drivers to quit the game on that track."

Burman was even more forceful, and in windy prose no doubt whipped up by Ernie Moross (Wild Bob's new press agent) said:

> Never before has such a condition arisen, and I believe that the automobile drivers should feel that President Fisher and other officials of the Speedway in even giving publicity to such a project should be the objects of censure at the hands of white men who make a business of automobile racing. I have heard several others say that they will not appear at Indianapolis in September if Johnson is allowed on the track, and although I won many victories at the last Indianapolis meeting and am confident that the Buick would make another sweep there in September, I shall refuse to be a party to any meeting in which Jack Johnson or any other colored driver is allowed to participate.

The controversial race was ultimately held on October 25 of that year at the Sheepshead Bay track, in Brooklyn, with Oldfield driving his Blitzen Benz and Johnson in an expensive Thomas car. Things went poorly from the start. Johnson, seeing an unauthorized movie camera, demanded that its operator stop cranking, and when the man refused, the champ picked up the camera by the tripod and smashed it to the ground, causing the thousand or so spectators to gasp. According to the agreed-upon format for the competition, the winner was to be the first driver to take two 5-mile heats, but during the prerace discussions Johnson learned that Oldfield was reneging on his promise to let him win at least one heat, and this upset the pugilist to the point where he could not concentrate on his driving. Oldfield got away so fast in the first heat that Johnson was splattered with mud from the Benz's tires and struggled to stay close, ultimately finishing about a half-mile behind his more experienced foe. The second heat was a replay of the first, with the margin of victory even wider.

Johnson, despite being double-crossed, was gracious in defeat, saying, "I may be able to drive a car fast on a straight road, but I never will take any chances on the turns like Oldfield does. . . . He has had so much experience in that sort of work that he made a monkey out of me." Oldfield, in contrast, was a jerk: "I am glad if my victory of Johnson today will have any effect on the 'white man's hope' situation," he said. But it didn't have an effect on anything, if only because virtually no one ever saw the film of the one-sided showdown, which stirred no interest in theater operators.

DECLINING ATTENDANCE AT the Speedway did not of course please Fisher, who with his co-founders had sunk an additional $200,000 or so into the venture in 1910, adding a grandstand and modifying the grounds for the disastrous air shows (besides the June event, there were two balloon races on September 17 that supposedly drew a total of six thousand paying spectators). But it was not the throwing of good money after bad that most concerned Crazy Carl. "I don't think he was ever interested in money as a particular goal," said his longtime friend and lawyer Bill Muir, as quoted in Polly Redford's book *Million Dollar Sandbar: A Biography of Miami Beach.* "Carl could just pull a deal out of the air, he could combine things that would stagger the average person, and I think he was just interested in the excitement of having these ideas and accomplishing them." The worst-case scenario for Fisher, and probably his co-founders as well, would be to be stuck with a commitment to a project that had fallen flat but not quite expired, a dreary monument to mediocrity. He craved stimulation—if Prest-O-Lite wasn't a glamorous business, at least it gushed cash, and produced fiery explosions—and the ego boost that comes with pronounced business success.

And so it was inevitable that as the Speedway showed signs that it might top out as something less than a world-renowned attraction his attention showed signs of wandering. Fisher around this time became fascinated by the claims of a McKeesport, Pennsylvania, chemist named John Andrus, who said that he had developed a tiny and ridiculously cheap little pill—"made from certain chemicals," according to the *New York Times*—that turned water into an automobile fuel much more powerful (but easier on engines, and cleaner-burning) than gasoline. Fisher would eventually get Howard Marmon involved in the venture, and sink more than $100,000 of his own money into the miracle product called Zoline—only to discover a few years later that Andrus was pulling a sleight of hand trick, and substituting cans of gasoline for Zoline-treated water at all of his demonstrations. It was Miami, though, that would become Fisher's biggest distraction. The same year he met the shady Mr. Andrus, 1910, he discovered that tropical backwater of 5,471 and became, according to Jane Fisher, "enchanted with the jasmine-scented moonlight and the soft warm air." To hear her tell it, the challenge of developing Miami into what today would be called a tourist destination grabbed hold of him the moment he first looked through his bottle-thick glasses at Biscayne Bay.

Fisher had happened upon Miami by chance. In early 1909, a few months before getting married, he commissioned a yacht that he might have christened *Jane*, to honor his young bride-to-be, but instead named *Eph*, after his dog. In November the *Eph* set off down the Mississippi River on what became a honeymoon cruise only after Jane insisted on coming along with Crazy Carl, two of his male friends, and the ever-present butler Galloway. It was an unhurried and in some ways memorable journey. If Jane Fisher's account can be believed, Fisher was not at the Speedway for the first testing of the brick surface at the frigid time trials of December 1909; instead, on Christmas Eve, he and his cronies went ashore at New Orleans. When they returned two days later they smelled of bacon grease and burbled with apologies for losing the roast pig they had bought for Jane while playing football with the carcass in the French Quarter. Sometime later Jane went into town with the men, and noticed that a madam standing under a red light outside her establishment smiled when she saw Carl and greeted him by name. In her book, Jane chalks up such behavior to her husband's "lusty and incomprehensible personality."

Not long after that, writes Jane, the *Eph* ran into a hurricane—apparently one of those sneaky ones that do not show up in the records of the National Weather Service—and they had to continue their Southern trek by train, eventually winding up in Miami's seductively balmy embrace. From that year on, Fisher would spend ever more time there, building hotels and buying and selling property—although never, if he could help it, to blacks or Jews. The standard language in his real estate contracts said, "Said property shall not be sold, leased or rented in any form or manner, by a title either legal or equitable, to any person or persons other than of the Caucasian Race, or to any firm or corporations of which persons other than of the Caucasian Race shall be a part or stockholder." As Gerald Posner notes in his book *Miami Babylon*, Fisher did not consider Jews to be Caucasian—although if they were particularly rich or prominent in their fields, he did allow them into Le Gorce, his otherwise restricted country club.

YET FOR ALL the attention he lavished on Miami, Zoline, and a few other projects, Fisher was not yet completely disenchanted with his sprawling auto racing plant. By the time of the July 1910 meet, he and his co-founders, James Allison, Frank Wheeler, and Arthur Newby, knew that they had a business problem of the sort that wasn't going to solve itself, and the question of what to do next at the Speedway became part of a freewheeling discussion that occupied the founders throughout the summer of 1910. By then three of the four lived in close proximity to each other on Cold Spring Road, then known as Millionaire's Row or the Newport of Indianapolis. Fisher had been the first of the founders to move to the area, about halfway between the city and the Speedway, buying a small house already on the site in 1909 and expanding and reworking it into what eventually would come to resemble a Miami Beach mansion. That same year Frank Wheeler, the Manchester, Iowa–born Carburetor King, built a few hundred feet away an eleven-thousand-square-foot home that was an impressive example of Arts and Crafts architecture. Allison constructed his sumptuous twenty-five-thousand-square-foot Prairie-style mansion just to the other side of Fisher's house in 1910. Only Newby, who never married and was rarely in robust health, stayed in town, in what Deborah Lawrence, the vice president of development for Marian University, a Catholic school that has owned the Cold Spring Road properties since 1967, described to me as "a comfortable but less flamboyant place" on Indianapolis's Meridian Street. "The three who moved here," she added, "had a very strange setup. They lived rather insane lives."

The adjoining estates reflected each man's definition of pleasure. Fisher's place, which he called Blossom Heath, had twelve bedrooms, because he liked to invite a lot of people over (and then ignore them), a five-car garage, a polo field, and a smaller, separate home in the garden out back where he brought his mother to live, at least in part so she could keep his wife occupied when he was out gallivanting, or gallivanting in some other part of the house, or in one of the other founders' basements. Wheeler, who christened his home Magnolia Farms, had a strange Gothic tower over his garage where, with the apparent knowledge of his wife, he kept a beautiful young Japanese mistress. The original pagoda structure at the track (built in 1913 and replaced several times since) is believed by some local historians to be, says Ms. Lawrence, "a tribute to Mr. Wheeler's girlfriend."

Allison's was the most elaborate of the mansions: Riverdale, as he called it, cost $2 million to build—the main house had elevators, wood paneling carved by a famed European craftsman, a Tiffany glass ceiling, a huge aviary, and, perhaps owing to the resulting bird seed and feathers, central vacuum cleaning, a most avant-garde convenience. Trails and waterways laced Allison's sixty-four-acre "backyard," which was tended by twenty-seven gardeners. For the Speedway co-founders, however, the house's most beloved feature was its dark, leather-lined rathskeller, into which they descended frequently for spouseless, but not necessarily stag, evenings. A century later, it remains intact. Walking past side-by-side cabinets for guns and liquor, one enters a small chamber in which the ceiling and upper walls have been richly decorated with German heraldic symbols, scenes from Teutonic myths, and caricatures of Allison, Wheeler, and Fisher wearing old-fashioned pointy beards, forest-gnome outfits, and carrying horns, crossbows, and other antique hunting paraphernalia.

"Kind of strange, no?" Lawrence said, as she was giving me the tour. "God only knows what went on down here."

Allison, who died, officially of a bad cold but, according to Lawrence, most probably of syphilis, in 1928 at the age of fifty-six, was not the most colorful of the founders, but he was the most accomplished.

"Fisher was the dreamer," their common business associate, Lem Trotter, once said (years later, after Wheeler had blown his brains out in his master bedroom, apparently distraught over the death of a business associate), "but Allison had the most brilliant mind of any man I ever knew. He was the industrialist." When his father died, eighteen-year-old James Jr. took command of the Allison Coupon Company of Indianapolis and, while he was managing it to record profits, designed the Allison Perfection Fountain Pen, which would become a huge seller. After meeting Fisher at the Zig-Zag Club, and lucking into the Prest-O-Lite deal with him, and then investing in the Speedway, he founded the Allison Engineering Company, which a year after his death was acquired by General Motors for the bargain price of $592,000. Allison's first wife, Sarah, always maintained that it was her husband, and not Fisher, who first suggested that the founders scrap the idea of holding several auto race meetings at the Speedway each year, each one encompassing two or three dozen races, and instead roll the dice by having one big day featuring a single race that would be the richest, most demanding, and most coveted auto racing prize in the world.

We will never know who said what exactly to whom in Allison's rathskeller, or some other setting, of an Indiana evening in the late summer of 1910. But even if Sarah Allison is correct, it must be said that her husband was articulating an idea that had been taking shape in Fisher's brain for at least two years, even as he kept indulging his own inclination to complicate and overdo matters. In any case, Fisher liked the thought of upsetting the AAA pooh-bahs who wanted to keep race distances down to what they considered sensible lengths. His initial suggestion was that they stage a 1,000-mile race, or maybe a 24-hour one, but the partners talked him down from these, noting that races that long merely continued the practice of asking the audience to endure an overly long show. "Let's give people something they can see start to finish in a reasonable amount of time," Allison supposedly said as they stayed up late one night, hashing things out. And so it was that on September 7, 1910, a press release went forth: "Officials of the Indianapolis Motor Speedway today announced plans for an automobile race to be run May 27, 1911 [it would soon be pushed back to the 30th], in which American cars will be pitted against the best of Europe for a purse of

$25,000. The contest as announced will be for 500 miles and is to be known as the 'Indianapolis Motor Speedway 500-mile International Sweepstakes.'"

Originally, the Fourth of July had been considered as a date for the race, but on further consideration late May looked preferable because of an annual pause in the farming cycle, a brief, relatively unbusy period known as "haying," that would allow more rural families to attend. Likewise, the change from the 27th, a Saturday, to the Tuesday holiday was eventually made when someone realized that potential spectators would find it hard to get away on Saturday, then still a full or partial workday for many. Some civic and church leaders criticized the Speedway founders for horning in on a holiday that had been set aside for visiting battlefields and laying wreaths, but their cause was already lost. Even with many Civil War veterans still hobbling around, Decoration Day was already well on its way to becoming what it mostly is today, an excuse for cookouts and commerce.

NO ONE WAS more excited about the idea of the 500-mile sweepstakes than Howard Marmon. As soon as Fisher phoned him with the news, and told him that the race would be a "free-for-all" in which his one-off Wasp would be accommodated (the only requirements were that cars have a CID maximum of 600 and weigh a minimum of 2,300 pounds), he rushed to the basement drafting room at his plant, looking for Harroun. "I know what you've said about retirement," Marmon told him, "but I'd like you to drive the Wasp just one more time in this new 500-mile race."

Harroun looked up blankly, and sighed his annual sigh.

Seven weeks later, when he went to the Atlanta Speedway to finish out his 1910 commitments for Marmon by driving in the fall meet there, Harroun still had not made up his mind about whether he would compete in the big race. The prize for the 500-mile sweepstakes—$10,000 in gold to the winner—was tempting, but as long as he remained a driver, the specter of death was never far away. On Tuesday, November 1, during practice for the Atlanta races, Al Livingston, "The Pacific Coast King of the Dirt Track," spun out and flipped over after his National's right rear tire blew while he was traveling 90 miles per hour; as his parents, wife, and sister watched from the stands, he flew thirty feet and landed on his head, fracturing his skull. He died seven hours later.

At just after 11:00 A.M. on Thursday the 3rd, as Livingston's funeral was in progress across town, the nine drivers in the meet's first race pulled their cars up to the starting line at the Atlanta Speedway, cut their engines, and, said the *New York Times*, "stared hard with tear-dimmed eyes at the hoods of their vehicles" while a band played "Nearer, My God, to Thee" in Livingston's memory. The hymn was followed by an extended silence.

Everyone agreed it was a striking scene, a truly moving tribute. And then, after about a minute, said the *Times*, the band started up "a lively two-step."

In short span, the newspaper noted, Livingston "had passed forever from automobile racing. New speed kings were throwing the clutches into position, and the big race was on."

14

HOWARD MARMON MAY have been excited about it, but the announcement of a 500-mile sweepstakes made something less than a medium-size splash in the local papers, and many who heard what Carl Fisher and his Speedway co-founders were planning must have filed the idea under "balloons," "motorcycle races," "taroid," "subzero time trials," "Zoline," and similar Crazy Carl brainstorms. To the automobile cognoscenti, the timing of the news seemed especially, exquisitely awful.

It was a passing feeling that tends not to get noted in history books, but a lot of people in and out of the car business in late 1910 were starting to believe that the party was over and that the auto boom had run its course. We can see from here that America's famous love affair with the automobile was just beginning—and yet it's true that the relationship had reached an awkward and tender juncture. As the first decade of the automobile age came to a close, a levelheaded assessment seemed in order in the wake of what had been such a whirlwind romance.

But that is hardly the same as an industry-wide recession. The closest thing to hard evidence of the car market going soft was a small but decided dip in sales across a number of brands as the 1911 model year drew near. Whether or not this was the tip of an ugly trend no one knew, but car makers, nervous men in a nervous age and cowed in particular by the success of Henry Ford, reacted in ways that were not likely to boost consumer confidence. Instead of trying to better understand the changing nature of demand, they lashed out stridently at critics and naysayers, some of whom they had to construct out of straw. "Conservative businessmen have for years predicted our failure," said Alfred Reeves, general manager of the Licensed Automobile Manufacturers. "Yet each year has seen more and better motor cars produced and more men employed." In a speech delivered before industry representatives and the press at a Brooklyn YMCA, Reeves pointed out that "motor cars are used the world over"—everywhere, he said, curiously, except Bermuda, where "the roads were so narrow as to make motoring unsafe." The *Indianapolis Star* backed him on the car's near-universal acceptance, running, above its account of his talk, a photo of five smiling Chinese auto salesmen comically packed into a Detroit-made EMF car, an image that might seem unfortunate enough without the headline: "Slant-Eyed Motorists Prefer American-Made Autos."

Discreetly alluding to the sag in spirits that these positive words attempted to mask, the weekly trade journal *Motor Age* reminded its readers that "enthusiasm is the life blood of a new industry," that "France has lost her premiership in the motor business through lukewarmness," and that U.S. manufacturers "should not let their enthusiasm wane, no matter what the cost." Indianapolis automakers, at least, took the advice to heart. Smiling a little too broadly in the face of what they saw as hard times ahead, they recast their annual automobile show, held in late February and early March of 1911, as a "Gasoline Carnival of Mirth." The event kicked off with fireworks and a "Mardi Gras parade" of flower-covered cars that rolled through the downtown streets in what the boosterish *Star* described as "barbaric splendor." Sounding a bit like Steve Carell in *The Office*, or maybe even Kim Jong-il, the head of the local Automobile Trade Association ordered his members to turn out for the spectacle wearing "fantastic costumes and masks" and to attend the "Brain Sandwich banquet" (so named, apparently, because of all the wise speakers and toastmasters on hand), at which King Motor would be crowned, advising that "every man will be required to sing songs [extolling the virtues and potential of the auto industry] between courses, whether he has a cultured voice or not."

Shoppers, meanwhile, could stop by various showrooms in town and hear a live orchestra play "Ta-Ra-Ra-Boom-Di-Yay," "My Gal Sal," and "Stop Your Tickling, Jack," and get a free cigar or fresh carnation with their sales pitch. Goodyear passed out potted plants. The Gibson Automobile Company hired a turbaned "Hindoo seer" named Odan to greet passers-by and "issue prophesies" about the company's future, all of which proved to be positive. As Gasoline Carnivals of Mirth go, it was truly grand. Yet its message was never fully accepted by its own speakers, who continued to wring their hands and moan about the state of the industry—and to be told by their trade journals to knock it off already, or they'd start scaring people away.

The worries that infected the manufacturing end of the auto business—all the more insidious for being based on misconstrued or imaginary information—soon spread to the racing garages that were, in the end, part of each company's marketing division. Some of the sport's most prominent drivers, the same men who not long ago were crowing about their "addiction" to speed, and shrugging off death as just another part of their glamorous trade, moped openly in the wake of the Speedway's sparsely attended 1910 meets, and expressed angst. Racing had failed at the box office, they maintained, and it could only be resuscitated by instituting a national circuit with a set annual schedule and standardized rules, the way harness racing (the most popular sport in America in 1900) and baseball had done years earlier. Auto racing still would not survive, though, said these nabobs of negativity, unless promoters made tracks and road courses less dangerous and manufacturers systematically cut the drivers in on the purse money, the way jockeys were. As 1910 drew to a close, DePalma, Bruce-Brown, Disbrow, and a few others talked in the press about forming a union to be called the Automobile Race Drivers Association and bargaining collectively with car makers and race promoters—stating at every opportunity that unless their suggestions were taken, their gravely ill game would soon vanish. The *New York Times* even reported on March 19, 1911, that such an organization was launched. (Nothing seems to have come of it, however.)

Barney Oldfield, who was then under an indefinite suspension from the AAA following his race against Jack Johnson, was not part of this particular group of gloomy and disgruntled drivers—but only because it was too moderate for his tastes. Around that time he wrote, or allowed his name to be attached to, a strongly worded article in *Popular Mechanics* that castigated the public for its morbid preference for crashes over clean races. "I was never famous," Oldfield said bitterly, "until I went through the fence at St. Louis. [After that] promoters fell over one another to sign me up." The article included a photograph showing teenage boys gathered around a cigar store in Los Angeles where a "24-hour Race Bulletin" posted news of accidents—but, significantly, not running order, or results—at the local track. ("6:40 P.M.: Car #4 ran into Car #7. Two men hurt. Come out and see the spill.") The last ten years, Oldfield said, "has been a decade of incessant slaughter, of many broken machines and a few broken records. It's been a decade replete with black headlines and black mourning. Much money has been made by the sport-governing association; a little has been made by drivers. It has also been a source of income to hospitals, undertakers and cemetery societies." Ultimately, Oldfield said, in a line that would be widely quoted, "the game is not worth the candle." Other drivers, even if they weren't quite as bitter and pessimistic as Oldfield, seemed to agree on the last point. Ralph Mulford, Louis Chevrolet, "Farmer Bill" Endicott, Herb Lytle, and Johnny Aitken all announced their retirement from racing during the winter of 1910–1911, and Harroun, as late as March 1, was still insisting that he was gone for good.

It was at this doom-laden moment that the founders of the Indianapolis Motor Speedway chose to announce an event predicated on America's fascination with automobiles and automobile racing. Their insensitivity struck some people in the industry as ridiculous, pathetic, almost comic—and not entirely out of character, given the place's penchant for disastrous and poorly attended events. Because virtually all their correspondence from that era has been lost, we cannot say how risky a move Fisher and his cohorts felt their new idea was or wasn't—and if they did see it as a do-or-die gamble, how nervous or thrilled they were to be rolling the dice. But this much we do know: if the Speedway founders *were* worried about the 500-mile race catching on with the American public, they weren't worried long.

PART THREE

MAY 1911

15

I would rather win that race than anything in the world. I would rather be Ralph DePalma than president.

—ERNIE PYLE

THE START OF the first Indianapolis 500-mile race is naturally viewed as the beginning of new era in American sport, and it certainly was, in a way, but in spirit it more properly fits with the thirty or so days that preceded it than with the 6 hours, 42 minutes, and 8 seconds that followed in its wake. The race itself was problematic, a riddle wrapped in a mystery inside an enigma, as Winston Churchill would later say of Russia (and like Russia, it remains a subject likely to drive its would-be decipherers to drink). The first "rolling start" ever attempted in an automobile race, on the other hand, was simply the most spectacular thing that anyone who was there to witness it had ever seen. "I remember that the excitement and the tension of that 40-car start was almost unbearable even to a spectator," Waldo Wadsworth Gower, thirteen years old at race time, wrote in a 1959 letter. It was Crazy Carl Fisher in a cocked hat leading eight rows of five cars each—no previous track race had ever had more than twenty-six starters—around the two-and-a-half-mile rectangle. The entries (most of them red, but two yellow and black, several gleaming white, a few bright green, and one vermilion) were aligned in rakishly ragged formation, champing at the 40-miles-an-hour prerace speed limit that had been negotiated during numerous rehearsals, billowing smoke, kicking up a monsoon of dust, and creating such a cacophony that one columnist wondered in all seriousness if the roar could be heard on the moon.

With the snap of a red flag and an inaudible shout of "Go!" starter Fred Wagner got the field away while putting a punctuation mark on a month during which Indianapolis had been (said Barney Oldfield in the nationally syndicated column he was writing because the AAA wouldn't let him drive in the sweepstakes) "race mad." The newspapers, Oldfield (or his ghost) went on, "have forgotten Madero and Díaz [key figures in the then ongoing Mexican Revolution]. The extras may tell of a horrible railroad wreck with many lives lost or some other calamity, but the youngsters are yelling out only what is new in Speedway happenings. On the bills of fare they have 'Omelette a la Burman,' 'Filet Mignon Bruce-Brown,' and so on."

Two years before, the town had come alive in anticipation of the Speedway's inaugural meeting, but this was success on a fiercer, almost force-of-nature scale. Said the *New York Times*, "This is the first time that Indianapolis has been overtaxed." The leading press clipping service of the day predicted, a few weeks out from the event, that the race ultimately would generate more coverage than the Jack Johnson–Jim Jeffries bout in Reno the year before—and that "Fight of the Century" had been by a wide margin the most written-about sports event in history up to that point. The *Sun*'s description of the visitors drawn by such hype makes them sound like the swells who later turned up for championship fights: "Speed-lust kings and queens, trimmed in gold and perfumed with gasoline and lubricating oil, gowned in sables and rare gems, smoking black cigars and dainty cigarets, sipping the amber nectar, laughing at nothing and ribald with the joy of living." These rarefied beings were seen "sweeping down upon the city in a cloud of dust; bussing, sputtering, droning; leather capped, goggled, ulstered and grimy—for all the world like the old-time Kansas grasshopper army, which darkened the sky as it swooped across the plains, carrying all before it."

The Claypool Hotel (495 rooms) and the Dennison (five hundred) had been sold out for race week since New Year's Day, and many respectable people were sleeping under trees in public parks or on side streets ("Gods of gold laid themselves down upon the cool green grass to snooze," said the *Sun*. "Their long white coats shimmered through the gloom beneath the trees like the slain of a battle laid out in silent rows") or alongside strangers on cots set up in the hallways of private homes or in the public rooms of hotels. "Cots in Every Nook," read one headline. Said the *Sun*: "Beggar and prince, rich man and 'dip' rolled about and kicked each other in the ribs midst playful and unconscious slumber." In the week after that was written still more people tried, with varying degrees of success, to squeeze themselves into Indianapolis. A swollen schedule of extra-long trains bore down on the city from Chicago, New York, Los Angeles, Canada, and Mexico, and, said *Motor Age*, "people slept in the train cars once they arrived in town." The *Indianapolis News* reported that passengers on some local Speedway-bound rail lines "fearful of failure to get on board because of the dense throngs around the steps of every car occasionally clambered into trains through open side windows, though station employees and trainmen tried to thwart their efforts."

The town fathers were flummoxed. Faced with a solid month of what we would now call gridlock, and having no experience with automobile traffic (who did?), they turned for help to the Speedway founders, who, perhaps sobered a bit by what they had wrought, sat down together and sketched out a scheme for rerouting several downtown streets, presumably using the same prodigious capitalist intellects that had earned them mansions and mistresses. Like the timing system at the racetrack, it didn't work, not even in the slightest, but having a plan made everyone feel better. On Illinois Avenue, stalled streams of vehicles constantly "vomited forth thousands of dirty but happy passengers" who proceeded to their destinations on foot, said *Automobile Topics*.

Fisher seems to have lent the city an undeveloped parcel of land near his Stoddard-Dayton dealership on Capitol Avenue for use as a temporary municipal lot—though this was not an ideal solution to the parking space shortage, given that cars were mostly open to the elements in those days (hence the proliferation of garages in cities large and small), and that joyriders armed with hand cranks and a bit of hot-wiring savvy could (and did) easily steal unattended vehicles. A sense of lawlessness pervaded the city, coupled with a sense that, whatever your inconvenience or your outrage, the police were otherwise engaged. "The underworld is in evidence," said one paper, with "both sexes plying their trade and playing on incautious and careless visitors." Saloons stayed open past mandatory closing times and on the Sabbath, and bookies sat on barstools, openly taking illegal bets, the money for which could be obtained by applying to the loan officer sitting one stool over. Official starter Fred Wagner, who also had a syndicated newspaper column, warned that wagering on the sport could lead to race fixing, and noted that "Wrestling died out because of fakery."

In most such places Spencer Wishart and his Mercedes stood as the three-to-one favorite, and (in a much more popular proposition) five would get you ten that two or more men would die during the race. Small wonder that respectable people referred to these establishments as gambling "hells." *Hell* might have been the operative word in Indianapolis, given the severe bed shortage, the baking heat, and what *Automobile Topics* called "the fine, penetrating dust that has made its way everywhere." And yet the mood was, if not exactly upbeat, decidedly giddy, bordering on hysterical. The *Star* advised readers to brace themselves for "the largest slumber party in history." Wherever you went in town, it seemed that everyone was laughing—at death, at dirt, and, as the *Sun* noted, at "nothing."

One hundred years of calculated, corporate-sponsored hoopla at Olympic, Final Four, and Super Bowl sites may dull our sense of how simultaneously exciting and unnerving this all was, even to the very people clinking their highball glasses in Indianapolis. Until then no big city had ever spent such an extended period heaping significance on something as demonstrably trifling as an automobile race. A new, silly, or at least very un-Hobbesian era was clearly at hand. To old-timers who could remember when "sports" meant sweaty, backroom cockfights and bareknuckle brawls (often between men who were nasty, brutish, and short), the idea of a town turning itself upside down for four weeks or more in preparation for a single afternoon of family-oriented fun seemed utterly ridiculous. The younger generation did not disagree, but thought "ridiculous" not a bad word or an unworthy aspiration.

■ ■ ■

GIVEN THE SINKING spirits and attendance figures that had characterized car making and car racing just a few months before, it's tempting to see Fisher as a man who, stumbling around in the dark with an electrical plug, takes one desperate stab at making a connection—and turns on a carnival. It wasn't just the hotels, restaurants, and whorehouses that were doing what the papers liked to call a "land office business" (the cliché was slightly fresher perhaps in the days still redolent of the Western rush). Outside of the hospitality industry, boxing promoters probably skimmed the most from the sojourning swells, staging dozens of shows throughout May, the climax being the welterweight clash between "The Italian Pittsburgh Dynamiter" Banana Diamond and Eddie Webber at the Indianapolis Athletic Club on the night before the race. Working stiffs benefited from the tourist boom, too. Ads in the "Wanted-Male" section of the classifieds screamed for 500 SALESMEN FOR THE SPEEDWAY ON MAY 30 TO SELL LEMONADE AND ICE CREAM CONES AND LUNCHES. CALL PAYNE'S BUSY BEE LUNCH, 44 N. ILLINOIS AFTER 8 P.M. BRING $1.70 FOR FIRST LOAD. This turnaround to sticky-sweet prosperity and automania was Carl Fisher's victory to claim, some local Republican kingmakers duly noted, if he ever wanted to try stuffing the skeletons to the rear of his closet and running for, say, governor.

While the Speedway president was open to the idea of public service, and the practical business benefits it had to offer, the sublime madness of May 1911 speaks less of a miraculous, or even miraculously lucky, maneuver by Fisher than of a fundamental miscalculation (or two) finally corrected. Take, for starters, the auto industry as a whole. It was not dying in late 1910 as many of its leading lights feared; the doldrums of those months signaled, rather, that it was growing and changing, and in some ways pausing before it surged forward. Consumers at that very moment, in fact, were converting to autoism in what might have been reassuring droves. A study released on May 1, 1911, showed that New York State residents already owned more than 780,000 cars, and while the rural states were still lagging in terms of automobile ownership (Indiana had only 35,000), they were catching up quickly. Clearly there could be no going back to the already quaint horse-drawn days as depicted on Currier and Ives prints: cars had been acquired, beloved steeds sold or put down, grooms fired, chauffeurs hired. To many Americans, the idea of having animals—brutish, needy, constantly defecating and urinating *animals*—haul you to work, to church, or to Grandma's house already seemed as weird and medieval as it does today.

The real—and only—problem was that for the most part the first generation of automakers clung too long and too fiercely to the notion that cars were a wealthy man's conveyance. Henry Ford—who believed motoring belonged to the masses, and that modest, dependable vehicles were what was needed most—sold nearly twenty thousand Model Ts in 1910, twice as many as the year before, and because of ever-improving assembly-line methods, the price for these "Tin Lizzies" was constantly dropping (from $850 in 1908 to $290 in 1927). All these years later, one almost winces at the evidence of his rivals repeatedly refusing to get the message. During the 1911 Indianapolis car show, for example, the Indiana Automobile Company, agents for the high-end, Detroit-made Chalmers, took out newspaper ads framed as "shopper's guides" advising what to look for when venturing into the motor market. Safety and reliability are barely mentioned, and price never once comes up. Instead, virgin car buyers are advised to look for "beauty first," and then focus on "the matter of comfort." Such ads no doubt attracted a trickle of well-off customers. Meanwhile, though, Ford brought in floods of common folk with his beautiful and comfortable price tags, and his famously frank assurance that "You can have any color you want, as long as it's black." (In fact, prior to 1913 Model Ts were available in green, red, blue, and gray as well as black.)

As for the racing side of the business, there, too, one could find baffled and depressed decision makers stubbornly sticking with a formula—lots of shorter races with fields defined by unsexy piston-displacement numbers—that clearly wasn't finding traction with the public. In the case of Carl Fisher we can see something even more regrettable—a dazzling flash of insight allowed to fade and become forgotten. Consider that when James Allison suggested in mid-1910 that the Speedway founders take a gamble on one marathon race, he was actually just bringing Fisher back around to a brainstorm that Crazy Carl himself had had two years earlier. The chief lessons Fisher took from the blood-soaked 1909 meet, let us not forget, were that longer races were the way to go, probably the *only* way to go if you put aside auto industry politics and make spectator pleasure your measure of success — and that the problem inherent in long races, the rather inconvenient fact that after a few minutes no one could make sense of them, could be addressed (that is, appear to be solved, though not really solved) by the Warner Horograph, a timing system even more complicated than this sentence.

The Speedway president, however, had failed to follow through, and while that, from a business standpoint, is unfortunate, to say the least, it is hardly surprising. Fisher always had trouble staying focused, and his attention deficit was doubly tested by a project like the Speedway, which had turned out to be mostly work and worry and disappointingly little fun. Rather than rolling up his sleeves and retooling the place's approach to racing, he let other things — auto industry pressure and newer projects like the development of Miami Beach — distract him from going forward with the single best idea he ever had, until attendance dropped alarmingly and Allison had to remind him that there was a reason they had gotten involved with Warner's harebrained timing scheme in the first place.

It is to Fisher's continuing credit that he didn't just change the frequency or distance of the races, he changed the terms: instead of being about prestige or an eight-foot-tall trophy, winning was suddenly all about winning *money*. It would be difficult to overstate the impressiveness of the sweepstakes' $25,000 purse, from which the winner would realize $10,000, plus another possible $10,000 or $15,000 in "manufacturers' prizes" put up by sponsors for cars using their tires, brakes, magnetos, shock absorbers, and such. Mere cash seemed too vulgar a manifestation for such an exalted pile; payouts would be made, the Speedway announced, in the form of "solid gold bars" — or if you chose to believe a later press release, "gold nuggets in leather sacks bearing the winners' names in gold letters."

Today even a $40,000 pot seems paltry, not just because of inflation, but because our culture rewards athletic success seemingly without limit. In 1911, apart from a few small fortunes purportedly paid to certain prizefighters — Johnson was said to have earned $65,000 for beating

Jeffries—there was little precedent for heaping life-changing amounts of money upon sports stars. The thoroughbred colt Meridian earned about $4,000 for winning that year's Kentucky Derby, then the nation's premier sporting event, and the highest-paid major-league baseball player, Ty Cobb, made $10,000 a year, or about thirteen times the salary of the average American worker. Today the Derby is worth $1.425 million to the winner and the *average* baseball salary ($3.3 million) is about eighty times the typical fan's. True, the sweepstakes purse would be divvied among the first ten finishers, and in many cases subdivided again among driver, riding mechanic, and car maker, but even so the figure was impressive, and the idea of men risking their lives in public for money—or anything other than honor or country—made everyone feel decadent and giddy and grand.

It would be coy to say that the 500-mile sweepstakes had a vivifying effect on the sport. No one was more eager to pack their jammies and join the big Indianapolis slumber party than the auto racers themselves. Mulford, Louis Chevrolet, Bill Endicott, Lytle, and Aitken all un-retired, more or less immediately after the announcement of the race was made, and began making plans for Indianapolis. The first entry form hit Fisher's desk on October 2, long before anyone had expected to see one, with the full $500 fee attached, though only a $100 down payment was necessary. (The drivers and car makers either didn't seem to notice, or if they did, didn't seem to care, that they were racing for a pot composed entirely of their entry fees.) It was from the J. I. Case Threshing Machine Company of Racine, Wisconsin, nominating a car to be driven by the great Lewis Strang. In the press notice announcing his participation, publicist Shuart, who adored nicknames—his own was Heinie—dubbed him "The Clicquot Kid" because of his alleged affinity for Veuve Clicquot champagne. Strang's little red and gray Case got the pole position, as starting spots (and car numbers) were assigned that one year based on the order in which the applications arrived. Having a "mount" in the sweepstakes made Strang the envy of his fellow driving stars. Ralph DePalma, then an unsigned free agent, piped up immediately to say, "I will be a starter even if I have to drive a wheelbarrow!" He wound up in the second car entered, a barely legal (at 597 CID it was a mere three cubic inches under the limit) New York–made

Simplex, painted red and white, fitting colors for an Italian-American who could not escape the descriptive "spaghetti fiend."

Did bigger necessarily mean better in a long race? If it did then Strang wasn't likely to be quaffing much Veuve Clicquot on May 30; his engine measured a mere 274 CID, meaning that it shared the distinction of being (along with the two other Cases that were eventually entered) the smallest machine in the sweepstakes by that widely accepted standard. Still, as Oldfield noted, with variables such as weight and number of pistons also in play (five of the cars had six cylinders, the rest four), the relationship of size to power was slippery and there was no consensus on the best approach.

"One can listen for hours to the arguments they put up in the hotel lobbies or around the repair pits," wrote Oldfield, who was not known for listening to anyone. "One great pilot will tell why he chose a heavy car with great power and large tires. Another equally famous will tell how he cannot lose with his light-powered car, close to the maximum weight limit and with small tires. The third noted fellow laughs at both the others and tries to convince his auditors that his medium-powered car is simply perfect for the race from a scientific standpoint." Cubic inch displacement had to count for *something*, though, or the founders, who initially pitched the sweepstakes as an "international" event meant to decide whether European cars were still superior to American ones, would not have drawn the admission standards in a way that effectively eliminated most of the powerful German, French, and Italian entries that Americans supposedly no longer feared. Fisher, who had the provincial's distaste for foreigners, would have been sickened to see his trophy go overseas, or for that matter across state lines.

A quick scan of the entry list would have told Fisher that only a good deal of luck, coupled perhaps with some strenuous string-pulling, could ensure that the bragging rights to "the greatest race of all time" (as it was already being called) would be retained by in-state interests. What was probably the best of the Indiana cars, the Marmon Wasp, had developed engine trouble after 150 miles in one previous race, at the Atlanta Speedway, and though it had won anyway and Harroun had been working on it steadily, some of the bigger bettors were skeptical. In all, only thirteen of the forty starters were Indiana-made, and several of the most formidable entrants came from elsewhere. Deep into May, Wishart and Bruce-Brown were still in Europe, tinkering with the Mercedes and Fiat they intended to drive in the sweepstakes, and getting their expensive engines down to 583 and 589 CID, respectively. Ralph Mulford, the cheerful, blond, part-time choirmaster who had dominated road racing in 1910 the way Harroun had ruled the "circular" tracks, had a powerful, pure-white, Detroit-made Lozier (544 CID) that impressed connoisseurs of fine engineering (one of the few true stock cars in the race, it cost about $5,000 retail) and looked like it could handle the distance. The equally fancy albeit medium-sized (390 CID) Pope-Hartford, a product of Connecticut, also loomed as a serious threat, because it had displayed so much raw speed during practices, and because it was driven by Louis Disbrow, whose coldhearted determination, it was thought, would make him laugh, or more likely sneer, at the challenges posed by what Oldfield called "the simply too-long" sweepstakes.

Disbrow, too tough and grouchy to exalt openly in being an autoist, nevertheless showed his enthusiasm for the big race by preparing for it diligently. "Gymnastics won't do a race driver much good," he told the *Coatsville* (Indiana) *Herald* in mid-April. "Neither will any specified course of exercises. There is one thing alone which will make a man fit to sit behind the wheel through the strain of seven hours such as the 500-mile race will mean. That is taking a daily course of hard knocks over the country roads in a racing car at a fairly good rate of speed." Disbrow said he planned to drive two or three hundred miles a day on rough Midwestern roads for at least thirty days before the race, "and in this way harden myself so that the 500-mile drive will be nothing unusual for me." He even worked his trip to Indianapolis into his training regimen. He and his trusty riding mechanic left Hartford, Connecticut, in a bright red "practice car" on May 6, Speedway-bound. The journey, which MapQuest says today should take 13 hours and 46 minutes, took them six days because of bad and circuitous roadways. As he passed through upstate Le Roy, New York, the fire alarm sounded and Disbrow, after learning that the town had only one horse-drawn "hose wagon," wound up hauling the necessary reel to the scene of the blaze, with "the entire fire company draped over his car and hanging on wherever they could get a footing," said the *New York Tribune*. After he hit a bump near the Jell-O factory (now the home of the Jell-O Museum), "most of the men went sprawling to the street," the paper noted, "but Disbrow kept right on and beat the horse engine to the fire by four minutes."

Mulford set out in his race car from the new Lozier factory in Detroit on the 14th of May, with his shortish, plumpish wife, Ethel, in the riding mechanic's seat. Smiling Ralph was a true superstar, famous enough to have spawned an imposter who went around the country telling young women he was Ralph Mulford and wanted to marry them. The real Mulford had joined Lozier in 1901, when he was sixteen and Lozier was making boats, not automobiles, at its headquarters in Plattsburgh, New York. Three years later, though, when Lozier got into the car business—using an engine that it had essentially cloned from Mercedes and selling its wares in a glittering showroom on 42nd Street opposite Grand Central Terminal—Mulford was picked to be a driver. He had no street license at the time, but he did have a knack for mechanics and could be counted on to be courteous to potential customers, who he hoped would be attracted by his racing success. And succeed he did. In his first race, a 24-hour grind at the Point Breeze horse racing track outside Philadelphia, he and a partner not only won, trading off three-hour shifts, but he proved his mettle on a track that all-night rains had turned to what he called "oily, liquid mud." With the tires of the other cars constantly throwing up gunk, "it was," he recalled, "impossible to drive with goggles and pretty painful to drive without them. So for most of the race we drove with one hand and peeked between the fingers of the other."

Because of the rutted, muddy roads along their route from Detroit to the Speedway it could not be said that he and Ethel traveled in comfort, but they did travel in style: he sported his gleaming-white Lozier sweater and matching sharply creased summer-wool slacks while she wore the khaki men's overalls she favored, no doubt in part because she was her husband's de facto mechanic—except of course when he was driving in races from which, for the offense of being a woman, she was explicitly banned. (Mulford's actual riding mechanic, who had set out from Detroit in another Lozier two days before him, was Billy

Chandler, a boyhood friend from Brooklyn who chain-smoked and chain-cussed and added some badly needed grit to the operation. "He was a jolly good fellow," Mulford said of Chandler. "Full of jokes, laughing all the time. His only fault was the smoking. I saw him smoke fifteen packs of cigarettes in a day. During races, he just had to smoke. He even had a cigarette company make him up cigarettes with a kind of built-in match at the end, and I actually saw him take one out and light it at 100 miles an hour. It finally killed him," Mulford added, "but he just didn't seem to care.")

The Mulfords had a special, almost storybook relationship. Ralph took Ethel to all of his races, including the 24-hour Brighton Beach grind that had occurred on their wedding night in June of 1910. Ethel was a good sport about that unfortunate scheduling conflict—they had to rush to the track directly from the altar—and even sat in the stands for the entire marathon, waving to Ralph every time he passed, except for those relatively short stretches when she dozed demurely beneath the veil of her dark green bridal headdress. Every one of her greetings was reciprocated by her husband with a wave and one of his big, gummy smiles. To reporters, Mulford frequently waxed enthusiastic about his missus, adding, "and I'm not afraid I'm going to get tired of watching her in the 500-mile race at Indianapolis, either." Indeed, Carl Fisher may well have had the Mulfords in mind when, at a drivers' meeting the evening before the sweepstakes, he said that he would fine any man $50 who took his hands off the wheel during the competition to wave at someone in the grandstand.

LET US RETURN for a moment to the question of the sweepstakes' extraordinary length. In his short-lived but widely read newspaper column, Oldfield repeatedly stressed the dangers of the distance, saying ominously that "the Indianapolis race was certain to take drivers, cars and spectators beyond their limits."

Was 500 miles beyond the limit of human endurance, given the rough-riding, stiff-steering cars of the day? The question of how far a man could drive without passing out—or away—had been posited before races of 50, 100, and 250 miles, and it never failed to stir passionate debate. It's worth remembering, as we attempt to understand the prerace sentiment, that except for the occasional 24-hour "novelty" grind, usually staged as more of a stunt than a serious competition at some gaudy resort area like Brighton Beach, 500 miles was the longest event ever scheduled for a racetrack. After half that distance, most of the participants would enter uncharted regions.

Among the drivers questioned that May, opinion was almost equally divided on whether 500 miles was too long for any one man to stay behind the steering wheel. The macho traditionalists, the men who swore they would never use a relief driver (almost never the riding mechanics, who figured to be too worn out themselves to take charge), included Ralph DePalma, who said he would have no problem with 500 miles because of his exercise regimen and abstemious ways. "Many of the biggest races in the sport have been lost the night before," he explained. "By that I mean that inexperienced drivers have given way to temptation and have indulged in intoxicants to an extent that rendered them incompetent to sit at the wheel." DePalma was one of the bravest and most beloved drivers of the early times, but when he talked like this, you sometimes wished he would blow a tire and crash—ideally into Joe Dawson, his fellow Goody Two-shoes. Dawson, the aggressively clean-cut driver of the "other" (non-Wasp) Marmon, told the *Indianapolis News* that he believed he was capable of going the entire race without help because "I have been a member of the Y.M.C.A. for four years, and during that time it has been rare for me to miss a turn in the gymnasium with the class that meets three nights a week." (Almost needless to say, he used a relief driver in the race.) Mulford, meanwhile, said he needed no help beyond gumdrops, which he kept in a paper bag between his thighs, and consumed by the pound. The always imaginative Heinie Shuart christened him "The Gumdrop Kid."

Anyone wanting to test the limits of human or personal endurance now had the full permission of the sport's chief governing and sanctioning body. The AAA, which apparently never met an interest group or influential executive it didn't cower before, had passed a rule after the bloody 250-mile Wheeler-Schebler race of 1909 limiting a driver to three consecutive hours in the cockpit. Back then the organization was trying to mollify civic and religious leaders who equated long-distance racing with certain death. Fred Wagner, an AAA honcho who would be the official starter of the first Indy 500, said in 1909 that "Fatalities are caused by holding too long races on a track. When you ask a driver to whirl round and round for over two hundred miles, seeing nothing but a white band on either side, you are demanding too much of his nerves. With the nervous breakdown he loses control of the car and an accident results."

The AAA must have believed that in two years human beings had evolved to a point where they could handle a lot more whirling, for in January of 1911 it threw out its old law and substituted a seven-hour maximum. By some bizarre coincidence that was the projected duration of a certain just announced 500-mile sweepstakes that was being aggressively boosted by a powerful automaker named Howard Marmon, a member of the AAA's rules committee. It's funny how things work out sometimes, but what was even more surprising, given the masculine codes of the day, and the fact that they now had official permission to keep going until they had a nervous breakdown or whipped themselves into butter, like the tigers in the then best-selling children's book *Little Black Sambo*, was how many men were *not* planning to drive the full distance without help.

That list, not unexpectedly, started with Harroun, who had made the hiring of a relief driver one of the primary conditions of his comeback. But it also included the swashbuckling Bruce-Brown, who announced in late May that talented newcomer Joe Matson would spell him in his red Fiat (which Shuart had taken to calling "Le Diable Rouge"). Strang at first said he was using "the well-known aviator" E. M. Harrison as a backup, then switched to Charles "Kid" McCoy, a Hoosier light heavyweight famous, like Strang, for his convoluted love life (as well as his invention of the corkscrew punch). The Cole company signed former lightweight contender Johnny Jenkins for a relief role, while Firestone-Columbus brought in twenty-one-year-old Eddie Rickenbacher (he would change the spelling to Rickenbacker in the Army), a car-crazy kid from a German-speaking household in Columbus, Ohio, who had studied automotive engineering via correspondence course. Accounts vary, as they do with virtually every aspect of the 1911 race, but it seems that about half of the forty-car field employed standby drivers, and as many as sixteen teams actually used their services.

Yet if the drivers were becoming a little more sensible about their personal safety, they were a no less colorful group, prone to flaunting their emotions, especially the joy of being a professional race car man. "Danger is fun!" Frank Fox, driver of one of the three Pope-Hartfords in the race, declared upon his arrival at the Speedway. Reporters usually loved the chatty Fox (information that would temper their affection would soon emerge), who kept breaking his left leg in wrecks, long after he'd had the original limb amputated and replaced. "Don't worry, it's not painful," he assured listeners with a shrug each time he pulverized another prosthetic. "It's just that I can't get myself another leg until I get home!" Said Oldfield: "A grouch would not last long in one of these racing camps."

Despite the heat, masks of cloth and leather were all the rage that year as a way of protecting one's face from dust and flying brick-slivers. "Hooded and begoggled, [the drivers] look more like deep-sea monsters or nightmare fancies than like men," said the *Oakland Tribune*. Joe Jagersberger, pilot of the No. 8 Case, stalked around pit row in a tightly fitting cotton hood so liberally festooned with odd little flaps it might have served as the scaly inspiration for the Creature from the Black Lagoon. "Boo!" he kept saying. Wacky headgear is always good for a laugh. One hot day when the sun was beating on the drivers' heads during practice, somebody had the idea of borrowing a hat from one of the farm ladies in the crowd, and soon there were dozens of men zipping around the track in gingham bonnets. Laughing at themselves and one another, men who might have been bitter rivals steadily bonded. On most evenings, after the work was done and the sun was setting behind the grandstand, one could find America's elite autoists and their crewmen gathering on the infield to play baseball, laughing and applauding teammates and opponents alike as, to quote Oldfield, "they turn to smiting the horsehide."

Baseball, which had held its first World Series eight seasons earlier, was then a fashionable, fast-growing pastime whose leading citizens could be counted on to lend a touch of glamour to any occasion. The twenty-four-year-old Ty Cobb, who'd won a luxurious Chalmers car for being the 1910 American League batting champ, came by on May 15 to make an "assault" on Barney Oldfield's one-mile record of 35.53 seconds in a straight-from-the-showroom National supplied by Speedway co-founder Arthur Newby. On a rainy afternoon, the Georgia Peach burned rubber but missed the mark by about 7 seconds. Eleven days later the guest of honor was Hal Chase, the first baseman and manager of the New York Highlanders, a superb all-around player but a man destined to be remembered as a fixer of games and a layer of wagers. Chase took a spin in Joe Dawson's Marmon with Highlanders pitcher Russ Ford, the inventor of the emery or "scruff ball," in the riding mechanic's seat. The shady duo made one circuit of the course, noted the sarcastic *Richmond* (Indiana) *Item,* at "an amazing five miles an hour."

From the world of show business—as boxing announcers say when introducing luminaries before a title fight—came Miss Jane Wheatley, then in rehearsals for her leading role in a rustic comedy of manners called *Mary Jane's Pa* set to open soon at Indianapolis's Murat Theater. A large, strapping woman more opera diva than ingenue, Wheatley pleasantly but firmly told her chauffeur for the day, the diminutive Knox driver Fred Belcher, that instead of merely going in circles around the racetrack, she wanted an "auto tour" of the downtown district as well. He drove as instructed, then brought her back to the Murat, where she had one further request. "Can you run this car backward?" she asked. Belcher, by way of demonstrating, threw his racer into reverse, but according to the *Star,* "failed to calculate exactly a turn in the boulevard and the machine crashed into a lamp post." The pole snapped in two and crashed down on Wheatley's leonine cranium. "Companions who were following in another car," said the *Star,* "were much frightened when they saw the blood trickling down her forehead." Playing the consummate trouper, Wheatley laughed off her "flesh wound," and vowed to "wear the Knox colors on Decoration Day," though she apparently left town before the race and canceled her run in the play.

NOT EVERYTHING ABOUT the prerace scene was so zany or so innocent. In the middle of May it came to light that just before he'd arrived at the Speedway, the usually carefree Frank Fox had been arrested for kidnapping. His victim: John J. McNamara, secretary-treasurer of the International Association of Bridge and Structural Iron Workers. In a bloody and complicated case then making national headlines, McNamara (along with his brother, James) had been indicted in California in connection with the October 1910 bombing of the virulently anti-union *Los Angeles Times.* To avoid extradition, John McNamara had been holing up in Indianapolis, site of his union's headquarters, at least until he was apprehended by the well-known private detective William J. Burns, then working for the National Erectors' Association. Fox got involved when Burns, needing a fast and daring driver, hired the racer to take him and McNamara from Indianapolis to Chicago, where the detective and the suspected bomber boarded a train for L.A.

There was nothing remotely lawful about this operation, which seriously jeopardized the case against the McNamaras, whose terrorist act was responsible for twenty-one deaths and some one hundred injuries, but Fox, though financially well-off, took the job anyway, because, he said, he was excited by Burns's instructions to "ignore all speed limits" along the route and to "be prepared for accidents." The driver was free on $3,000 bail at the time of the sweepstakes, and charges against him would eventually be dropped. In the midst of their "Trial of the Century," James and John McNamara pled guilty and received prison sentences of life and twenty years, respectively. But Fox was hardly a hero for his role in the affair, and wooden-leg jokes notwithstanding, his presence was a decidedly sour note in the Indianapolis overture. Most newsmen steered clear of his pit.

Logic, or journalistic instincts, did not always dictate where the reporters went, however—or the dullest driver would not have received the most prerace ink. Of course, there are some good reasons why Ray Harroun might have been approached for interviews: he had had the best record on racetracks (as opposed to roads) during the previous year and his car stood out for being a pointy-tailed single-seater. Yet the sheer amount of attention the bogus Bedouin received is startling: many scrapbooks could be filled with May 1911 articles in which Harroun reveals that he rides with a hot water bottle to combat aches and cramps, uses a "somewhat simpler" set of hand signals than most drivers to communicate with the pits, and plugs his ears with wads of cotton to deaden the loud noise made by the other cars. Combing through the embarrassment of clips in my own bulging Harroun file, I see that his never-changing racing strategy was to avoid macho speed duels, and thus go easy on his machine and especially his tires, thereby making as few pit stops as possible. Like the gradual accumulation of mutual funds through payroll deduction, this was a fundamentally sound but wearisome strategy that hardly seemed to merit all the attention it received.

The mystery dissipates when we stop seeing Harroun as a male Siren, pulling in slack-jawed reporters with his dull yarns, and start to see the fine hand of Heinie Shuart gently guiding newsmen (who had not paid Harroun any special attention before this) to the Marmon pit, perhaps even as his other fine hand slipped nice fat Cohibas into their breast pockets. Providing such publicity services for Team Marmon was the least that Carl Fisher could do to repay his good friend, business partner, and Columbia clubmate Howard Marmon for defending him in public after the disasters of 1909, and for helping him promote the 500-mile sweepstakes within the industry.

This was not the first instance of favoritism shown by Fisher to Marmon. In February, when Howard Marmon formally entered the race, his company was heavily promoting the model 32—a kind of less racy, "stock" version of the Wasp. Given what was happening in the luxury auto market, Marmon was especially anxious about the 32's success, and he had invested heavily in an advertising campaign in which 32 was writ large in print ads and on billboards and posters. Everything, it seemed, bore the number 32—except, alas, his two sweepstakes cars, which, because they had been entered early, had been assigned numbers 11 and 12. Could something possibly be done, Howard Marmon asked Fisher, so that the Wasp, the stronger of his two sweepstakes entries, could be designated the No. 32 car, in order to provide a publicity boost? Seeing no problem with the request, Fisher said he would simply withdraw the Marmon cars from the race, then "hold them aside" until they could be "dropped back in" as the legitimate 32nd and 33rd entries.

The special handling of Howard Marmon went on almost without limit. Fisher came to Marmon's aid yet again about ten days before the race, when a group of drivers and rival car owners showed up at Fisher's office at the Speedway to complain about the Wasp, saying that as the only entry in the race without a riding mechanic, it not only enjoyed an aerodynamic advantage, it did so at the expense of safety, since

Harroun would have no one to warn him of cars approaching from the rear. The way this story is sometimes told, Fisher is pressured into at least temporarily suspending the Wasp—until Ray Harroun goes back to his garage and invents the rearview mirror, which the other drivers then marvel at and celebrate like South Seas islanders bedazzled by the shiny sextant of Captain Cook.

It did not happen that way. Fisher may have mentioned the mirror as he shooed the protesters away, telling them to stop whining about the Wasp and start concentrating on their own damn automobiles. But it didn't play a significant role in the first Indy 500—and in any case, Harroun didn't invent it.

Every time I see Harroun credited with inventing the rearview mirror, and I've seen it a lot, I think of W. C. Handy, the composer who spent a fair part of his later life denying that he "invented" the 12-bar blues. Handy had to explain over and over that the form wasn't original to him, that in 1903 he had heard a "lean, loose-jointed Negro" at a train station in Tutwiler, Mississippi, singing in a strange, new way, and adopted the man's music to his own sophisticated purposes, coming up with "St. Louis Blues" and other tunes from the early "standards" canon. But though his story was self-effacingly honest, people tended to tune it out and stick with their somehow more satisfying belief that everything has an identifiable inventor.

So it is with Harroun, who after the race said more than once that he had long ago seen rearview mirrors on horse-drawn carriages, and that he had merely imitated those when he fitted a small looking glass into a metal cowl and attached it to his car above the dashboard sometime in early May of 1911. His denial of paternity is supported by pre-1911 auto accessory catalogues that show rear- and side-view mirrors for sale, as well as a 1908 article in *Popular Mechanics*, which states that "One of the numerous ways by which autoists succeed in foiling the attempts of the police to catch them exceeding the speed limit is a large reflector fastened to the dashboard of their automobile." Moreover, in a May 14 interview with the *Star*, Harroun mentions, in an offhanded way, that he will use what the reporter refers to as "a dumb mechanician," that is, a rearview mirror, in the race. There had been no organized protest about the Wasp at that point.

In any case, the device, by any name, was ultimately useless. It vibrated so badly that Harroun could see in it only a kaleidoscopic blur, and soon gave up even glancing in its direction. Harroun admitted this, too—until he realized people preferred not to be proffered this truth, either. For the remaining fifty-odd years of his life, he would silently and smilingly accept being introduced at industry functions as "the man who won the first Indianapolis 500 thanks to his invention of the rearview mirror." If that was what the world wanted, he would take his speaker's fee, roll with the back-pats, and smile.

THE ANTI-WASP PROTESTERS had barely been ejected from Carl Fisher's office when basically the same bunch was back to complain about something else. The source of their displeasure now was Ernest A. Moross. The former "director of racing" had resurfaced at the Speedway that spring as the "personal manager" of Bob Burman as well as the owner of Burman's car, the huge Blitzen Benz that had once been driven and owned by Barney Oldfield (at a time when Moross was *his* manager). At 1,300 CID, the Blitzen was far too big for the sweepstakes, but Moross aimed to have Burman drive it in a series of time trials on the morning of May 30, during which Burman would attempt to lower Oldfield's Speedway records for the mile, kilometer, and half-mile. These were precisely the sort of sterile car-versus-clock exercises the public had yawned at over the past few years. Yet Fisher went along with the stunt, probably because he was trying to please Firestone, a powerful presence in the industry and one of Burman's sponsors. Moross, in any case, had sold Burman on a complete makeover, starting with his famous nickname. Instead of "Wild Bob," Moross preferred "The King," a reference, in Moross's mind anyway, to Burman's having become the "fastest man alive" on April 23, when he traveled 141.73 miles per hour in the Blitzen Benz at Daytona. Assuming the assaults at Indianapolis were successful, Moross planned to immortalize the new moniker by presenting his client with "a $10,000 crown of gold inlaid with pearls and similar in design to the crown of the reigning house of England," all of this to happen perhaps an hour before the sweepstakes.

Many of the entrants in the big race, however, thought the staging of this event impinged on the powerful simplicity of race day as it had been originally conceived. Why should they have to share the spotlight—and why should Moross and Burman benefit from the presumably gigantic, captive crowd? Fisher let the dispute fester a while, then on May 28 promulgated a compromise whereby Burman would make his speed run on the day *before* the sweepstakes, attempting to lower all three marks in one dramatic whoosh, and receive whatever honors he might be due the following morning.

The time trial turned out to be more exciting than anyone expected. Burman's Benz blew its right front tire coming into the homestretch turn, and for a few seconds it looked, said the *News*, like Burman "would not be able to hold the lurching white monster" on a track that had been made wet by morning rains. The *Star* reported that the driver went "high on the turn" and "nearly rolled over." Such blasts and swerves were part of the game, of course. But what made this particular time trial so curious was that even though Oldfield had made his run without incident, and on a dry track, in the same car, Burman had broken his records. Burman's times were 16.83 seconds for the half-mile, 21.40 for the kilometer, and 35.35 for the mile, as compared to Oldfield's of 17.00, 21.45, and 35.53. Both drivers employed a "flying start." When something as unlikely as that happens at your racetrack, you don't put a crown on the driver's head, you take a long, hard look at your timing.

Indeed, somebody at the Speedway should have checked on the Warner Horograph a few days earlier, during the qualifying rounds. Qualifying in those days was a more pro forma affair than it is today: to certify its starting spot in the race each car needed to demonstrate only that it was capable of averaging 75 miles per hour for one lap, for most an easy feat. Following each qualifying run on May 26, entrants and reporters were told whether the car in question had made it into the sweepstakes or not, but, noted the *Star*, "officials refused to give out any times in the trials." The field was reduced from forty-four to forty cars by this method.

Why would the Speedway not divulge such basic data? Since some cars were in fact eliminated from the race this way, didn't the autoists and fans have a right to know the clockings? Clearly, the Warner system was having problems even when its only task was to time one car at a time. But it seemed no one was addressing the issue, perhaps because the hour was late and a fix would have been daunting—or more likely because no one really expected the system to function properly or quite understood how it *did* function. On race day, at least two hundred "timing judges"—many of them prominent men-about-town, chosen for their connections to Indianapolis business and society, with no consideration given to prior auto racing experience—would be called upon to simultaneously clock and record the running order of a forty-car field going 500 miles. How skillfully would these men employ the strange array of tools that inventor Charles Warner had assembled for their task: miles of wire, four Burroughs adding machines, two Columbia Dictaphones, the actual Horograph, several telephones, thousands of marbles, and a "telautograph" (defined by Warner as "an electrical device which reproduces the handwriting of the operator at 12 different stations on the grounds")? The simple answer was that nobody knew.

Decades later, when he wrote a memoir of his life in engineering, Charles Warner did not mention that he invented the system used to time numerous races at the Indianapolis Motor Speedway, including the first 500-mile sweepstakes. A curious omission, to be sure. But once the race was started, the reason he failed to memorialize his contribution would be clear.

16

The most wonderful thing in connection with the 500-mile race is the feeling that bad accidents will occur. The very atmosphere is filled with fear and many are trembling at the possibilities held out by this contest.

—HOMER C. GEORGE, *Atlanta Constitution*

THE SOBER, SCIENTIFIC men of the early-twentieth-century motor press sometimes referred to the 13th circuit of an automobile racecourse as "the hoo-doo lap," not because more bad stuff tended to happen at that point, but because for professional reasons they fervently wished that it would. And so it was that on May 30, 1911, a dozen reporters leaned forward anxiously—their straw boaters tilted backward, their pencil points whetted and wetted—to watch the forty-car field for the first Indianapolis 500-mile race power past the start line for the 12th time and roar yet again into turn one.

A wreck just then would be good for all concerned—except of course the drivers and RMs involved and their families and friends, as well as any spectators who happened to find themselves in the vicinity, and, naturally, *their* pals and kin. A wreck, in other words, would be good for the reporters. Coming at that point, it would play nicely into the tabloid trope that superstitions are not to be flouted, and it would give the contest some much-needed narrative cord, thus helping the scribes shape their stories. And God knows those men required—and by some standards of judgment deserved—all the help they could get. Many by then had been in Indianapolis for a month or more, pumping up the importance of the Speedway and the Circle City via the dispatches they filed for their far-flung dailies. They had recorded the arrival of virtually every "sweepstakes pilot" in the race, interviewed drop-by celebrities like Detroit Tigers outfielder Ty Cobb and "noted songstress" Alice Lynn, investigated the burgeoning supply of counterfeit $1 general admission tickets ("Remember to buy only in bona fide outlets like the Fox taxicab stand and the cigar store in the traction station"), and scrambled for miscellaneous stories like the Indianapolis house cat who "deliberately committed suicide" by jumping from a sixth-story window, the downstate chicken with fourteen toes on its left foot, and the rumored sightings of a Terre Haute–based, PG-rated pervert known as Jack the Hugger. For men accustomed to doing little more on a workday than walking the length of a boxing ring to ask one toothless man his opinion of another, this was arduous labor.

But the 500-mile sweepstakes, when it finally transpired on that surprisingly cool Tuesday morning, wasn't paying the pressmen back in kind. It was, like every other lengthy automobile contest these experts on baseball and boxing (but not car racing) had ever witnessed, damnably *confusing*. The race had gotten off to a thrillingly raucous start replete with aerial bombs and a grandstand (said an early edition of the *Fort Wayne Journal-Gazette*) "gay with tossing flags, roaring with cheers," but with every mile the storyline became more and more scrambled, the spectators more and more subdued, and those charged with describing the "excitement" to an eager audience of millions had felt the first damp signs of panic.

"Happy" Johnny Aitken, in the dark blue No. 4 National, had grabbed the early lead, only to be passed, after about 7 miles, by Spencer Wishart, the son of a mining magnate, who was driving a squat gray customized Mercedes that was said (by other newspapermen) to have cost him (or more likely his daddy) $62,000. Eight laps later, Wishart (who wore a custom-made shirt and silk tie beneath his overalls) suddenly pitted with a bad tire, leaving the lead to a big brown Knox driven by the unheralded working-class kid from Springfield, Massachusetts, Fred Belcher. Soon Wishart stormed back onto the course, but into what lap exactly no one, including the judges, could say for certain. The leaders, as mile 30 approached, were starting to lap the stragglers, so the field of forty was a snake eating its own tail. Belcher now found himself running second to a ball of smoke concealing, it was generally believed, the dark red Fiat of twenty-three-year-old David Bruce-Brown, whose family was even richer than Wishart's. A class-war theme might be emerging, the newspapermen thought—but then again, just as likely, perhaps not.

The crowd regained its focus and oohed audibly each time a scoreboard worker indicated a change in running order by manually removing and rehanging the numbers on their pegs. Still, the denizens of the infield press box—more skeptical than the average fan, and with a better perch—couldn't help noticing that the Speedway's four scoreboards were usually not in agreement, and that a crew from the timing department was frantically trying to repair one of the Warner Electric Timing System trip wires, which had been snapped by who knows which automobile a lap or two back (they succeeded, but it was immediately rebroken). Given such chaos, was it really so wrong to wish for a spectacular accident that would wipe away the muddle and allow the beleaguered scribes a second chance at getting a grip on the action?

Of course it was wrong, but moral questions wither in the face of a hoo-doo, even one conjured by a coven of pasty, ink-stained hacks. Right on cue, the No. 44 Amplex, a bright red car driven by Arthur Greiner and traveling in mid-pack, just ahead of a scarlet and gray Firestone-Columbus, lost its right front tire. The bare wooden wheel hit the bricks hard, causing Greiner's extralong auto to swerve crazily amidst the trailing cars and veer into the infield, where it plowed through tall meadow grass, then started to perform an end-over-end somersault. Rather than keep going, though, the car stopped in mid-maneuver, so that it stood straight up, balancing for a moment on its steaming grille. The twenty-seven-year-old Greiner was flipped from the cockpit like a shucked oyster, with the steering wheel somehow still in his hands. Riding mechanic Sam Dickson, meanwhile, remained more or less in his bucket seat, one hand planted on the dashboard, the other clutching a leather side-handle, his only restraining device. This was the sort of heart-stopping moment that only auto racing could provide. If the car fell forward it would drive Dickson's head into the ground like a tent spike; if it tilted backward, returning to its three remaining tires, he might get nothing worse than a jolt. The crowd fell silent. Dickson tensed. The Amplex rocked on its radiator.

It would be noted later with some justification that Greiner— somewhere in the tall bluestem, bellowing—and Dickson could have seen this disaster coming. But then so could anyone keeping close track of the daily newspaper dispatches. The pair was not only on the hoo-doo *lap*, for goodness' sake, they were riding in the hoo-doo *car*, a distinction bestowed by the very same reporters who were now suddenly on their feet, twisting backward toward the vertical vehicle and gasping at their good fortune.

It was only natural for these newsgatherers to refer to the 44 thusly after it had been wrecked in practice nine days earlier, then repaired and put back into service. That was, as everyone knew, the classic method by which a mechanical mode of transportation acquired a hoo-doo. But the reporters erred when they merely slapped that label on the 44 and moved on to write about other cars they considered more logical contenders. Had they stayed with the story and continued to haunt the Amplex pits until the morning of the race, they would have known better where to train their field glasses at the start of the 13th lap. And because local bookmakers were offering propositions on deaths and maimings as well as traditional win, place, and show, they also would have known better where to lay their bets.

The tale of the two Amplexes in the 500-mile sweepstakes illustrates how a forty-car race can have an overarching narrative supported by many potentially intriguing subplots—and how the mostly generalist sportswriters assigned to cover the event botched the coverage on every conceivable level, leaving posterity with virtually no reliable historical record.

What many dailies reported on Thursday, May 25, was that the 44 had been wrecked in practice by a second-string Amplex driver named Joe Horan. Although this became one of the memes of race week, very little about the bulletin was true.

To understand what happened on the 13th lap of the 500-mile sweepstakes, one must go back to the practice sessions that took place on the morning of Sunday, May 21. At just after 10:00, the 44 car, with Gaston Morris in the cockpit, blew a tire, skidded on the oil-coated brick surface, and crashed into the outer backstretch wall. Morris, a veteran French autoist brought over by Amplex to serve as a backup driver, broke numerous bones and suffered internal injuries, and the chassis was seriously mangled. At least a few reporters must have witnessed the accident, or heard it happen, or heard accounts of it from other drivers or mechanics, but for several days, not a word about it was published. Why this was so we can only guess, though both the Speedway and the American Simplex Company (the manufacturer of Amplexes) had reasons to hush up the affair, and back then much was possible with the promise of a whiskey highball or the presentation of a Havana cigar. Still, all we know for certain is that a corps of supposedly story-hungry writers—there were more than a hundred in town by race day—thought the accident unworthy of mention. As a result, they never questioned why it was Morris being palleted off the Speedway course and not Walter Jones, the New York City kid who recently had been hired as the 44's main pilot. If they had, they would have been rewarded with a newsworthy tale. Jones wasn't driving because he was being held against his will at an unknown location by a group of his fellow autoists.

The circumstances of this abduction remain murky. It did come to light afterward, though, that for the previous week or more, Jones's mother, fearing for her son's safety, had been beseeching Speedway and AAA officials in telegrams, phone calls, and personal visits to bar him from the race. Since there was an unwritten law that obliged drivers and mechanics to help the distraught mothers and wives who regularly came forward to plead for their husband's or son's exclusion from auto races, it's possible that the autoists who kidnapped Walter were trying to do Mrs. Jones a favor by keeping him away from the track. It's even possible that Jones, unnerved by her morbid maternal premonitions and wanting to bow out, went along with the scheme to save face. (Released in time for race day, he seemed to harbor no hard feelings, since he spent May 30 standing by with other relief men in the Amplex pits.) In any case, although Amplex immediately decided to patch up the car and put it back in the race, the 44 had no pilot for several days—until Joe Horan, a mechanic with designs on being a race driver, stepped forward to take the assignment.

To help Horan acclimate himself to the course, American Simplex arranged for him to take a few practice spins, on May 24, in its *other* sweepstakes entry, the compact and more manageable No. 12 Amplex, which was to be driven in the sweepstakes by William H. "Wild Bill" Turner. The 12 wasn't manageable enough for Horan, though, who on one of his very first circuits of the Speedway came out of turn four too fast, skidded, overcorrected, and wound up crashing into the inner homestretch rail, breaking his left leg and at least temporarily putting the second Amplex car out of commission. It was on the next day, May 25, that most papers carried their garbled reports of Horan wrecking the 44. American Simplex felt confident that it could fix both of its entries in time for the race, and in expressing this it seemed to acknowledge that there were two damaged vehicles, yet reporters stuck with their erroneous version of events.

Even more difficult than repairing the vehicles in time, though, was finding another top-flight driver. Turner was unwavering in his commitment to steer the theoretically just-as-jinxed No. 12, but with the race just five days away, American Simplex once again needed to find a pilot for the 44, if only because failing to do so would mean losing the $500 entry fee, which for a company of its size was no small consideration. Although many top men had been eager for a mount in the 500, a hoo-doo car was a hard sell: besides being superstitious, drivers frequently shied away from rebuilt vehicles over concerns about newfangled welding techniques, which they felt did not always work as effectively as advertised, and led to cars falling apart in mid-contest. Amplex needed someone not only competent but also a little crazy to take the wheel of the 44.

Enter Art Greiner. The high-living son of a Chicago leather goods king appeared at first glance to be just another semi-tamed trust fund kid with a need for speed and excitement (he had been briefly married to a sixteen-year-old actress-dancer named Margaret Boyer in 1907). But in fact he was no dilettante, being a successful amateur driver and the manager of the Falcar racing team. Greiner also had a history with hoo-doo autos, having once accepted (a bit too eagerly, some said) an assignment to drive the National in which Tom Kincaid had died during practice the previous year at the Speedway (Greiner totaled it at

Elgin, Illinois, a month later, but escaped serious injury). Just a few days before, he had begged Fisher to bestow the number 13 on the four-cylinder Falcar he had intended to drive in the sweepstakes (the Speedway president this time was not willing to bend the rules, as he had for Marmon).

When Greiner, at the last minute, had trouble securing the proper rear axles from his supplier, he was forced to pull both Falcars from the big race, and when Amplex team manager George Salzman heard he was carless, he sent him a wire offering a ride. Despite the inherent drawbacks of the 44 (which with its 123-inch wheelbase was the longest car in the race, and not a good fit for the Speedway's relatively tight turns), Greiner quickly accepted—and hopped a midnight train from Chicago. Arriving in Indianapolis very early on the morning of May 26, he went straight to the Speedway, where he encountered Harry Endicott, pilot of the No. 3 Interstate car, who was surprised to see him back on the scene. "Hello, Art," said Endicott. "What are you going to drive?"

"Me for the hoo-doo car!" Greiner said.

Besides being bold (or foolish) enough to take on the assignment, Greiner's other qualification was that he fit perfectly into the driving togs that had been custom-sewn for the kidnapped Walter Jones. On the morning of the race, he arrived at dawn, decked out in his Amplex uniform, and in the bracingly cool first light he and Dickson "ran a good many fast [practice] laps," according to a letter Waldo Wadsworth Gower, the boy who had witnessed the race, wrote in 1959 to Sam Dickson's niece. In Gower's still vivid memory, the occupants of the 44 cut exceedingly fine figures, carrying themselves in a way that reflected the importance of their endeavor.

"It was an unforgettable sight to see Greiner and Dickson in the great long red monster charging down the bricks that morning," Gower wrote.

The old car was freshly painted, the two men were dressed up in style! White cloth racing helmets, with long white silk scarves tied in loops on the top of the caps and streaming out behind them . . . bright red turtle-neck jerseys with "Amplex" in script across the front . . . fine check riding pants of the tight knee type, with leather puttees. Those men were right where they wanted to be, and they made an unforgettable sight, and they knew it. Who should feel sorry for Indianapolis drivers and mechanics? I never knew one that approached the race with any misgiving or any regrets if fate dealt him a bad hand. . . . All the color and glamour of life as a dangerous enterprise was wrapped up in that picture of the red Amplex flying over the bricks with its mighty humming roar that sounded more like the biggest bumble bee in all imagination doubled and tripled.

Dickson may have felt, to borrow a phrase from William James, "dilated with emotion" at that moment—but it is not accurate to say that he had no misgivings. In a 1980 *Indianapolis News* interview, Col. Edward J. Towers, then ninety-two and the last living participant in the first Indianapolis 500 (he was the riding mechanic and a relief driver for the No. 12 Amplex driven by Wild Bill Turner), said that Dickson approached him on the morning of the race, sometime between the practice laps and the start, and struck up a conversation, seemingly for the purpose of conveying that he'd had a restless night and "a premonition" about something bad happening. When Towers shot him an annoyed look—the RM was violating another unwritten rule by alluding to possible disaster—Dickson said, "You know, Ed, we're a pair of damn fools."

"How come?" Towers said.

"Because we don't know whether we're going to get our ass broke, or we're going to make a buck."

"Sam," Towers remembered saying, as he picked up a tool and stepped away from his pessimistic colleague, "you should have thought of that before you left the factory."

By then, it had actually been quite a while since Dickson had toiled in "the factory." A tall, handsome charmer (a six-footer in a family of five-foot-four men) with black hair and piercing blue eyes, the twenty-four-year-old RM was then in the midst of a meteoric rise at American Simplex—which Gower in another letter describes as "a little pepper-tree automobile company housed in a droopy little brick building in Mishawaka [Indiana]." Amplexes, which featured an innovative valveless design, were expensive cars, costing about $4,500, yet American Simplex was such a shoestring operation that its president drove an Overland because it was more fuel-efficient than his own vehicles, which got only 5 miles to an 11-cent gallon of gas.

Dickson joined the firm in 1908 as a mechanic making $1.50 an hour. A week later he got bumped up to $2.00, or as much as many common laborers made in a ten-hour day. After a year at that job, and still only twenty-two, he was asked to be the manager of the company's new Boston branch. Dickson loved everything about cars, but it was driving that he loved most, and no matter what the occasion or the distance he always drove fast. A family legend has it that one night when he was bringing a girlfriend back to her Chicago home he skidded wildly while making a turn onto her block, got his tire caught in the streetcar tracks, and wound up putting his Packard on her front porch. Down in Florida for one of his first races, he started on the course but somehow ended up in the ocean. In another such tale, he spun off the racetrack—and into the hay-padded embrace of a wide-open cow barn.

For Sam that day the risks were considerable. As Gower writes in yet another of his letters, "After Greiner had run so many miles in the car that morning, somebody [just before the race] got the bright idea of changing the right rear tire." This was a typical precautionary move, because the right rear tire always got the most wear on a track where cars were constantly making hard lefts. But, as Gower notes dryly, the adjustment came "a little late." The "quick" demountable rims used in those days, he explains, "were not quick except compared to changing a tire outright. Before the lugs could be tightened," he notes ominously, "the race was started." Greiner later admitted that while the field was filing onto the track for the start, a fan had yelled at him from across the fence, saying that his right rear wheel looked wobbly, and that he, Greiner, had nodded to indicate that he already knew it was. He probably could feel the vibration right up through the steering column. His pit crew seems to have known about the loose lug nuts, too. Gower says that "Greiner was given direct orders to run one lap [in order to register an official start] and then come in for a tire check and a tightening of the rim lugs."

Ducking in that early would not necessarily have eliminated the 44's chance at the trophy; in those days, in a race of great length, a driver could spend as much as ten or fifteen minutes in the pits all told and still win, because everyone was doing the same thing (today an Indy 500 car typically spends less than five minutes in the pits). "But human nature being what it is," Gower writes, "Greiner never came in. The excitement of that start got to him," and he could not tear himself away from the race. Instead "he charged up through the pack, picking up and passing cars every second. I remember that the excitement and the tension of that 40-car start was almost unbearable even to a spectator. Coming out of the southeast turn on his 13th lap Greiner lost it when the whole tire and rim came off due to the loose lugs."

In real time, the upended Amplex probably didn't take more than 10 seconds to fall. And when it did, it fell forward, killing Dickson. The daily press and weekly automotive journals provide many diverse accounts of this accident, some saying that Dickson was thrown twenty feet and hit a fence, others saying it was more like thirty feet but failing to mention a fence, and still others saying he was crushed when the car rolled on its side. The most reliable, though, seems to be the eyewitness account of Towers, who spoke with great certainty and in exquisite detail about the crash. Dickson's body—"horribly mangled," said the *Star*—was taken with dispatch to the Speedway hospital where "the smell of medicine mingled with the smell of burning rubber from tires" and a crowd of gawkers, who had run over from the grandstand, gathered. The race continued without interruption.

17

Down to the Gehenna, or up to the throne,
He travels fastest who travels alone.

—RUDYARD KIPLING

IT DIDN'T TAKE long for things at the Speedway to return to their confusingly normal state following the crash of the Amplex. Twenty-five minutes after the No. 44 drove Sam Dickson headfirst into the earth, in much the same unsatisfactory way that a hammer "drives" a six-inch nail "into" concrete, the several hundred people who had overwhelmed the "Speedway militia" and swarmed the infield to get a closer look at the bodies had been dispersed; the greater mass of attendees had stopped screaming and resumed its distracted rumble; and young Waldo Wadsworth Gower, whose letters I have thrice quoted from, was standing alone over the wreck of Dickson and Art Greiner's red race car, snapping a picture with his trusty Kodak. In the thoughts he put down toward the end of his life and sent, from his home in Los Angeles, to one of Sam Dickson's relatives, Gower remembered the piercing sadness brought on by the sight of the mangled auto that he had seen being painted and polished to a high gleam two months before at the little factory in Mishawaka. Energy and optimism had surged through the plant that morning when the entries were posted, he recalled, with "everybody hoping that a good showing would help them sell automobiles." About six weeks after that, the two Amplexes had left Mishawaka for the four- or five-hour trip on dirt roads to Indianapolis. With "a nice shiny coal oil lantern hung on the radiator cap" and "some help from a bright moon," he said, they had found their way to the city of big dreams.

This is all very touching, I thought, while reading the letters that had been passed along to me in photocopy form by Dickson's nephew Scott—but I also couldn't help but wonder why this kid was standing out there in the middle of the infield getting all Proustian instead of watching the race. Gradually, though, as my research deepened and the scene came into focus, I came to realize that except in sporadic moments of crisis very few spectators were following the action. Newspapers and auto industry magazines both noted that for most of the day many seats in the grandstand, though sold, went unoccupied, and lines at lavatories and concession stands stayed serpentine. About an hour into the event, Lewis Strang, who had brought in his Case for engine repairs, was seen crouching down in the pits and playing with a stray kitten.

Few watched for the simple reason that no one could tell what he was seeing. The opening half-hour had been bewildering enough, with all forty racers on the track passing and being passed as they scrambled for early position, but at least it was fairly apparent in those first 30 miles who at any one time held the lead. As the field approached 40 miles, tires started to blow—or as *The Horseless Age* tended to phrase it, with perhaps more precision, blow *up*. The Wasp, Belcher's Knox, Wishart's Mercedes, and several other cars were among the first to hobble into the pits. It took some crews two minutes to change a tire, others eight or ten or fifteen, and no one was timing these stops officially, so the already debatable running order became utterly inscrutable. To compound the chaos, some cars were crossing the finish line, then *backing up* to their pit, causing themselves to (perhaps inadvertently) get credit for a whole additional lap when they emerged and traveled a few feet back across the line. And the worst breaches of order and continuity were yet to come.

What makes all this especially maddening was that the race was proceeding exactly as everyone had expected it would, given the natural antagonism between bricks and tires: the smarter drivers were adopting the Harroun style of curbing their aggressiveness and instead hanging back and going at the relatively easy pace of 75 miles an hour or so in an attempt to keep pit stops to a minimum, just as they had said they would. ("I don't think the winner will take the lead until about 400 miles," Mulford had predicted, and Harroun had said in at least one of his prerace interviews that the engineers at Firestone had warned him to stay below 80 at all costs, because to go even 5 miles an hour above that would halve the lives of his tires.) You might think that such a conservative and formful contest would help the hundreds of clocking and scoring officials in their labors. But no. As *The Horseless Age* put it, "The system planned . . . did not work as expected, merely because the cars were so numerous and tore around so fast." In other words, if only there hadn't been a car race at the Speedway that day, the Warner Horograph would have functioned just fine.

They constituted a largely ignored minority, to be sure, but a few writers and publications were frank about the problems in their accounts. "The workers at the great score boards . . . keep very bad tally on the laps that each car makes," said the syndicated writer Crittenden Marriott, whose on-deadline dispatch holds up well over the years. "Hundreds of amateur mathematicians do sums upon their cuffs and find that the pace is 70 to 75 miles an hour, a speed that the survivors maintain till the end." Said the *New York Times*: "It was acknowledged that the timing device was out of repair . . . for an hour during the race." (Actually, some sources had the downtime as considerably longer than that.) *Cycle and Automobile Trade Journal* found that "Cars were bunched so closely and came across the wire so continuously that it was absolutely impossible to tell who was ahead and who was running behind." But no one sounded more exasperated than the influential weekly *Motor Age*, which dismissed the sweepstakes as "a spectacle only, rather than a struggle for supremacy between great motor cars." There were, said the weekly, "too many cars on the track, and no one could follow the race. . . . [The event] was robbed of that great interest that is ever present when everyone knows at all times exactly how the different cars are running. The race did not tire the drivers perhaps as much as was expected, but it did tire thousands of spectators."

Most reporters, however, took a different tack, and chose not to peek around the edges of Carl Fisher's Potemkin timing system. Realizing that a conventional story was easier to compose on deadline than an exposé, that their readers preferred a winner to a whine (and, no doubt, that Heinie Shuart had been covering their drink tabs since they arrived in Indianapolis), they acted as if the race had a coherent storyline that could be grasped by an eyewitness, written down, and passed along to readers, the way a journalist might do with, say, an account of a fire or a baseball game. The writers did this partly by guessing at what they were seeing, and by agreeing to agree on certain premises. But mostly they wrote their stories by accepting the Speedway's official version of events as disseminated by Shuart—even though that did not always jibe with the venue's scoreboards, and would change substantially when the judges issued their Revised Results early on the morning of June 1. What any one of these spoon-fed reporters had to say about the running order is for informational purposes mostly worthless. But by braiding their accounts, and occasionally referring to the Revised Results, we can perhaps begin to re-create a very rough version of the race and also see why so many sweepstakes spectators got up so frequently to get a bread ham sandwich.

The dashing David Bruce-Brown, we can say with a fair amount of certainty, played an important role in the proceedings. Virtually all newspaper and industry-magazine writers agreed that his Fiat, in the lead when the Amplex plunged into the infield on lap 13, was still ahead a few minutes later, when the field began to stream past the 40-mile mark. At 50 miles, though, accounts diverge. Most dailies said "the millionaire speed maniac" remained on top, but *The Horseless Age*, in an issue that appeared the day after the race, had Johnny Aitken and his big blue No. 4 National back in front at this point, with Bruce-Brown 2nd and DePalma 3rd. The Speedway's Revised Results, meanwhile, put DePalma's Simplex in the lead at mile 50, followed by Bruce-Brown, then Aitken.

Virtually all sources converge again at mile 60, where they have DePalma ahead, and most also say that soon afterward Bruce-Brown reclaimed the lead and held it for a good long while. (Speedway workers were shoveling sand on the track all afternoon to offset the increasing oiliness of the bricks, and some of that sand had worked its way into DePalma's wheel bearings, giving him fits for most of the race.) Bruce-Brown reached the 100-mile mark first, according to the Warner

System, in 1:22:16—though upon further review but without explanation that time was lowered in the Revised Results *by nearly 4 minutes.* At mile 140, some sources placed Bruce-Brown a full three laps, or 7.5 miles, ahead of DePalma, with Mulford and his Lozier holding down 3rd. As for Harroun, he had been riding as far back as 10th place for most of the race by some estimates, but he moved into 2nd place at mile 150. Or so said some sources.

The second significant accident of the day occurred at mile . . . well, here we go again. The *Star* said it was the 125th mile, *The Horseless Age,* "between the 150th and 160th miles," when Teddy Tetzlaff, a California driver on Mulford's Lozier team, blew a tire and crashed into Disbrow's Pope-Hartford, seriously injuring the Lozier riding mechanic, Dave Lewis, and taking both cars out of the competition. In case you're wondering, the Revised Results are useless in determining when this actually occurred. They have Disbrow *dropping out* of the race after 112.5 miles, and Tetzlaff leaving with mechanical problems after a mere 50. So by the Speedway's lights the participants weren't even racing when their accident occurred and Lewis did not officially fracture his pelvis.

Harroun, it seems, was the first to reach for a relief driver. At mile 158, he pitted for the second time and turned his car over to an unassuming fellow Pennsylvanian named Cyrus Patschke. Some 26 miles later, or at about mile 185, Bruce-Brown blew a tire, made his first pit stop of the day, and the Wasp, with Patschke at the wheel, inherited the lead. In the opinion of every reporter at the Speedway, and according to the initial data provided by the Warner System, Patschke reached the 200-mile mark first. The Revised Results, however, have it Bruce-Brown, DePalma, Patschke.

THE BUFFS AND nerds who still chat about such matters know that May 30, 1911, was not the steering knuckle's finest hour. Several had given way early in the day, and, at about 205 miles, Eddie Parker broke the one on his No. 18 Fiat and spun out into loose sand on the inside of the track at the top of the homestretch. Though not a serious mishap—no one was hurt and Parker got out and with a few others pushed his car a few hundred yards into the pits—it set the stage for what steering knuckle historians know as The Big One.

As the leaders, whoever they were, came down the homestretch on what is officially said to be mile 240, Joe Jagersberger suddenly realized he had no control over his red and gray No. 8 Case. The car bounced off the concrete retaining wall on the outer part of the track, then skidded diagonally toward the infield, traveling perhaps 100 feet. Jagersberger's riding mechanic, Charles Anderson, fell or perhaps jumped in panic out of the vehicle and somehow wound up underneath it, lying on his back; the right rear wheel of the Case passed directly over his chest. He was able to get up, however, or at least begin to—when he saw Harry Knight bearing down on him in the battleship gray No. 7 Westcott.

Knight, as the reader will remember, was a rapidly rising young pilot (the previous year he had worked as the chauffeur of Col. Russell Harrison, son of former president Benjamin Harrison) trying to win enough money in the sweepstakes to marry Jennie Dollie, the beautiful "Austro-Hungarian dancing sensation," who ranked as the morning line favorite among his several simultaneous fiancées. She had at first balked at his prerace proposals, saying, "No haphazard racer for my life's companion!" via her hopefully not very expensive interpreter, but then had come around and proffered a tentative yes after, said the *Star*, "she found out Knight was a man of good habits and devoted to his mother," and he presented her with a diamond solitaire. All Knight had to do was to pay for the ring, but here now was Anderson literally standing between him and a possible share of the purse. Should he mow down the hapless riding mechanic and perhaps improve his position in the running order—or swerve violently, spare the RM, but quite likely wreck?

His love for Miss Dollie notwithstanding, he chose the latter course, crushing the brakes and veering toward pit row—where he crashed into the vermilion and white No. 35 Apperson, taking his own and Herb Lytle's car out of the race. In an article called "Who Really Won the First Indy 500?" by Russ Catlin in the September 1969 issue of *Automobile Quarterly*, and in a very similar piece (it even has the same title) by Russell Jaslow that appeared in the February 1997 *North American Motorsports Journal*, each author states that Jagersberger's careening Case hit the judges' stand, causing the timing officials to scramble for their lives and, in the process, abandon their record-keeping duties. The incident those authors describe is consistent with the sometimes slapsticky nature of the day, yet there is no evidence of a crash. The official historian of the Indianapolis Motor Speedway, Donald Davidson, a revered figure in motor sports and staunch defender of the official results of the race, maintains that Catlin got this wrong, and that Jaslow merely repeated the untruth, both operating from a simple desire to stir controversy, and perhaps undermine the credibility of the IMS at a time (in the case of the Jaslow article) when the Indy Racing League was battling an upstart rival group called CART that had recently split from the Speedway. Davidson notes that the smashing of the judges' stand is something that surely would have been mentioned in the newspaper accounts of the race, especially since the structure was located just a few yards from the main press box, but that no reference to a smashup is made in any daily or weekly journal. He is right about that, and what's more, a brief film clip of this portion of the race, available on the Internet (www.youtube.com/watch?v=DObRkFU6-Rw), appears to bear out Davidson's contention that there was no contact between the Case and the judges' structure.

Ultimately, though, the question of a crash is moot because Jagersberger's car came close enough to their stand to send timing officials running, and there *are* contemporary reports stating that in the wake of the chain reaction of accidents on mile 240, no one was keeping track of the timing and running order for at least ten minutes. If the operators of the Warner Timing System hadn't lost the thread of the race narrative before that moment, they would have done so then, abandoning their telephones, Dictaphones, adding machines, Horograph, marble chutes, and telautograph as the cars continued to whiz by and to enter and exit the pits. One can easily imagine scoring sheets fluttering away in the breeze. In any case, with the halfway point of the marathon approaching, the *Indianapolis News* said, "So much excitement was caused in the judges' and timers' stands that the time for the 250 miles was overlooked" (the Revised Results have it as 3:17.49). As far as placement went, *The Horseless Age* said that Harroun's reliever, Patschke, had the Wasp ahead at the halfway point; the *Indianapolis Star* said that Harroun himself had the No. 32 car in the lead; and the always entertaining

Revised Results said it was Bruce-Brown, followed by the Wasp, then Mulford's Lozier.

Taken to the Speedway hospital for a quick look-see, all of the men involved in the incident at mile 240 checked out fine, but one reporter noticed a curious sight: Art Greiner reading an extra edition of the *Star* that had been dropped off at the Speedway just minutes before. "Bruce-Brown Has Early Lead," said the main headline on page one of the paper, which contained an account of the lap 13 accident. After being carried to the enclosure, Greiner had received the standard Speedway hospital treatment: his wounds and cuts had been packed with black peppercorns as a deterrent to infection, and he had been bandaged with strips of old bed linen donated by local citizens and hotels. He had probably been given a few stiff belts of rye whiskey as well—in any case, he seemed serene and reflective when the reporter approached and, despite the roar of the race going on all around them, broached the subject of the fatal crash.

"Poor Dick," Greiner said, putting the paper down in his lap and shaking his head. "I was conscious the whole time, but I guess Dick didn't know what hit him." Then, ticking off the names of Gaston Morris, Joe Horan, and Dickson, he said of the 44, "I'm convinced now that it really does have a hoo-doo."

Greiner might have included himself on that list of people adversely affected by the Amplex. He was then just beginning a run of bad luck that would knock him off his already loose hinges. At the very hour he was being interviewed, in fact, his secret wife of five months, the twenty-year-old Ziegfeld Follies dancer Gladys Sykes, had rushed to his family home in Chicago after hearing erroneous reports that he had been fatally injured. When she introduced herself to Greiner's parents, they were appalled to learn of their son's second showgirl marriage; as soon as it was clear that he would live, they said they would cut him off without a cent. Greiner never seriously pursued racing again; he started a car dealership, which was not successful, and he began drinking heavily, and acting bizarrely, delivering long, semicoherent speeches in Chicago barrooms, sometimes about current events but more often about the lowdown ways of sundry women, some known to him, some not, and getting beaten up for his orations. In the five years following the first 500-mile race, he divorced, remarried, and redivorced Gladys, married and divorced another woman, then got married yet again to a woman he immediately accused of adultery. In late 1916 his family had him committed to a Milwaukee insane asylum, where several months later, at the age of thirty-four, he died.

ALSO AROUND THE 250-mile mark, Patschke pulled in to the pits and hopped out of the Wasp, and Harroun grabbed his hot water bottle and hopped back in. If the 32 Marmon truly had the lead, then it was Patschke who had put it there and kept it there, probably, for roughly 40 laps. Patschke was not finished for the afternoon—he would relieve Joe Dawson from mile 400 to 440—but at about 1:30 P.M. on May 30, 1911, he was as famous as he would ever be. In newspaper accounts and post-race ceremonies his name would seldom be mentioned.

All sources had Harroun ahead at 300 miles, but now Mulford was making his move. In *The Fastest of the First*, an odd but well-written book published by the Belcher Foundation, an organization apparently dedicated to preserving the memory of the man who finished 9th in the first sweepstakes (and didn't accomplish much else of historical import), the anonymous author notes that "One of the most exciting artistic works in racing history is . . . artist Peter Helck's painting of the close battle between Harroun's yellow 32 Marmon and Mulford's white No. 33 Lozier for the 1911 Indianapolis 500." The syndicated writer Marriott said that the Lozier hovered 30 seconds behind the Wasp from mile 300 to 350, and *The Horseless Age* made the gap only slightly larger. For what it's worth, the Revised Results have Mulford *in front* at 350 miles—though the *Star* spoke for most journalists when it said that "Harroun was never headed from the 250th mile to the finish of the race."

At mile 340 or thereabouts the aptly named No. 27 Cutting sliced through one of the timing wires again.

At about 400 miles, the drivers stopped being cautious and started to position themselves for the final push. DePalma bore down so furiously that he was forced to come in for tires three times over the course of 18 laps. Mulford's Lozier also was having trouble with tires as the pace quickened: late in the race, he pitted for a replacement that took a shockingly brief 23 seconds, then came in again only a few laps later for a stop that didn't go so well and consumed several minutes. The crowd sensed the gathering intensity on the track and in the pits and, said *Motor Age*, "realized that it really was a race. They forgot their morbid curiosity in accidents and studied the scoreboards." Fisher's favorite hot-air balloonist, Capt. George F. Bumbaugh, chose this moment to launch what *The Horseless Age* called "a huge bladder carrying four men and a label from which one would infer that it was intended to advertise somebody's brand of lager beer." The ascension, said the *Star*, was "roundly ignored."

But what exactly did the crowd see when they gazed upon the scoreboards? The Lozier team would insist that its car was listed first on at least one of the scoreboards after 450 miles, and that officials even had assured team manager Charles Emise (exactly how is not clear) that that was one of the rare scoreboard postings people could trust. As a result of this assurance, Emise said he had through hand signals told Mulford that he should ease off as much as possible in the last 10 or 20 miles to ensure that he would finish first.

Several members of the Lozier camp would later swear that Mulford saw the green one-lap-to-go flag first, at which point he was running comfortably ahead of Bruce-Brown, with Harroun third. A mile or so later, Bruce-Brown's Fiat developed sparkplug problems that caused it to drop back behind Harroun.

Mulford, in this version of events, crossed the wire first, and, as was the custom among many drivers of that day, ran an "insurance lap" (or two) after getting the checkered flag, just to be doubly certain that he had covered the required distance. When Mulford finally came back to the winner's circle to claim his trophy, he found Harroun there, surrounded by multitudes.

18

THE RACE, WHICH had started just after 10:00 A.M., ended at about 5:37 that evening when the 11th-place finisher, the No. 10 Stutz driven by Gil Anderson, was shown the checkered flag. By 7:30 P.M. the Speedway was empty and quiet, except for the mop-up work being done by the remaining crewmen along pit row, and the sun was setting behind the main grandstand. Harroun, who earned a total of $14,250 in purse money and "accessory prizes" for his victory, had long since scarfed down a sandwich, showered, and been whisked off the grounds, to attend a banquet sponsored by the Dorian Tire Rim Company at the Claypool Hotel, where the numerous speakers never once uttered the phrases "Warner Timing System" or "Cyrus Patschke." The "Conquering Sheik" was the toast of Indianapolis in what would have been a landmark moment in Arab-American relations if Harroun had been the slightest bit Bedouin. Though the praise was premature—the result of the race had not been declared official yet—and the statements made about him often inaccurate (besides not being an Arab, he was neither a "local boy" nor an actual professor), the guest of honor contradicted no one who had something complimentary or colorful to say about him. As a race car driver who came of age in the era before the windshield, Harroun understood the advantages of keeping his mouth shut.

Howard Marmon, however, was having a different sort of evening.

In *The Marmon Heritage*, a dense tome that is the closest thing we have to a scholarly treatise on the company and its products, the authors, George Philip Hanley and Stacey Pankiw, give great credence to an obscure but richly detailed report of the race published in the August 1971 issue of *Car Classics.* The writer of the magazine piece, Napoleon Boz, depicts Howard Marmon as "wandering about the track all night worrying until the final announcement," and quotes Harroun as telling a reporter years later, presumably with a chuckle, "I guess I was the only member of the Marmon organization that was sure who won." Howard Marmon, according to the Boz piece, had strong doubts about the outcome. He had been concerned since the midpoint of the race that Mulford's Lozier was actually several laps ahead of his Wasp—in other words, he shared the view of the Lozier team—though most sources had the Wasp leading Mulford's auto from mile 250 onward. Now that a call for a reexamination of data had been made by an ad hoc group of dissatisfied car manufacturers and drivers, and the judges were poring over records of various sorts, Marmon worried that the trophy—which had been thrust upon him with unseemly haste by Shuart, then pulled back at least temporarily at the instructions of the presiding AAA officials—would be presented to his Detroit rivals.

Here, before I begin a brief description of the protests that followed the race, would be a good place to acknowledge what might be called the protest deniers. In the small world of people who still discuss and debate the first Indianapolis 500, there is a subset of buffs that maintains there was no rising up of voices in the wake of all the timing and scoring problems, or at least no significant one, because no mention of a protest occurs in the *Indianapolis Star*, then and now the city's leading newspaper. This is the same logic employed by Speedway historian Donald Davidson to successfully establish that Joe Jagersberger's car did not crash into the judges' stand at mile 240—but in this instance I believe it inadequate to the task. The protest deniers are right about the *Star*'s shamelessly provincial perspective on any controversy that might possibly reflect poorly on Indianapolis or any of its citizens or institutions, but wrong not to look further into, for example, the somewhat harder-to-find *Indianapolis Sun*, where the late-afternoon debate was covered in detail—or to papers like the *Washington Post* (which ran a story headed "Tangle in Auto Race Result") or the *New York Tribune* ("Protest in Auto Race"). To read just a bit more widely through the coverage is to see without question that the confusion didn't stop when the checkered flag came out, and that protests were if not "filed" formally, then at least energetically voiced. From scanning these non-*Star* sources, we can actually learn quite a bit about the mostly behind-the-scenes drama that, if only because it is more comprehensible, seems at least as intriguing as anything that happened that day on the track.

While Harroun was still in the winner's circle, trembling with hunger and fatigue despite the substantial spelling he received from Cyrus Patschke, a number of drivers, crewmen, and auto manufacturers stalked up to A. R. Pardington, a once and future crony of Fisher's who was serving as the AAA referee, and who had positioned himself not far from all the hoopla. This coterie of competitors, now united in anger, complained that they had not been credited for laps they had in fact traveled during the race, and demanded to know how the scorers were dealing with periods when there had been broken timing wires and an empty judges' stand. Pardington, always sympathetic to whoever was standing in front of him, had no ready reply, other than to decide on the spot that, if only for appearances' sake, he would hold up formal presentation of the race trophy. Instead of celebrating with Harroun in the Claypool's Grand Ballroom, the AAA referee and his associates repaired—along with Speedway publicist Shuart, who held no position in the AAA and thus had no business being there—to Pardington's Claypool suite, where they pored over scoring sheets and other data. The officials ordered dinner in their suite at 8:00 P.M., and at midnight called for the Warner Timing System Dictaphones to be brought from the racetrack. They would not emerge, Pardington promised the assembled press (who were not allowed to witness the deliberations), "until we can prove beyond a shadow of a doubt the result."

Anyone who heard even a snippet of the Dictaphone tapes, which were supposed to record the running order of the race as shouted in the heat of competition by various judges, knew it was going to be a very long night. For upon playback it was impossible to distinguish between, say, "20, 4, 7" and "24, 7," or between "30, 2, 3" and "32, 3."

(Even though the scoring system would change, cars were not assigned the numbers 20, 30, or 40 again until the 1960s.) Never mind that the investigating officials did not even have a full 500 miles' worth of this muddled material, or how many hours it might have taken to listen to and review all the ultimately inconclusive evidence that they did possess.

At 3:00 A.M., a haggard-looking Pardington poked his head out to tell reporters dozing in the hallway that deliberations would be continuing into the next day. Since it already was the next day, this was not exactly stop-the-presses stuff—but then he added something strange that *would* make headlines. The official order of finish might well change when the final results were announced, Pardington said, but whatever happened, Harroun would remain in first place.

"OH, YES, SIR, there was some hometown scoring!" Edward Towers, the riding mechanic in the No. 12 Amplex, would say many years later, when he reflected upon the race.

To say that the Wasp's placement was immune from revision when it had traveled so close to both the No. 31 Lozier and Bruce-Brown's Fiat for most of the final 50 laps, and when there had been so many scoring problems, was unmitigated chutzpah. Pardington's brazenness, though, was rooted in fear. He did not have the will or the nerve to "reverse" the popular semiofficial "decision" and deprive the rich, Indianapolis-based and Speedway-friendly Howard Marmon of a victory the auto maker not only wanted but felt he needed badly for business reasons (Marmon had a major advertising campaign, in which he boasted about the victory for "the Marmon 32," ready to go). Nor did the referee, who was beholden to Fisher for his Speedway post, need to be told where Fisher, who was beholden to Marmon for so many things, came down on all this. By proclaiming the Wasp the undisputed winner, Pardington, ever the people-pleaser, wasn't pretending to proffer a conclusion based on the comparison of different scoring methods—the ostensible work of the men behind the hotel room door—he was simply signaling to the powers that be, and the hometown fans, that he wasn't going to do anything stupid.

One must expect men to put their sense of self-preservation before their sense of justice, but Pardington's lack of subtlety was positively unseemly, and the favoritism he would show Marmon blatant to a degree that tainted the victory he was attempting to bolster. Harroun didn't even need such ham-handed help. A strong case could—and still can—be made for his being the winner; after all, most eyewitnesses assumed that he had crossed the finish line first. By most accounts, Harroun had made the fewest number of pit stops—four—of any of the twenty-six cars still running at the finish (Mulford made a more typical eleven), and the thousands of newspapers already had variations on "Harroun Wins!" in banner headlines; in a lot of minds, of course, print equals proof.

Still, Pardington's crew, when it finally announced its Revised Results at 7:00 A.M. on Thursday, June 1, did not merely keep the Wasp in first place as promised (albeit while raising Harroun's official time by one minute to 6 hours, 42 minutes, and 8 seconds, an average of 74.6 miles an hour, with Mulford 2 minutes and 43 seconds back in 2nd place, a decrease of nearly 3 minutes from his initial timing, and Bruce-Brown 3rd—the same 1-2-3 order as originally announced). The judges also upgraded the status of the *other* Marmon car in the sweepstakes, Joe Dawson's four-cylinder 31, from "Did Not Finish" to 5th place, making him eligible for $1,500 in prize money—and giving Howard Marmon two cars to brag about in his ads. The official explanation of Dawson's ascension must have been especially galling to Mulford, since the judges said that in the case of the smaller Marmon, they had initially miscounted the laps, and that the No. 31 was already somewhere beyond 500 miles when its radiator started leaking and it was forced to stop.

Mulford's response to all the post-race mischief is a subject that often comes up when the first Indy 500 is discussed. That's because the second line of defense for those who support the notion of Harroun as winner, but feel they must acknowledge the overwhelming evidence that post-race grousing was rampant, is often to say that the manipulation of the scoring data, and the maneuvering of the Marmon Wasp into the winner's spot, could not be as egregious as some people (like me) make it sound, or Mulford would have complained louder and longer than he did that day. Indeed, one can make a case for Smiling Ralph being not at all vexed by the proceedings. For one thing, though he did not enjoy the services of a relief driver for the complete run of the race, he never stopped smiling. For another, when interviewed not long after the finish by a reporter from the *Star*, he said, "I had a great time today" and "I feel so good right now I could go and play a baseball game!" This, you have to admit, does not sound like a man who had just been screwed out of glory, job security, and several gold nuggets in a monogrammed leather sack. (His prize for second place was $5,000, and he received another $200 for using a Bosch magneto.)

But to correctly judge Mulford's reaction we must consider the special kind of man he was. Ralph DePalma called him "the most modest of drivers" and "a true gentleman." No one who knew him thought his choirboy image was a public relations pose or a remnant of his innocent youth. Auto racing's choirboy, it turned out, actually sang in a church choir in Fair Haven, New Jersey, abstained from alcohol and tobacco, openly cherished his wife—and practiced sportsmanship, positivity, and politeness as if his immortal soul depended on it. Mulford was polite even to his sometimes temperamental automobiles. "Ralph nurses his car along," DePalma said, "and yields more to the whims of his machine than any pilot now racing for fame or fortune." Mulford constantly spoke to his cars, said one reporter, "as if they were a family horse or a household pet." On the rare occasions when he did get a bit peeved with his vehicle, he would wait until his anger subsided before dealing with the mechanical problems, "so as not to speak too sharply to his engine."

The Gumdrop Kid's good nature sometimes bordered on gullibility. "Isn't it a shame," a mechanic identified only as "Stevens" told a reporter from *Motor Age* in 1915, "that everything Ralph takes hold of is unlucky?" According to one source, in the 1920s a business associate cheated Mulford out of his life savings in a scheme to finance an automobile company that unbeknownst to Mulford never really existed. But Mulford never made a public statement about the swindler, just as, in the heat of the moment and over the years, he had only good things to say about Ray Harroun ("a fine gentleman, a champion driver") and no comment at all on Carl Fisher. When asked, as he was on various occasions after his retirement in 1922, if he harbored resentment toward the Indianapolis Motor Speedway, he always said, "No, not a bit," and never failed to mention that Tony Hulman, then the president of the IMS, "always treated me nicely and took care of me at Christmas time." Although this statement has raised eyebrows because it sounds to some like an allusion to hush money, IMS historian Davidson dismisses that notion, saying that Mulford merely was referring to a set of souvenir drinking glasses that Hulman sent out annually to the people on his holiday gift list. Davidson, in his defense of the official result, gives the Warner Timing System, I dare to say, infinitely more credit than it is due. But I do buy this business about the glasses because Mulford was not the sort of man to sell his silence at any price.

In any case, he didn't keep silent about the matter, even if he did have the wisdom and grace to refrain from taking his anger public through the press. In the same interview in which he mentioned being fresh enough to play baseball, Mulford tactfully but matter-of-factly gave himself credit for being the only one of the top five finishers to go the distance without a relief driver, and noted that his Lozier had been a true stock car racing against mostly souped-up competition. One of Lozier's pit mechanics that day, William Giblin, used to tell his grandson that Mulford was certain he had been cheated out of the victory. "My granddad would say, 'They completely screwed us up with the counting of the cars—it was total mayhem!'" Bill Nitschke told me. "Then he'd add, 'Mulford knew exactly what was going on, and don't ever believe anyone who tells you any differently.'"

Mulford, who died in 1973 at the age of eighty-eight, has two grandsons, neither of whom for some reason warms to the subject of his ancestor's exploits, but one of whom, William Mulford of Worcester, Massachusetts, did tell me in a brief phone conversation, "All I can say is that he contended that he won the race until the day he died." This is indeed true. In a brief memoir Mulford wrote in the September 1969 *Automobile Quarterly* (the same issue of *AQ* in which the original "Who Really Won the First Indy 500?" article appeared), he says tersely of the first 500, "The argument is over who really won the race. I still think I did, and so did a lot of other people." Then, referring to the Russ Catlin piece that lies a few pages ahead, he declines to go into detail. The truth is, by then he was sick to death of giving his opinion on the judging controversy, because when journalists and racing fans sought him out, it was usually the first thing that they asked. I must suppress a snicker at his understandable snappishness when I look at a June 1954 Associated Press piece about Mulford, which appeared in the *Idaho Falls Post Register* under the headline "Auto Dealer Says He Won 1911 Speedway." He was not the crank that that headline conjures, but all those years later, what happened in the hours following the first sweepstakes would still rankle him. ("The Case car broke a steering knuckle in front of the grandstand, but I saw an opening and zigzagged through," Mulford told the reporter, explaining how he picked up at least one lap that went unrecorded. "The timers and judges didn't see me, and they scattered to keep from getting hurt.")

Not just Mulford, but anyone who cares about the Indy 500 has the right to be furious at Carl Fisher for his final decree in regard to the inaugural race of 1911. This was to tell Pardington that he wanted all of the records—every scoring sheet, Dictaphone and adding machine tape, Horograph strip, and random judge's note—destroyed before the AAA referee announced the Revised Results. Even Donald Davidson calls this "the thing that's hardest to reconcile" with the idea of a fair decision. To those who disagree with Davidson's opinion of the outcome, the reason Fisher issued this order was obvious: to leave Warner's scattered and scrambled numbers open to scrutiny would be to show how meaningless his system, and thus how valueless the official result, was.

Timing official Harry Knepper defended his cohorts as best he could, saying the judges locked in Pardington's suite that night actually had four sets of records for each car, which they mixed and matched for hours on end, even if they could see from the score sheets that "it proved impossible for the human hand to keep these records up to date." Pardington proffered an equally inept stab at an explanation for the AAA's methods, saying, "Lap positions and lap times will never be divulged on those cars forced from the race. We consider it unfair to such as the Apperson which was withdrawn through no fault of its own." Neither, however, said anything about why data of more widespread and more pressing interest was dragged to the Claypool's dumbwaiter shaft in the early-morning hours, like an inconvenient corpse. All that was later found in the AAA's "confidential" file for the 1911 race was a note-to-self from the organization's chairman, Sam Butler, saying, "Mechanical devices for scoring should be avoided at major contests. They can break down and at best are only as good as the operator."

Mulford no doubt sensed the futility of fighting back. He had as much chance of overturning the unofficial decision as the anti-car lobby had of pushing through laws that lowered the speed limit to 5 miles an hour and forced autoists to attach a rendering of a bucolic scene to their bumpers so as to camouflage their appearance from skittish horses. The world may have had to view the race through the cracked lens of the newspaper coverage, but it had been galvanized by the images of Harroun in the winner's circle, surrounded by happy faces, saying he would never race again "because it is simply too dangerous," and smiling gallantly as a cup of water is held to his cracked and grease-smeared lips. To no one alive, but to many now gone, it was an indelible memory.

IN AN ESSAY published in *Natural History* magazine in November of 1989, "The Creation Myths of Cooperstown," paleontologist Stephen Jay Gould mused on the powerful attraction of creation myths. "For some reason," he wrote, in a piece that discusses the public's preference for the apocryphal story of Abner Doubleday over "evolutionary explanations" for the origins of baseball,

> we are powerfully drawn to beginnings. We yearn to know about origins, and we readily construct myths when we do not have data (or we suppress data in favor of legend when a truth strikes us as too commonplace). The hankering after an origin myth has always been especially strong for the closest subject of all—the human race. But we extend the same psychic need to our accomplishments and institutions—and we have origin myths and stories for the beginning of hunting, of language, of art, of kindness, of war, of boxing, bowties, and brassieres.

And, of course, auto races. It is not difficult to see why people prefer dramatic, relatively concise creation myths to the more diffuse, often less titillating truth, Gould said. Creation myths "identify heroes and sacred places," while evolutionary stories "provide no palpable, particular thing as a symbol for reverence, worship, or patriotism."

Carl Fisher didn't think in terms of creation myths, but he understood viscerally what Gould meant, and he knew, as we all do, that no truly glorious undertaking starts with a stumble. The 1911 Indianapolis 500-mile sweepstakes was, as *Motor Age* had said, a tremendous spectacle, but as an automobile race it was far beyond a stumble, or even a face-planting pratfall; it was that rare thing so wrong, so utterly off the mark—a nearly seven-hour race without a result!—that *it simply could not be what it was.* It had to be transmuted into something acceptable. The public wanted a winner, or to put it in Gould's terms, a nice clean creation myth. Fisher wanted a winner from Indiana, ideally driving a Marmon. The principals were never that far apart. And so it came down to the Wasp and Ray Harroun, the combination of which made the most people happy.

In the remaining sixty-two years of his life, the closest Ralph Mulford ever came to letting his anger boil over was probably during the 1912 Indianapolis 500-mile race. Driving a Knox that year—Lozier got out of racing at the end of 1911—he experienced numerous clutch problems and was running 10th and last among the remaining vehicles when Joe Dawson took the checkered flag with his National in 6:21:06. As the 10th-place finisher, Mulford was entitled to about $500 in purse money but under a new rule he couldn't collect it unless he completed the full 500 miles. Mulford thought this was fundamentally stupid, and while a crowd of eighty thousand looked on, at least for a while, he figured he would show the AAA, and Carl Fisher, just why. Alone on the track with riding mechanic Billy Chandler, Smiling Ralph slowed down, then slowed further, to a 20- to 25-mile-an-hour crawl. At one point he pitted, picked up fried chicken dinners for himself and Chandler, then resumed his torpid trek as both men painstakingly sucked the bones clean and tossed them from the cockpit. When their main course was consumed Mulford pitted again, for ice cream. By the time he hit his 500th mile, in 8 hours and 53 minutes, still the slowest time ever recorded by an Indy finisher, virtually every spectator, as well as starter Fred Wagner and Carl Fisher, had left the grounds, the latter two, it was said, more than a little perturbed.

To delve into the 1911 race is, I think, to sympathize with Mulford, yet we cannot simply say that he was cheated out of victory. We cannot *simply* say anything about the first Indianapolis 500. A year later the sweepstakes would have a glorious reincarnation. With improvements in the scoring and timing, and the field reduced to a saner twenty-four cars, the race righted itself in 1912 and took off toward its destiny as one of America's premier sporting events. But the 1911 edition was something else—a weird mashup of cars, money, and misdirection that was, for better or worse, symptomatic of the new American century. From it we can learn . . . well, what, exactly? Maybe only that there are things more hotly desired than truth. Against the need for heroic men and sacred places, truth doesn't stand a chance.

EPILOGUE

RIDING HIS STODDARD-DAYTON in the rolling start of the 1911 Indianapolis 500 was probably the high point of Carl Fisher's life. He was then just beginning his Miami adventure, for which he is probably as well known as for his Speedway days, but Miami would turn out to be a soul-numbing and ultimately wallet-emptying exercise. He and Jane had a son, Carl Jr., on November 13, 1921, but the child died a few weeks later of malnutrition, the parents apparently not realizing he wasn't drawing sufficient nourishment from the bottle or breast. That sad event effectively signaled the end of their marriage—Carl was not attentive to the boy Jane adopted a short while later, as she was about to set off on a round of affairs. Both married again several times and Fisher kept coming up with schemes, many of them large in scale but flawed in conception, like his 1913 plan for the Lincoln Highway, a privately financed road connecting America's east and west coasts. Booze, an abortive attempt to develop Montauk, Long Island, and the Great Depression ultimately did Fisher in. He died, bloated and broke, in a small shack in Miami where a friend was letting him live, on July 15, 1939, at the age of sixty-five. Barney Oldfield was one of his pallbearers. Fisher is buried in an elaborate mausoleum, purchased, as they say, in happier times, in Indianapolis's prestigious Crown Hill Cemetery.

When I sat down in the shadow of Lucas Oil Stadium with Dennis Horvath, an expert on Indiana automobile history, in the course of researching this book, he made a point of noting that the old-time racers themselves tended to wind up with relatively humble headstones. As an example he cited the Chevrolet brothers, bearers of a name that would probably not pass muster with a twenty-first-century focus group (*Too hard to pronounce!*) but which, in the old Dinah Shore jingle, rhymed quite nicely with "U.S.A." The Chevrolets rest eternally in the scruffy Catholic cemetery on the wrong side of the Indianapolis tracks. But at least we can visit their graves and think about Louis, a man principled (and hotheaded) enough to storm off without compensation from the company he founded. Plenty of others from that era have made a hard left into the abyss of history. Whither Howard Hall, driver of the No. 41 Velie in the first Indy 500—and Bert Adams of the No. 23 McFarlan?

Of the forty drivers in that 1911 race (fifty-six if you count relief men), Ray Harroun and Ralph Mulford lived the longest, reaching eighty-nine and eighty-eight, respectively. Johnny Aitken (No. 4 National) died in the Spanish influenza epidemic of 1918; he was thirty-three. Charlie Merz (No. 7 National) became a real estate agent, Bill Endicott (No. 42 Cole) a traffic cop; both died in their sixties of natural causes.

Most of the men in that first field stayed in racing, and nine of the forty starting drivers died on the track. Some of their deaths have been noted in the preceding pages. Of the rest, Harry Endicott (No. 3 Interstate) was killed while practicing in Jackson, Michigan, in 1913. Spencer Wishart (No. 11 Mercedes) hit a tree and died during a national championship road race at Elgin, Illinois, in 1914. Harry Grant (No. 19 Alco) was killed in practice for the 1915 Astor Cup. The next year in Uniontown, Pennsylvania, Hughie Hughes (No. 36 Mercer) crashed and died on a board track. Howard "Howdy" Wilcox (No. 21 National) died in the Altoona 200 of 1923.

David Bruce-Brown's death made page-one headlines in October of 1912. He and his riding mechanic, Tony Scudalari (sometimes rendered as "Scudellary"), were practicing for the American Grand Prize, a road race held that year in Milwaukee. They had brought their Fiat into the pit area for fuel and Fred Wagner, the famous starting judge, had noticed that its tires looked like they needed changing, and told them so. But Bruce-Brown chided Wagner for his mother-henness and took off anyway. A few minutes later he suffered a violent blowout and turned turtle several times. When the big car finally stopped rolling it was right side up but both men inside were dead.

The dubious honor of being the first Indy 500 driver to die belongs to Lewis Strang. On July 20, 1911, about seven weeks after steering knuckle problems had knocked him out of the big race after 210 miles, the twenty-six-year-old Clicquot Kid was taking his Case car on the Wisconsin Automobile Association's annual reliability run, a low-key event meant to demonstrate a vehicle's dependability and usefulness under a variety of quotidian conditions. He had his pal and fellow sweepstakes veteran Joe Jagersberger in the seat next to him and two Case executives in the back. At a narrow spot in the road near the town of Blue River, they encountered a farmer slowly driving his hay wagon in the opposite direction. Strang and the farmer both bore to their right and tried to squeeze by each other, but the racer went a bit too far and began to slide down a modest-size embankment. His three passengers hopped out to safety, but Strang stayed put, and the car flipped over and killed him. The *Marshall* (Michigan) *Evening Statesman*, and other papers, raised the possibility that Strang's strange lack of action amounted to suicide, saying that he had been despondent and at times reckless "since he was sued for divorce by his wife, the beautiful actress Louise Alexander." In his obituary, *The Horseless Age* said, "This driver's career was marked with numerous narrow escapes," and that "he had often declared that death would never get him in a speed contest." Technically speaking, he was right about that. The police report said that at the time of his death he had been traveling 4 miles an hour.

ACKNOWLEDGMENTS

ON AN EVENING he probably doesn't remember, Jeff Ballow helped me more than he knows. When my wife and I arrived at the home that Jeff, a consultant in the nonprofit sector, shares in Brooklyn with his wife, the esteemed yoga teacher Stephanie Creaturo, and their year-old son, Beckett, I was distracted by my own professional problems, as writers often boringly are. But what irritated me was not the usual stubborn knot of words or swampy stretch of chapter that I had once deemed brilliant; no, this was a gnawing dissatisfaction with, and even a feeling of anger toward, a reality my research had made plain—namely that the first Indianapolis 500 race had been neither an all-out assault on the speed records of the day nor a motorized chess match, but rather six-plus hours of chaos and confusion. As some contemporary publications had noted, it could not rightly be called a race. "How can I build a story around *that*?" I had said to Jeff quite a few minutes after he made the mistake of asking how the book was going.

His comeback was not immediate. Jeff paused, frowned, paused a bit longer, then said, "You know, I don't really see this as a problem. I mean, suppose one car had led from start to finish, or suppose the lead had changed hands a few times, and at the end one of those cars, or some other car, was ahead? Suppose it had been a conventional race.

Then you'd be stuck with describing that and, you know, so what? Isn't it more interesting that things should go so wrong, and that people should try to cover that up—and that so many other people would be willing to believe the so-called official version?" Another pause, another frown. "Honestly, I think you're lucky to have that to work with."

Jeff's cold splash of common sense shut me up, and by the time we finished an excellent homemade pizza, I was, no pun intended, back on track. As his wife had done in yoga class so many times, Jeff helped me see that if you don't accept things as they are in the world, you're turning something that's difficult enough into something impossible.

Getting the order of the thank-yous right *is* impossible. Some of my first and most pleasant days on this project were spent with Donald Davidson, the official historian of the Indianapolis Motor Speedway. Donald is often called a walking encyclopedia, but he is a much more inviting presence than a book with legs. On my first visit to the Speedway in connection with *Blood and Smoke*, he gave me a personal tour of the museum, schooled me in the basics of early motor sports, and introduced me to Ron Rose of the Indiana State Library, himself a student of Indianapolis history and a 500 buff who was generous with his time and advice. Over the course of several other trips, Donald talked to me at length about the IMS founders and the controversy surrounding the first 500-mile race and pointed me toward some valuable research materials. As I say in the text, he cannot be held responsible for my conclusions, but he did encourage my interest in the Speedway and always made well-reasoned arguments in defense of the official results of the first 500.

The writer and bon vivant J. Michael Kenyon, who has read deeply and thought long about the early motor age, gave me help with the broad strokes and the telling details, and pointed me toward fascinating sources, all out of the goodness of his heart. It was John Capouya, the writer and professor of journalism, who put me in touch with him.

I had help from two first-rate researchers. Mark Schneider, a student at Indiana University for most of the time I was writing this book, provided me with a smart overview of the one hundred years of 500s and haunted the libraries of Indianapolis for many months on my behalf. Michael Shea, a graduate student in the Research Internship Program of the Writing Division of the School of Arts of Columbia University, run by Patricia O'Toole, creatively searched for newspaper and magazine clippings, as well as obscure books and long-lost relatives of the participants in the 1911 race. He was indispensable to this project.

One of the people Mike found for me was Scott Dickson, the nephew of Sam Dickson, the riding mechanic killed in the first 500. Before he died in November 2009, Scott provided me with clippings, photos, letters, and family lore that I found extremely useful. Scott's niece, Janice Frazier, was also helpful, as was his wife, Martha Dickson. Through Mike I also tracked down Johnny Rutherford, who spoke to me about his experience driving the Marmon Wasp, and other matters.

I owe thanks to Gregory Hendricks, president and CEO of the ESM group, for allowing me to see the unpublished Louis Schwitzer memoir and to quote from it. Mark Dill, who became the vice president for marketing and public relations for the IMS while this book was in progress, gave help and advice. His Web site, firstsuperspeedway.com, is an invaluable source for information, photos, and film clips on early auto racing and Indy 500 history. Mary Ellen Loscar at the Speedway Photo Operations Department helped me gather the images. I am also grateful for the interviews granted me by Dick Harroun, Dennis Horvath, and William Nitschke, whose grandfather William Giblin was part of Ralph Mulford's 1911 Indy pit crew, as well as for the help of photographer Diana Eliazon and researcher Barb Nicolls.

Herb Lederer gave me a ride in his 1912 Mercer Raceabout, which was scary fun. Thanks are also due to John Fierst and Susan Powers at the Clarke Historical Library at Central Michigan University, as well as Dawn Hugh and Patricia Bannhona at the Historical Museum of Southern Florida, and the entire staff of the Science, Industry, and Business branch of the New York Public Library, on Madison Avenue.

I am grateful for the support and counsel I received from my agent at ICM, Kris Dahl, and from Bob Bender, my editor at Simon & Schuster, superstars both. Kris's assistant Laura Neely and Bob's colleagues at S&S, Johanna Li, Victoria Meyer, Danielle Lynn, Jonathan Evans, and Ruth Lee-Mui have also enriched my book writing experiences. As always, my friend the writer Karen Schneider was an early reader of the manuscript and encouraging presence.

Then there are these people: Erica Leerhsen, Deborah Leerhsen Amundsson, and Nora Leerhsen, whose names tell the story. Thanks to Frankie the Dog, I was forced to get up every four or five hours and go for a walk, which is good for the writing process and the glutes.

My wife, Sarah Saffian Leerhsen, happens to be a wonderful editor as well as the love of my life. Who do I thank for that?

APPENDIX

THIS LIST WAS released to the press at 7:00 A.M. on Thursday, June 1, more than thirty-six hours after the race ended. In response to numerous complaints about the timing and scoring on the original order-of-finish list, a committee of officials reviewed the available data and adjusted several finishing times and made one change in the running order, moving Joe Dawson's No. 31 Marmon from the "Did Not Finish" category to 5th place. How the committee reached its conclusions is not known, since Indianapolis Motor Speedway president Carl Fisher ordered all records of the race immediately destroyed.

Position	No.	Driver	Relief Driver	Car	Time
1	32	Ray Harroun	Cyrus Patschke	Marmon Wasp	6:42:08
2	33	Ralph Mulford		Lozier	6:43:51
3	28	David L. Bruce-Brown		Fiat	6:52:29
4	11	Spencer Wishart	Dave Murphy	Mercedes	6:52:57
5	31	Joe Dawson	Cyrus Patschke	Marmon	6:54:34
6	2	Ralph DePalma		Simplex	7:02:02
7	20	Charlie Merz	Len Zengel	National	7:06:20
8	12	W. H. Turner	Walter Jones	Amplex	7:15:56

Position	No.	Driver	Relief Driver	Car	Time
9	15	Fred Belcher	John Coffey	Knox	7:17:09
10	25	Harry Cobe	Louis Schwitzer	Jackson	7:21:50
11	10	Gil Anderson		Stutz	7:22:55
12	36	Hughie Hughes		Mercer	7:23:32
13	30	Lee Frayer	Eddie Rickenbacher	Firestone-Columbus	flagged
14	21	Howdy Wilcox		National	flagged
15	37	Charles Bigelow	W. H. Frey, E. H. Sherwood	Mercer	flagged
16	3	Harry Endicott		Interstate	flagged
17	41	Howard Hall	Rupert Jeffkins	Velie	flagged
18	46	Billy Knipper		Benz	flagged
19	45	Bob Burman		Benz	flagged
20	38	Ralph Beardsley	Frank Goode	Simplex	flagged
21	18	Eddie Hearne	Edward Parker	Fiat	flagged
22	6	Frank Cox	Fred Clemons	Pope-Hartford	flagged
23	27	Ernest Delaney		Cutting	flagged
24	26	Jack Tower	Robert Evans	Jackson	flagged
25	23	Bert Adams (started), Mel Marquette (finished)		McFarlan	flagged
26	42	Bill Endicott	Johnny Jenkins	Cole	flagged
27	4	Johnny Aitken		National	Did not finish
28	9	Will Jones		Case	Did not finish
29	1	Lewis Strang	Elmer Ray	Case	Did not finish
30	7	Harry Knight		Westcott	Did not finish
31	8	Joe Jagersberger		Case	Did not finish
32	35	Herbert Lytle		Apperson	Did not finish
33	19	Harry Grant		Alco	Did not finish
34	17	Charles Basle		Buick	Did not finish
35	5	Louis Disbrow		Pope-Hartford	Did not finish
36	16	Arthur Chevrolet		Buick	Did not finish
37	39	Caleb Bragg		Fiat	Did not finish
38	24	Fred Ellis		Jackson	Did not finish
39	34	Teddy Tetzlaff		Lozier	Did not finish
40	44	Arthur Greiner		Amplex	Did not finish

A NOTE ON SOURCES

NO TRUTH WAS injured intentionally in the creation of this work of nonfiction. No quotes are made up, no scenes manufactured. Conflicting and misleading contemporary accounts are reported as such. The information is drawn from thousands of newspaper articles dating back to the nineteenth century as well as long since defunct automobile magazines that simultaneously served the fledgling industry and the consumer. I also relied on books, Web sites, miscellaneous material found in libraries, and interviews that I conducted. Rather than use footnotes or ask the reader to flip between the text and a back-of-the-book notes section, I identify the sources as the information occurs.

My search for information about the early auto industry and the racing scene of a hundred years ago led me directly to the Science, Industry, and Business Library, a branch of the New York Public Library on Madison Avenue and 34th Street, where I spent many happy and dusty days poring over *The Horseless Age, Motor Age, The Automobile, The Motorcycle,* and several other ancient weeklies and monthlies that can be found almost nowhere else. I also worked in the Detroit Public Library and the library at Central Michigan University, which contains some of the personal papers of Ernest Moross, the first director of contests at the Indianapolis Motor Speedway. The books on the history of the car and the car business I found especially useful were *Indiana Cars: A History of the Automobile in Indiana* and *Cruise IN: A Guide to Indiana's Automotive Past and Present*, both by Dennis E. Horvath and Terri Horvath; *The People's Tycoon: Henry Ford and the American Century* by Steven Watts; *The Automobile Age* and *America Adopts the Automobile, 1895–1910*, both by James J. Flink; *The Golden Age of the American Racing Car* by Griffith Borgeson; *The Story of the American Automobile* by Rudolph E. Anderson; *Barney Oldfield: The Life and Times of America's Legendary Speed King* by William F. Nolan; *A Hoosier Holiday* by Theodore Dreiser; *Chrome Dreams: Automobile Styling Since 1893* by Paul C. Wilson; *Pioneers, Engineers, and Scoundrels: The Dawn of the Automobile in America* by Beverly Rae Kimes; *Billy, Alfred and General Motors* by William Pelfrey; *One Hundred Years of Motoring: An RAC Social History of the Car* by Raymond Flower and Michael Wynn Jones; *Road Trips, Head Trips, and Other Car-Crazed Writings*, edited by Jean Lindamood Jennings; *The Checkered Flag* by Peter Helck; *American Automobile Racing: An Illustrated History* by Albert R. Bochroch; *Unforgivable Blackness: The Rise and Fall of Jack Johnson* by Geoffrey C. Ward; *Any Color So Long as It's Black: The First Fifty Years of Automobile Advertising* by Peter Roberts; *Eat My Dust: Early Women Motorists* by Georgine Clarsen; *Race of the Century: The Heroic True Story of the 1908 New York to Paris Auto Race* by Julie M. Fenster; and *Excuse My Dust* by Bellamy Partridge.

The first two books I read (actually reread) to get a sense of the times were the autobiographical classic *The Education of Henry Adams* and *The Vertigo Years: Europe, 1900–1914* by Philipp Blom. I also read Mark Sullivan's *Our Times* series; *The Age of Reform* by Richard Hofstadter; *Going Out: The Rise and Fall of Public Amusement* by David Nasaw; and *Horses at Work: Harnessing Power in Industrial America* by Ann Norton Greene.

On the subject of Carl Fisher these are among the books I consulted: *Castles in the Sand: The Life and Times of Carl Graham Fisher* by Mark S. Foster; *The Pacesetter: The Untold Story of Carl G. Fisher, Creator of the Indy 500, Miami Beach and the Lincoln Highway* by Jerry M. Fisher; *Fabulous Hoosier* by Jane Fisher; *Billion-Dollar Sandbar: A Bi-*

ography of Miami Beach by Polly Redford; and *Miami Babylon: Crime, Wealth, and Power—A Dispatch from the Beach* by Gerald Posner.

Information on the Circle City came largely from the Indiana State Library in Indianapolis. I also found *Indiana: An Interpretation* by John Bartlow Martin especially interesting and went often to the *Encyclopedia of Indianapolis*, edited by David J. Bodenhamer and Robert Graham Barrows; *Indianapolis Then and Now* by Nelson Price; *Lost Indianapolis* by John P. McDonald; *Indianapolis: An Illustrated History* by Bill Harris; and *Milestones 2000*, a publication of the *Indianapolis Business Journal*.

For a good overview of the first century at the Indianapolis Motor Speedway I would recommend the *Autocross Official History of the Indianapolis 500* by Donald Davidson and Rich Schaffer, as well as the several substantial articles in *Automobile Quarterly* that I mention in the text. Mark Dill does an excellent job of finding and presenting information on the early days of racing in Indianapolis and elsewhere at his First Super Speedway Web site (firstsuperspeedway.com). Other books on the Speedway that I found useful (and occasionally maddening in their willingness to traffic in cliché and to put politeness ahead of truth) include *Indy: Racing Before the 500* by D. Bruce Scott; *Indianapolis 500 Mile Race History*, edited by Floyd Clymer; *500 Miles to Go: The Story of the Indianapolis Speedway* by Al Bloemker; *Indianapolis Motor Speedway: 100 Years of Racing* by Ralph Kramer; *The Indianapolis 500* by Brock W. Yates; *The Fastest of the First: A Complete History of the Inaugural 1911 Indianapolis 500*, presented by the Belcher Foundation; and *Indy: The Race and Ritual of the Indianapolis 500* by Terry Reed.